Children and Adolescents

INTERPRETIVE ESSAYS ON JEAN PIAGET

THIRD EDITION

DAVID ELKIND

New York   Oxford
OXFORD UNIVERSITY PRESS
1981

The section on Conservation in the Introduction is from *Childhood Education*, January 1968, Vol. 44, No. 5. Reprinted by permission of the Association for Childhood Education International, 3615 Wisconsin Ave., N.W., Washington, D.C.

"Jean Piaget" (originally entitled "Giant in the Nursery") and "Children's Questions" © 1968 by the New York Times Company. "Of Time and the Child" © 1970 by the New York Times Company. Reprinted by permission.

"Misunderstandings about How Children Learn" from *Today's Education*, March 1972. Reprinted by permission.

"Egocentrism in Children and Adolescents," and "Cognitive Structure and Experience in Children and Adolescents," from "Egocentrism in Adolescence," *Child Development*, 38, 1967, 1025–34. Reprinted by permission of the Society for Research in Child Development; and from "Cognitive Structure and Adolescent Experience" from *Adolescence*, 1967–68, 427–34. Reprinted by permission of Libra Publishers, Inc.

"Piaget and Montessori," from *Harvard Educational Review*, 37, Fall 1967, 535–45. Copyright © 1967 by the President and Fellows of Harvard College. Reprinted by permission.

"Two Approaches to Intelligence," from "Piagetian and Psychometric Conceptions of Intelligence," *Harvard Educational Review*, 39, Spring 1969, 319–37. Copyright © 1969 by the President and Fellows of Harvard College. Reprinted by permission.

"Reading, Logic, and Perception," from *Educational Therapy*, Vol. 2, 1969, 195–207, Special Child Publications, Seattle, Washington. Reprinted by permission.

"Beginning Reading: A Stage-Structure Analysis," from *Childhood Education*, 1979, 55, 248–52. Reprinted by permission.

"Piaget and British Primary Education," from *Educational Psychologist*, 1974, 11. Reprinted by permission.

"Adolescent Thinking and the Curriculum," from *New York University Education Quarterly*, Winter 1981. Reprinted by permission.

Library of Congress Cataloging in Publication Data

Elkind, David, 1931–
    Children and adolescents.

    Bibliography: p.
    1. Child psychology. 2. Adolescent psychology.
3. Educational psychology. 4. Piaget, Jean, 1896–1980.
I. Title.
BF721.E36   1981   155.4'13'0924   80–17476
ISBN 0–19–502820–1
ISBN 0–19–502821–X (pbk.)
Copyright © 1970, 1974, 1981 by Oxford University Press, Inc.
Printed in the United States of America
987654

In loving memory of my parents,
Peter and Bessie

Preface to the Third Edition

It is both a pleasure and a responsibility to introduce still a third edition of *Children and Adolescents*. The pleasure, of course, comes from the continued friendly reception the book has received from a wide variety of audiences. It really is pleasing to know that readers still find the book an interesting introduction to Piaget and the implications of his work for educational and clinical practice. On the other hand, the responsibility comes from having to add to the book in such a way as to bring it a little more up to date while retaining the qualities which accounted for the positive reception of the earlier editions.

Therefore, I have added four new pieces. Article 13, entitled "Work Is Hardly Child's Play," is an attempt to compare Piaget's theory of play with that of Montessori, Freud, and Erikson. This is a needed addition because I have not dealt with Piaget's theory of play before. The aim of the piece, however, is practical as well as theoretical. The equation of work and play in early childhood education has been, to my mind, unfortunate. Particularly in early childhood education, work and play serve different functions and need to be dealt with differently in the classroom. The article suggests what those functions are and how the two forms of activity can be recognized and supported.

A second addition, Article 14, written with Donna Hetzel and John Coe, relates Piagetian theory to British primary education.

The article argues that the informal programs in the British infant schools are a concrete embodiment of Piagetian theory applied to education. I must confess that the piece has been included in part for political purposes. The move toward child-centered education, as described in this piece, has lost much ground since its heyday in the late sixties and early seventies. In the conservative climate of today, it seems worthwhile to re-assert the values of child-centered, informal education.

The other two pieces also deal with education. Article 12, entitled "Beginning Reading: A Stage-Structure Analysis," is a more detailed working out of the theory of beginning reading presented in the earlier editions. It also includes a survey of recent research that supports that theory. I have left the original article on reading, logic, and perception in as well to show the continuity in the development of the ideas. The whole thrust of Piaget's psychology is that learning and understanding take time and involve much relearning and reunderstanding. Perhaps the two pieces, separated by almost a decade, will highlight the progressive restructuring of ideas.

Article 15, entitled "Adolescent Thinking and the Curriculum," reflects the current interest in Piaget's work at the level of secondary education. Oddly enough, perhaps because of the misuse of Piaget in the elementary curriculum movement of the sixties, one hears little of Piaget in contemporary discussions of elementary school curriculum. But at the secondary level it is another story and there is a kind of grass roots interest, particularly by science and math teachers, in the relation of curriculum materials to adolescent mental abilities. The paper outlines some concepts that would seem to be essential for the successful analysis of curriculum materials from a Piagetian perspective.

In making these additions I realize that I have emphasized the education implications and interpretations. This is not meant to slight the clinical implications of Piaget's work, because I believe that they are of great importance. It is just that the clinical implications are more involved and take longer to work out. Perhaps, if there is a fourth edition, I will be able to balance the scale.

D.E.

Medford, Mass.
November 1980

Preface to the First Edition

Jean Piaget, the Swiss psychologist, has been studying the development of children's thinking for more than fifty years. Only in the last decade, however, has American psychology and education come to recognize that Piaget is in fact one of the giants of developmental psychology. As the late J. Robert Oppenheimer wrote on the occasion of Piaget's seventieth birthday:

> It is clear to me that in its scope and in its conceptions [your work] is both a product of our times and the source of great changes coming into being in the way we think of nature and of ourselves as part of nature and ourselves as knowers of it. You have been an inspiration to your colleagues and have brought enlargement to man's understanding and his methods of seeking understanding.

The impact of Piaget's thinking upon present-day child psychology and education is becoming increasingly evident. He is the subject or partial subject of a growing number of books (three in the last year) and articles (30 in 1956; 80 in 1961; and 193 in 1966) in psychology, and is leaving an equally powerful impress on education. At the 1969 annual meeting of the National Educational Research Association in Chicago, eleven of the sessions dealt directly or indirectly with Piaget's research and theory. Piaget is, moreover, in very great demand as a lecturer in this country despite the fact that he speaks only French and must travel with an interpreter. Although he curtails his travel for reasons of health and because it interferes with his work, Piaget nonetheless man-

aged, in 1967, to lecture at the University of Montreal, as well as
at Clark University in February, to address the American Ortho-
psychiatry Association, and to give three talks at New York University in March, and to lecture at the universities of Minnesota
and Michigan in the fall.

Piaget's international reputation is also growing at a rapid rate
and his books have been translated into at least seven different
languages. He has even become an issue in the Sino-Soviet split,
for while Piaget is *persona grata* in the communist countries of
Eastern Europe, and has lectured in Warsaw, Prague, and Moscow,
he is called "the bourgeois psychologist Piaget" by the Chinese
Communists. A rough index of the growth of Piaget's international
fame is the list of his honorary degrees. Harvard gave Piaget his
first honorary degree in 1936. In the forties he received three degrees (from the Sorbonne, Rio de Janeiro, and Brussels) while in
the fifties he received four (from the Universities of Chicago,
McGill, Warsaw, and Manchester). In the past decade he received six (from the Universities of Oslo, Cambridge, Brandeis,
Montreal, Aix Marseille, and Pennsylvania). In 1952 he was also
made Professor of Child Psychology at the Sorbonne, the first
non-Frenchman to be given a chair at that University since De-
siderius Erasmus in 1530!

How can we account for the recent surge of interest by American psychology, and particularly American education, in Piaget
after the many years during which he worked in relative obscu-
rity? The answer is obviously a complex one, but it most certainly
involves the crisis in education which occurred in the mid-nineteen
fifties. The crisis was a product of many different factors including
the negative reaction to the "life adjustment" program of progressive education; the lack of teachers and facilities for the deluge of
"war babies" which suddenly inundated the schools; the demand
of an increasingly technological society for highly trained person-
nel; and the launching of Sputnik by the USSR in 1957 which
made competitive America aware of the fact that its major ad-

versary had drawn ahead in the race for technological achievements and innovation.

Even before Sputnik, however, a spate of books appeared that were highly critical of the educational establishment. Among these were Arthur Bestor's *Educational Wastelands*, Robert Hutchins's *The Conflict in Education*, Albert Lynd's *Quackery in the Public Schools*, and Paul Woodring's *Let's Talk Sense About Our Schools*. All of these books appeared in 1953 and they were followed by many more of the same genre. The brunt of the criticism contained in these attacks was that progressive education's concern with adjustment and educational professionalism had gone far beyond the mandate given to the schools. According to Arthur Bestor, the goal of education was not the personal adjustment of pupils, but rather "The deliberate cultivation of the ability to think." What was needed, the critics said, was to take educational planning out of the hands of the professional educators and to put it under the control of the scholars and scientists who knew their subjects at first hand.

As a consequence of this criticism and abetted by financial support of government agencies such as the National Science Fund and the U.S. Office of Education, centers for the study of curriculum were established at major universities across the nation. In many cases these centers were under the direction of a university professor who had proven himself a talented teacher and who was concerned with making his subject accessible and meaningful to children. Robert Karplus, the physicist who heads the Science Curriculum Improvement Study at the University of California at Berkeley, and Max Beberman, the mathematician who heads the University of Illinois Mathematics Project (and who is the major exponent of the "new math") are among the most prominent of the new breed of curriculum planners.

It is in the context of this search for what is now called "The New Curricula" that the surge of interest in Piaget must be understood. When the curriculum planners turned to psychology for guidance as to how the child acquires mathematical, scientific, and social science concepts they found little of value to them. Psychologists concerned with the learning process had, in order to study the process experimentally, turned to lower organisms, most notably the rat. Those psychologists who were concerned with children were, on the other hand, influenced by Freud and were primarily interested in personality and the effects of child-rearing practices upon child growth and development. To a large segment of the psychological community words such as "thinking" were ruled out as mythological, pre-scientific terms. For the new curriculum planners, who saw the goal of education as teaching children how to think, American psychology had very little to offer.

There was thus a tremendous need for information about children's thinking which would serve as guidelines for curriculum reform and which could not be satisfied by American psychology. As Lee Cronbach (professor of psychology at Stanford University and author of a standard text in educational psychology) said in 1964, "the learning theory that has been the preoccupation of the American psychologist since the days of Thorndike—SR theory—seems not to have had much impact on the curriculum work that has been going on." Fortunately, one of Piaget's later books, *The Child's Conception of Number* was translated in 1952 and this book together with the labors of psychologists such as Jerome Bruner at Harvard and the late David Rapaport at the Austen Riggs Foundation in Stockbridge, Massachusetts, helped to bring the scope of Piaget's contribution to the attention of American psychologists and educators.

As the significance of Piaget's work for psychology and education came to be recognized in this country, his books were translated at an increasing rate and many are now available in English. In 1963, John Flavell's scholarly and comprehensive summary and evaluation of Piaget's work and theory "The Developmental Psychology of Jean Piaget" provided a much needed introduction to Piaget's work for American psychologists. The ensuing years have seen the publication of a number of briefer summaries of Piaget's

work among which Hans Furth's "Piaget and knowledge" (40) *
and Ginsburg and Opper's "Piaget's theory of intellectual development" (42) are the most notable. Such summaries are required because Piaget is often difficult reading, even in English translation.

There is still a need, or so it seems to me, for a less technical
introduction to Piaget that would be appropriate to students of
education. The essays in the present book are directed to this audience. My aim in these essays is not simply to summarize Piaget
but rather to interpret the implications of Piaget's work for those
who are, or will be, teaching children. I have tried, as best I could,
to illustrate in non-technical language the basic findings and concepts of Piaget without, I hope, distorting his views. The book, it
should be said, is not meant as a text on Piaget, but rather as sup-
plementary reading for courses in educational psychology and
child development.

So many people have influenced and encouraged me that it is
impossible to acknowledge them all. Foremost among those to
whom I am indebted is the late David Rapaport, who first introduced me to Piaget and who encouraged my first research on
Piagetian themes. John Flavell, Hans Furth, Irving I. Siegel, William
E. Martin, Alberta Siegel, William C. Halpin, and Patricia Feeley
are among the many friends, colleagues, and editors whose support and confidence sustained me through those many periods
when I was sure that all I was saying was gibberish. I want to
thank, too, my secretary, Loretta Forbes Schafer, for the care and
speed with which she typed the manuscript. Most of all, of course,
I am indebted to the "Patron." His courage and steadfastness in
the face of a prevailing *Zeitgeist* condescending toward his methods, suspicious of his results, and hostile toward his theorizing
have been an example to all of his students of that independence
of mind and commitment to truth which is the motive force behind
all genuine scientific progress.

---

* The numbers in parenthesis here and throughout the text refer to entries
in the bibliography at the end of the book.

Contents

Children and Adolescents

It is probably fair to say that the work of Jean Piaget has revolutionized our ways of thinking about the mental growth of children. We now recognize that children not only have fewer ideas than adults, but also that the ideas which they do have are different in kind from those held by grown-ups. Much of the content of children's thinking that has been uncovered by Piaget's researches is described in the following chapters. This introductory chapter gives a brief précis of six basic Piagetian concepts and presuppositions that provide a framework for his empirical discoveries.

Introduction:
Six Basic Piagetian Concepts

CONSERVATION

"Always changing, always the same" is an expression which nicely captures the spirit of Piaget's notion of conservation. The child, to an even greater extent than the adult, is daily confronted with change. As he grows, and as his world expands beyond the home to school and community, the child repeatedly encounters new experiences and new challenges to his intellectual innocence. He is, moreover, himself a growing being so that he is progressively viewing the world from new heights and with increased sensitivity and acuity.

The ability and zest for coping with change rests, however, upon a foundation of stability. The faded, tattered blankets and dolls so cherished by children are but one manifestation of the need for constancy or conservation amidst a world in transition. And, more generally, it is the secure person who can most tolerate change while the insecure person shrinks back from new experience. Personal security in turn is based upon the assurance that something—and for the child this something is parental love and acceptance—will remain constant. A child in the presence of his parents will undertake adventures he would never contemplate in their absence.

What holds true on the level of personality holds equally true in the intellectual realm. The child's intellectual curiosity, his eagerness for new concepts and knowledge, is directly proportional to his awareness of constancies in the physical world. To discover such constancies the child must, however, learn to distinguish between reality and appearance, between how things look and how they really are. This is necessary because the child is confronted at every turn with apparent alterations which mask an underlying permanence. Such masks prevail on both the physical and social planes of reality. Whether the child is looking at a spoon that appears bent in water or is listening to a hostess pleading for him to stay when she really wishes him to go, he must distinguish between how things look and how they really are if he is to effectively adapt to his world.

How the child comes to distinguish between appearance and reality, the permanence within apparent change, is the issue which Piaget has attacked in his studies of conservation. In these studies he has explored the child's progressive solutions to problems, such as the numerical equivalence of six pennies in a pile and six pennies in a row, and the quantitative equivalence of substances in different forms, such as a ball and a sausage of clay. On the basis of these and a host of other researches, Piaget has evolved a general theory of intellectual growth. The essence of the theory can be simply stated: the child discovers conservation—permanence across apparent change—with the aid of reason. It is by reasoning about his experience that the child is able to overcome illusions and discover how things really are.

The simplicity of this conclusion should not detract from its significance or from its radical opposition to prevalent views about the growth of intelligence. Piaget is arguing that knowledge about reality is not attributable entirely to experience (the action of things upon us) but also to reason (our mental actions upon things). The permanence behind apparent change is therefore not thrust upon us from without, like the wail of a siren or the flash of lightning, but rather arises from within by the force of our own logic. Said differently, the reality behind appearance is never perceived by our senses; on the contrary, it is *conceived* by our intelligence.

The implications of this view for education are far-reaching. It is probably fair to say that the teaching of concepts is at the very heart of the educational enterprise. But education has most often focused upon the static aspect of concepts and has ignored their dynamic features. It is easy, for example, to teach a child that a Winesap, Pippin, and Golden Delicious are all "apples." But when is an apple no longer an apple? Across what transformations does it remain an apple and as a result of what transformations is it no longer a member of that class? Is it still an apple when peeled and quartered, when painted blue, or when made into applesauce? Such dynamic questions may seem trivial but are often of much more consequence to the child than is the static labeling of objects into one class or another. Yet the dynamic features of concepts are for the most part bypassed in the classroom. This is understandable. *The static features of concepts can be pointed to, while the dynamic features can only be reasoned about.*

We can help the child deal with the transformational character of his world both by providing the relevant forms of activity— allowing him to perform transformations of various kinds—and by engaging him with questions about states and transformations. By directing the child's actions and thought toward the transformations which alter things or leave them invariant, we can help him discover the constancies amidst his onrushing world. It is the child, however, who must discover conservations; we at best serve as guides who make the discoveries more possible. By abetting the child's discovery of conservations, we help him establish the intellectual security which is the necessary starting point for seeking out fresh encounters with the environment. The more the child

becomes aware of the truth inherent in the saying, "always changing, always the same," the more he will look upon new experience
as a challenge to his intelligence rather than a threat to his
existence.

ASSIMILATION AND ACCOMMODATION

In Piagetian terms, assimilation and accommodation are the invariant *modes* of knowing that occur at all age levels and at all
levels of mental development. Assimilation, the basic mode of
knowing, transforms incoming information so that it can fit into
existing forms of knowledge. For example, when a child has attained a concept of dog, he can then label as "dog" animals he has
never seen before, but which can be fit (assimilated) into his concept of dog. At a higher level, adults often read newspaper col-
umnists and listen to political broadcasters who reflect their own
opinions. Material consistent with one's own point of view is
easily assimilated.

In many ways, the accommodative mode of knowing reflects a
failure of assimilation. Suppose the child who has a concept of a
dog as a "four legged animal who barks" meets a Basenje (an
African dog that rarely barks). He will not be able to assimilate
this animal to his existing concept. Indeed, when one child first
encountered a Basenje, he said, "Some dogs go woof woof, some
dogs go bow wow, but this dog doesn't say anything at all." This
remark reflects the accommodative mode of knowing in that it
shows the child changing his concept of dog to include some that
"don't say anything at all."

EQUILIBRATION

Equilibration can be regarded as a higher order regulatory process
that governs the relationship between assimilation and accommo-

dation. In the example above, we actually see assimilation, accommodation, and equilibration in action. When the child says, "Some dogs say woof woof and some say bow wow," he is reflecting his tendency to assimilate dogs according to these criteria. When he says, "But this dog doesn't say anything at all," he shows accommodation to a new fact as well as a new higher level of assimilation because he still calls the animal a "dog." Equilibration, then, leads to expanded forms of thought and broader ranges of assimilation. It thus insures that new accommodations become integrated within existing forms of thinking.

Perhaps a different developmental example of assimilation, accommodation, and equilibration will help to make these concepts concrete. A child of four was shown Piaget's liquid conservation problem. Two glasses of equal size filled to the same level with orange juice were on the table. The child agreed that there was the same amount of orange juice to drink in each glass. When the juice in one glass was poured into a tall narrow glass and the child was asked whether there was as much juice in the tall, narrow glass as in the low, wide one he replied, "No, I have more because I want more." In this case he ignored the perceptual cues and his previous experience and assimilated the information according to an affective concept to the effect that "More is what I want it to be."

When at age five the child saw the same experiment, he reacted in a very different way. Confronted with the orange juice in the tall narrow container and in the low glass, he responded to the perceptual cues. He first said there was more in the low glass "because it is wider" and then he said there was more in the tall glass "because it is higher." Now he was responding in the accommodative mode and was forming a new, perceptual concept of "more" to the effect that "more is what it seems or appears to be."

At the age of six he saw the same experiment again. This time he said that both the low glass and the taller container had the same amount to drink. When asked why that was so he replied, "Because you didn't add any or take any away, it looks like there is more in the tall glass but there really isn't." At this stage his affective concept of more as "what I want it to be" and his perceptual concept of more as "what it seems to be" were subordinated to a higher level concept of more as "what I know (reason) it to be." This new, higher order concept of "more" made it possible for him to assimilate both the perceptual and affective concepts of "more" he had held before as well as to recognize that the rational "more" was most appropriate and adaptive.

It should be said that equilibration can be looked at as the dynamic, motivating force which brings about the resolution between assimilative and accommodative concepts and which makes new higher order assimilations possible. These newer, higher order assimilations will not always work, however, so that new accommodations and equilibrations will again be necessary. Mental growth can thus be seen as a progressive series of attempted assimilations, necessary accommodations, and new equilibrated assimilations at a higher level.

COGNITIVE STRUCTURES

The phrase cognitive structure is used in many different ways within Piagetian theory. Basically it refers to the mental organizations or abilities possessed by the child. Thus when Piaget talks about a child as being at the "concrete operational level" he is saying that the child has a unique set of mental abilities that distinguish him from younger children who do not yet possess them. The nature and content of these abilities is described in more detail in later chapters. Assimilation and accommodation operate through and with cognitive structures and can be considered their motive power.

An understanding of cognitive structure at different age levels can be a very powerful analytic tool in child rearing and education. At any given level of development it is the cognitive structures available to the child that determine what he can and cannot assimilate at that stage. An ability to diagnose cognitive structure is thus an asset when one is trying to instruct children in academic tool skills or in the rudiments of interpersonal graces. The ability to diagnose these structures is not acquired automatically, however, and is only attained after the expenditure of considerable time and effort. Once attained, this ability is invaluable in working with children.

To learn to diagnose cognitive structure one should first be familiar with the stages of development as outlined by Piaget and elaborated in later chapters in the book. Then, armed with these basic ideas, one has to observe children, lots of children, from a particular point of view. The point of view is that the child's cognitive structures will reveal themselves in any and all of his productions, his language, his play, his art productions and the way he approaches his learning tasks. In a sense, cognitive structures reveal themselves in the child's productions, in much the same way that an artist's style reveals itself in his creations. And if one really gets to know a particular artist one can recognize his work no matter what form it takes. Likewise, if one really knows say, pre-operational children, then one can always identify their productions whether they appear in language, art, or play.

Such insights are valuable in at least two ways. For one thing, they provide standards or guides according to which one can gauge the intellectual level of a wide variety of curriculum materials and their appropriateness for children at a given age. And, second, they allow one to determine where particular children are, cognitively with respect to their peers. Ability to diagnose cognitive structures is, then, beneficial to the selection of curriculum materials and to the individualization of instruction.

MENTAL OPERATIONS

Generally speaking, mental operations are the tools of thinking. They are, in effect, cognitive structures in action, that is, applied to real world problems. Whenever a child reasons he is, in effect, operating upon aspects of reality, language, or mental contents. Although infants have implicit reasoning abilities and can make intuitive deductions, they cannot reason with symbols, which is the evidence of mental operations proper. That is to say, in everyday practice it has become customary to reserve the term "operations" and "operativity" for the mental abilities of the school-age child.

SCHEMA

For Piaget a schema is a particular mental structure that is capable of generalization and transfer. Schemas occur at many different levels of abstraction. An early schema is that of the permanent object, which allows the child to respond to objects not present to his senses. Later, the child attains the schema of a class of objects which allows him to group objects within the class and to see the relation of the members of the class to other classes. In many ways Piaget's schema is like the traditional notion of the concept except that it is tied to mental operations and cognitive structures rather than to perceptual discriminations.

This chapter is meant as an informal introduction to Piaget, the man, as well as to his major discoveries about the development of children's thinking. Throughout the piece I allude to the similarities and differences between the work of Piaget and Freud. Despite the many parallels between these two giants of twentieth-century psychology, a fundamental difference should be kept in mind. Freud was primarily concerned with how thought, fantasies, and impulses become translated into action Piaget, in contrast, has been most concerned with how the child's actions become translated into thought.

1

Jean Piaget

In February, 1967, Jean Piaget, the Swiss psychologist, arrived at Clark University in Worcester, Massachusetts, to deliver the Heinz Werner Memorial Lectures. The lectures were to be given in the evening, and before the first one a small dinner party was arranged in honor of Piaget which was attended by colleagues, former students, and friends. I was invited to the dinner because of my long advocacy of Piaget's work and because I spent a year (1964–65) at his Institute of Educational Science in Geneva. Piaget had changed very little since I had last seen him, but he did appear tired and mildly apprehensive.

Although Piaget has lectured all over the world, this particular occasion had special significance. Almost sixty years before, in 1909, another famous European, Sigmund Freud, also lectured at Clark. Piaget was certainly aware of the historical parallel. He was, moreover, going to speak to a huge American audience in French and, despite the offices of his remarkable translator, Eleanor Duckworth, he must have had some reservations about how it would go.

His apprehension was apparent during the dinner. For one who is usually a lively and charming dinner companion, he was surprisingly quiet and unresponsive. About half way through the meal there was a small disturbance. The room in which the dinner was held was at a garden level and two boys of seven or eight suddenly appeared at the windows and began tapping at them. The inclination of most of us, I think, was to shoo them away. Before we had a chance to do that, however, Piaget had turned to face the children. He smiled up at them, hunched his shoulders and gave them a slight wave of his hand. They hunched their shoulders and smiled in return, gave a slight wave, and disappeared. After a moment, Piaget turned back to the table and began telling stories and entering into animated conversation.

Although I am sure his lecture would have been a success in any case, and that the standing ovation he received would have occurred without the little incident, I nonetheless like to think that the encounter with the boys did much to restore his vigor and good humor.

It is Piaget's genius for empathy with children, together with true intellectual genius, that has caused him to be regarded as the outstanding child psychologist in the world today, destined to stand beside Freud with respect to his contributions to psychology, education, and related disciplines. Just as Freud's discoveries of unconscious motivation, infantile sexuality, and the stages of psychosexual growth changed our ways of thinking about human personality, so Piaget's discoveries of children's implicit philosophies or systems of belief, the construction of reality by the infant, and the stages of mental development have altered our ways of thinking about human intelligence.

The man behind these discoveries is an arresting figure. He is tall and somewhat portly, and his stooped walk, bulky suits, and crown of long white hair give him the appearance of a thrice-magnified Einstein. His personal trademarks are his meerschaum pipes (now burned deep amber), his navy blue beret, and his bicycle.

Meeting Piaget is a memorable experience. Although he has an abundance of Old-World charm and graciousness, he seems to emanate an aura of intellectual presence not unlike the aura of personality presence conveyed by a great actor. While as a psychologist I am unable to explain how this sense of presence is communicated, I am nevertheless convinced that everyone who meets Piaget experiences it. In conversation, for example, he was able to detect, in what was implicit in my remarks, a significance and depth of which I was not consciously aware. Evidently one characteristic of genius is to search for relevance in the apparently commonplace and frivolous.

Piaget's is a superbly disciplined life. He arises early each morning sometimes as early as 4 A.M., and writes four or more publishable pages. Later in the morning he may teach classes and attend meetings. His afternoons include long walks during which he thinks about the problems he is currently confronting. He says, "I always like to think on a problem before reading about it." In the evenings, he reads and retires early. Even on his international trips, Piaget keeps to this schedule.

Each summer, as soon as classes are over, Piaget gathers up the research findings that have been collected by his assistants during the year and departs for the Alps, where he takes up solitary residence in a room in an abandoned farmhouse. The whereabouts of this retreat is closely guarded; only Piaget's family, his long-time colleague Bärbel Inhelder, and a trusted secretary know where he is. During the summer Piaget walks, meditates, and writes. Then, when the leaves begin to turn, he descends from the mountains with the several books and articles he has written on his "vacation."

Although Piaget, now in his seventy-third year, has been carrying his works down from the mountains for almost fifty summers (he has published more than thirty books and hundreds of articles), it is only within the past decade that his writings have come to be fully appreciated in America. Until fairly recently only a few of his books had been translated into English. Now the ideas that Piaget has been advocating for more than thirty years are regarded as exceedingly innovative and even as avant-garde.

His work falls into three more or less distinct periods, covering an enormous amount of psychological territory and developing a multitude of insights. During the first period (roughly 1922–29), Piaget explored the extent and depth of children's spontaneous ideas about the physical world and about their own mental processes. He happened upon this line of inquiry while working in Alfred Binet's laboratory school in Paris where he arrived, still seeking a direction for his talents, a year after receiving his doctorate in biological science at the University of Lausanne. It was in the course of some routine intelligence testing that Piaget became interested in what lay behind children's answers, correct and, particularly, incorrect. To clarify the origins of these answers he began to interview the children in the open-ended manner he had learned while serving a brief internship at Bleuler's psychiatric clinic in Zurich. The semiclinical interview procedure, aimed at revealing the processes by which a child arrives at a particular reply to a test question, has become a mark of Piagetian research investigation.

What Piaget found with this method of inquiry was that children not only reasoned differently from adults but also that they had quite different world views, literally different philosophies. This led Piaget to attend to those childish remarks and questions which most adults find amusing or nonsensical. Just as Freud found in seemingly accidental slips of the tongue and pen evidence for unconscious motivations, so Piaget found the "cute" sayings of children evidence for the existence of ideas quite foreign to the adult mind.

Piaget had read in the recollections of a deaf mute (recorded by William James) that as a child he had regarded the sun and moon as gods and believed they followed him about. Piaget sought to verify this recollection by interviewing children on the subject, and he found that many youngsters do believe that the sun and moon follow them when they are out for a walk. Similar remarks Piaget either overheard or was told about led to a large number of investigations which revealed, among many similar findings, that young children believe that anything which moves is alive, that the names of objects reside in the objects themselves and that dreams come in through the window at night.

Such beliefs, Piaget pointed out in an early article entitled "Children's Philosophies," are not unrelated to but rather derive from an implicit animism and artificialism with many parallels to primitive and Greek philosophies. In the child's view, objects such as stones and clouds are imbued with motives, intentions, and feelings, while mental events such as dreams and thoughts are endowed with corporality and force. Children also believe that everything has a purpose and that everything in the world is made by and for man. The child's animism and artificialism help to explain his famous and often unanswerable "why" questions. It is because children believe that everything has a purpose that they ask, "Why is grass green?" and "Why do the stars shine?" The parent who attempts to answer such questions with a physical explanation has missed the point. (My 5-year-old son asked me why we have snow and answered his own question by saying, "It is for children to play in.")

In addition to disclosing the existence of children's philosophies during this first period, Piaget also found the clue to the egocentrism of childhood. In observing young children at play at the Maison des Petits, the modified Montessori school associated with the Institute of Educational Science in Geneva, Piaget noted a peculiar lack of social orientation which was also present in their conversation and in their approaches to certain intellectual tasks. A child would make up a new word ("stocks" for socks and stockings) and just assume that everyone knew what he was talking about as if this were the conventional name for the objects he had in mind. Likewise, Piaget noted that when two nursery school children were at play they often spoke at rather than to one another and were frequently chattering on about two quite different and unrelated topics. Piaget observed, moreover, that when he stood a child of 5 years opposite him, the child who could tell his own right and left nevertheless insisted that Piaget's right and left hands were directly opposite his own.

In Piaget's view, all of these types of behavior can be explained by the young child's inability to put himself in another person's position and to take that person's point of view. Unlike the egocentric adult, who can take another person's point of view but does not, the egocentric child does not take another person's viewpoint because he cannot. This conception of childish egocentrism has produced a fundamental alteration in our evaluation of the pre-school child's behavior. We now appreciate that it is intellectual immaturity and not moral perversity which makes, for example, a young child continue to pester his mother after she has told him she has a headache and wishes to be left alone. The pre-school child is simply unable to put himself in his mother's position and see things from her point of view.

The second period of Piaget's investigations began when in 1929, he sought to trace the origins of the child's spontaneous mental growth to the behavior of infants; in this case, his own three children, Jacqueline, Lucienne, and Laurent. Piaget kept very detailed records of their behavior and of their performance on a series of ingenious tasks which he invented and presented to them. The books resulting from these investigations, "The Origins of Intelligence in Children," "Play, Dreams and Imitation in Children" and "The Construction of Reality in the Child" are now generally regarded as classics in the field and have been among the major forces behind the scurry of research activity in the area of infant behavior now current both in America and abroad. The publication of these books in the middle and late nineteen thirties marked the end of the second phase of Piaget's work.

Some of the most telling observations Piaget made during this period had to do with what he called the *conservation of the object* (using the word conservation to convey the idea of permanence). To the older child and to the adult, the existence of objects and persons who are not immediately present is taken as self-evident. The child at school knows that while he is working at his desk his mother is simultaneously at home and his father is at work. This is not the case for the young infant playing in his crib, for whom out of sight is literally out of mind. Piaget observed that when an infant 4 or 5 months old is playing with a toy which subsequently rolls out of sight (behind another toy) but is still within reach, the infant ceases to look for it. The infant behaves as if the toy had not only disappeared but as if it had gone entirely out of existence.

This helps to explain the pleasure infants take in the game of peek-a-boo. If the infant believed that the object existed when it was not seen, he would not be surprised and delighted at its re-emergence and there would be no point to the game. It is only during the second year of life, when children begin to represent objects mentally, that they seek after toys that have disappeared from view. Only then do they attribute an independent existence to objects which are not present to their senses.

The third and major phase of Piaget's endeavors began about 1940 and continues until the present day. During this period Piaget has studied the development in children and adolescents of those mental abilities which gradually enable the child to construct a world-view which is in conformance with reality as seen by adults. He has, at the same time, been concerned with how children acquire the adult versions of various concepts such as number, quantity, and speed. Piaget and his colleagues have amassed and processed in the last twenty-eight years an astounding amount of information about the thinking of children and adolescents which is only now beginning to be used by psychologists and educators.

Two discoveries made during this last period are of particular importance both because they were so unexpected and because of their relevance to education. It is perhaps fair to say that education tends to focus upon the static aspects of reality rather than upon its dynamic transformations. The child is taught how and what things are but not the conditions under which they change or remain the same. And yet the child is constantly confronted with change and alteration. His view of the world alters as he grows in height and perceptual acuity. And the world changes. Seasons come and go, trees gain and lose their foliage, snow falls and melts. People change, too. They may change over brief time periods in mood and over long periods in height, hair coloration, or fullness. The child receives a static formal education while living in a world in transition.

Piaget's investigations since 1940 have focused upon how the child copes with change, how he comes to distinguish between the permanent and the transient and between the appearance and the reality. An incident that probably played a part in initiating this line of investigation occurred during Piaget's short-lived flirtation with the automobile, he took his son for a drive and Laurent asked the name of the mountain they were passing. The mountain was the Salève, the crocodile-shaped mass that dominates the city of Geneva. Laurent was in fact familiar with the mountain and its name because he could see it from his garden, although from a different perspective. Laurent's question brought home to Piaget the fact that a child had difficulty in dealing with the results of transformations whether they are brought about by an alteration in the object itself or by the child's movement with respect to the object.

The methods Piaget used to study how the child comes to deal with transformations are surprisingly simple and can be used by any interested parent or teacher. These methods all have to do with testing the child's abilities to discover that a quantity remains the same across a change in its appearance. In other words, that the quantity is conserved.

To give just one illustration from among hundreds, a child is shown two identical drinking glasses filled equally full with orangeade and he is asked to say whether there is the "same to drink" in the two glasses. After the child says that this is the case, the orangeade from one glass is poured into another which is taller and thinner so that the orangeade now reaches a higher level. Then the child is asked to say whether there is the same amount to drink in the two differently shaped glasses. Before the age of 6 or 7, most children say that the tall, narrow glass has more orangeade. The young child cannot deal with the transformation and bases his judgment on the static features of the orangeade, namely the levels.

How does the older child arrive at the notion that the amount of orangeade in the two differently shaped glasses is the same? The answer, according to Piaget, is that he discovers the equality with the aid of reason. If the child judges only on the basis of appearances he cannot solve the problem. When he compares the two glasses with respect to width he must conclude that the wide glass has more while if he compares them with respect to the level of the orangeade he must conclude that the tall glass has more. There is then no way, on the basis of appearance, that he can solve the problem. If, on the other hand, the child reasons that there was the same in the two glasses before and that nothing was added or taken away during the pouring, he concludes that both glasses still have the same drink although this does not appear to be true.

On the basis of this and many similar findings, Piaget argues that much of our knowledge about reality comes to us not from without like the peal of a bell but rather from within by the force of our own logic.

It is hard to overemphasize the importance of this fact, because it is so often forgotten, particularly in education. To those who are not philosophically inclined, it appears that our knowledge of things comes about rather directly as if our mind simply copied the forms, colors, and textures of things. From this point of view the mind acts as a sort of mirror which is limited to reflecting the reality which is presented to it. As Piaget's research has demonstrated, however, the mind operates not as a passive mirror but rather as an active artist.

The portrait painter does not merely copy what he sees, he interprets his subject. Before even commencing the portrait, the artist learns a great deal about the individual subject and does not limit himself to studying the face alone. Into the portrait goes not only what the artist sees but also what he knows about his subject. A good portrait is larger than life because it carries much more information than could ever be conveyed by a mirror image.

In forming his spontaneous conception of the world, therefore, the child does more than reflect what is presented to his senses. His image of reality is in fact a portrait or reconstruction of the world and not a simple copy of it. It is only by reasoning about the information which the child receives from the external world that he is able to overcome the transient nature of sense experience and arrive at that awareness of permanence within apparent change that is the mark of adult thought. The importance of reason in the child's spontaneous construction of his world is thus one of the major discoveries of Piaget's third period.

The second major discovery of this time has to do with the nature of the elementary school child's reasoning ability. Long before there was anything like a discipline of child psychology, the age of 6 to 7 was recognized as the age of reason. It was also assumed, however, that once the child attained the age of reason, there was no longer any substantial differences between his reasoning abilities and those of adolescents and adults. What Piaget discovered is that this is not the case. While the elementary school child is indeed able to reason, his reasoning ability is limited in a very important respect—he can reason about things but not about verbal propositions.

If a child of 8 or 9 is shown a series of three blocks, A, B, C, which differ in size, then he can tell by looking at them, and without comparing them directly, that if A is greater than B and B greater than C, then A is greater than C. When the same child is given this problem, "Helen is taller than Mary and Mary is taller than Jane, who is the tallest of the three?" the result is quite different. He cannot solve it despite the fact that it repeats in words the problem with the blocks. Adolescents and adults, however, encounter no difficulty with this problem because they can reason about verbal propositions as well as about things.

This discovery that children think differently from adults even after attaining the age of reason has educational implications which are only now beginning to be applied. Robert Karplus, the physicist who heads the Science Curriculum Improvement Study at Berkeley has pointed out that most teachers use verbal propositions in teaching elementary school children. At least some of their instruction is thus destined to go over the heads of their pupils. Karplus and his co-workers are now attempting to train teachers to instruct children at a verbal level which is appropriate to their level of mental ability.

An example of the effects of the failure to take into account the difference between the reasoning abilities of children and adults comes from the New Math experiment. In building materials for the New Math, it was hoped that the construction of a new language would facilitate instruction of set concepts. This new language has been less than successful and the originators of the New Math are currently attempting to devise a physical model to convey the New Math concepts. It is likely that the new language created to teach the set concepts failed because it was geared to the logic of adults rather than to the reasoning of children. Attention to the research on children's thinking carried out during Piaget's third period might have helped to avoid some of the difficulties of the "New Math" program.

In the course of these many years of research into children's thinking, Piaget has elaborated a general theory of intellectual development which, in its scope and comprehensiveness, rivals Freud's theory of personality development. Piaget proposes that intelligence—adaptive thinking and action—develops in a sequence of stages related to age. Each stage sees the elaboration of new mental abilities which set the limits and determine the character of what can be learned during that period. (Piaget finds incomprehensible Harvard psychologist Jerome Bruner's famous hypothesis to the effect that "any subject can be taught effectively in some intellectually honest form to any child at any stage of development.") Although Piaget believes that the order in which the stages appear holds true for all children, he also believes that the ages at which the stages evolved will depend upon the native endowment of the child and upon the quality of the physical and social environment in which he is reared. In a very real sense, then, Piaget's is both a nature and a nurture theory.

The first stage in the development of intelligence (usually 0–2 years) Piaget calls the sensory-motor period and it is concerned with the evolution of those abilities necessary to construct and reconstruct objects. To illustrate, Piaget observed that when he held a cigarette case in front of his daughter Jacqueline (who was 8 months old at the time) and then dropped it, she did not follow the trajectory of the case but continued looking at his hand; she was not able to reconstruct the path of the object which she had seen dropped in front of her.

Toward the end of this period, however, Jacqueline was even able to reconstruct the position of objects which had undergone hidden displacement. When she was 19 months old, Piaget placed a coin in his hand and then placed his hand under a coverlet where he dropped the coin before removing his hand. Jacqueline first looked in his hand and then immediately lifted the coverlet and found the coin. This reconstruction was accomplished with the aid of an elementary form of reasoning. The coin was in the hand, the hand was under the coverlet, the coin was not in the hand so the coin is under the coverlet. Such reasoning, it must be said, is accomplished without the aid of language and by means of mental images.

The second stage (usually 2–7 years), which Piaget calls the pre-operational stage, bears witness to the elaboration of the symbolic function, those abilities which have to do with representing things. The presence of these new abilities is shown by the gradual acquisition of language, the first indications of dreams and night terrors, the advent of symbolic play (two sticks at right angles are an airplane) and the first attempts at drawing and graphic representation.

At the beginning of this stage the child tends to identify words and symbols with the objects they are intended to represent. He is upset if someone tramps on a stone which he has designated as a turtle. And he believes that names are as much a part of objects as their color and form. By the end of this period the child can clearly distinguish between words and symbols and what they represent. He now recognizes that names are arbitrary designations. The child's discovery of the arbitrariness of names is often manifested in the "name calling" so prevalent during the early school years.

At the next stage (usually 7–11 years) the child acquires what Piaget calls concrete operations, internalized actions that permit the child to do "in his head" what before he would have had to accomplish through real actions. Concrete operations enable the child to think about things. To illustrate, in one study Piaget presented 5-, 6-, and 7-year-old children with six sticks in a row and asked them to take the same number of sticks from a pile on the table. The young children solved the problem by placing their sticks beneath the sample and matching the sticks one by one. The older children merely picked up the six sticks and held them in their hands. The older children had counted the sticks mentally and hence felt no need to actually match them with the sticks in the row. It should be said that even the youngest children were able to count to six, so that this was not a factor in their performance.

Concrete operations also enable children to deal with the relations among classes of things. In another study Piaget presented 5-, 6-, and 7-year-old children with a box containing twenty white and seven brown wooden beads. Each child was first asked if there were more white or more brown beads and all were able to say that there were more white than brown beads. Then Piaget asked, "Are there more white or more wooden beads?" The young children could not fathom the question and replied that "there are more white than brown beads." For such children classes are not regarded as abstractions but are thought of as concrete places. (I once asked a pre-operational child if he could be a Protestant and an American at the same time to which he replied, "No," and then as an afterthought, "only if you move.")

When a child thought of a bead in the white "place" he could not think of it as being in the wooden "place" since objects cannot be in two places at once. He could only compare the white with the brown "places." The older children, who had attained concrete operations, encountered no difficulty with the task and readily replied that "there are more wooden than white beads because all of the beads are wooden and only some are white." By the end of the concrete operational period, children are remarkably adept at doing thought problems and at combining and dividing class concepts.

During the last stage (usually 12–15 years) there gradually emerge what Piaget calls formal operations and which, in effect, permit adolescents to think about their thoughts, to construct ideals and to reason realistically about the future. Formal operations also enable young people to reason about contrary-to-fact propositions. If, for example, a child is asked to assume that coal is white, he is likely to reply, "But coal is black," whereas the adolescent can accept the contrary-to-fact assumption and reason from it.

Formal operational thought also makes possible the understanding of metaphor. It is for this reason that political and other satirical cartoons are not understood until adolescence. The child's inability to understand metaphor helps to explain why books such as "Alice in Wonderland" and "Gulliver's Travels" are enjoyed at different levels during childhood than in adolescence and adulthood, when their social significance can be understood.

No new mental systems emerge after the formal operations, which are the common coin of adult thought. After adolescence, mental growth takes the form—it is hoped—of a gradual increase in depth of understanding.

This summary of Piaget's theory of intellectual development would not be complete without some words about his position with respect to language and thought. Piaget regards thought and language as different but closely related systems. Language, to a much greater extent than thought, is determined by particular forms of environmental stimulation. Inner-city Negro children, who tend to be retarded in language development, are much less retarded with respect to the ages at which they attain concrete operations. Indeed, not only inner-city children but children in bush Africa, Hong Kong, and Appalachia all attain concrete operations at about the same ages as middle-class children in Geneva and Boston.

Likewise, attempts to teach children concrete operations have been almost uniformly unsuccessful. This does not mean that these operations are independent of the environment but only that their development takes time and can be nourished by a much wider variety of environmental nutriments than is true for the growth of language, which is dependent upon much more specific forms of stimulation.

Language is, then, deceptive as an index to thought. Teachers of middle-class children are often misled, by the verbal facility of these youngsters, into believing that they understand more than they do. At the other end, the teachers of inner-city children are often fooled by the language handicaps of these children into thinking that they have much lower mental ability than they actually possess. It is appropriate, therefore, that pre-school programs for the disadvantaged should focus upon training these children in language and perception rather than upon trying to teach them concrete operations.

The impact which Piagetian discoveries and conceptions is having upon education and child psychology has come as something of a shock to a good many educators and psychologists. In contrast to psychological research in America, which relies heavily upon statistics, electronics, and computers, Piaget's studies of children's thinking seem hardly a step beyond the pre-scientific baby biographies kept by such men as Charles Darwin and Bronson Alcott. Indeed, in many of Piaget's research papers he supports his conclusions simply with illustrative examples of how children at different age levels respond to his tasks. Many of Piaget's critics have focused upon his apparently casual methodology and have argued that while Piaget has arrived at some original ideas about children's thinking, his research lacks scientific rigor.

Other critics have taken somewhat the opposite position. Jerome Bruner, who has done so much to bring Piaget to the attention of American social scientists, acknowledges the fruitfulness of Piaget's methods, modifications of which he has employed in his own investigations. But he argues against Piaget's theoretical interpretations. Bruner believes that Piaget has "missed the heart" of the problem of change and permanence or conservation in children's thinking. In the case of the orangeade poured into a different-sized container, Bruner argues that it is not reason, or mental operations, but some "internalized verbal formula that shields him (the child) from the overpowering appearance of the visual display." Bruner believes that the syntactical rules of language rather than logic can account for the child's discovery that a quantity remains unchanged despite alterations in its appearance.

Piaget is willing to answer his critics but only when he believes that the criticism is responsible and informed. Criticism of his methods, for instance, brings the response that they are not as casual as they seem. Before they set out collecting data, his students are given a year of training in the art of interviewing children. They learn to ask questions without suggesting the answers and to test, by counter-suggestion, the strength of the child's conviction. Many of Piaget's studies have now been repeated with more rigorous procedures by other investigators all over the world and the results have been remarkably consistent with Piaget's findings. Attempts are currently under way to build a new intelligence scale on the basis of the Piaget tests, many of which are already in widespread use as evaluative procedures in education.

When it comes to criticisms of his theoretical views, Piaget is remarkably open. He frequently invites scholars who are in genuine disagreement with him to come to Geneva for a year so that the differences can be discussed and studied in depth. He has no desire to form a cult and says, in fact, "To the extent that there are Piagetians, to that extent have I failed." Piaget's lack of dogmatism is illustrated in his response to Bruner.

Bruner does say that I "missed the heart" of the conservation problem, a problem I have been working on for the last 30 years. He is right, of course, but that does not mean that he himself has understood it in a much shorter time. . . . Adults, just like children, need time to reach the right ideas . . . . This is the great mystery of development, which is irreducible to an accumulation of isolated learning acquisitions. Even psychology cannot be learned or constructed in a short time.

Despite his disclaimer, Piaget has offered a comprehensive theory of how the child arrives at conservation and this theory has received much research support.

Piaget would probably agree with those who are critical about premature applications of his work to education. He finds particularly disturbing the efforts by some American educators to accelerate children intellectually. When he was giving his other 1967 lectures, in New York, he remarked:

If we accept the fact that there are stages of development, another question arises which I call "the American question," and I am asked it every time I come here. If there are stages that children reach at given norms of ages can we accelerate the stages? Do we have to go through each one of these stages, or can't we speed it up a bit? Well, surely, the answer is yes . . . but how far can we speed them up? . . . I have a hypothesis which I am so far incapable of proving: probably the organization of operations has an optimal time. . . . For example, we know that it takes 9 to 12 months before babies develop the notion that an object is still there even when a screen is placed in front of it. Now kittens go through the same substages but they do it in three months—so they're six months ahead of the babies. Is this an advantage or isn't it?

We can certainly see our answer in one sense. The kitten is not going to go much further. The child has taken longer, but he is capable of going further so it seems to me that the nine months were not for nothing. . . . It is probably possible to accelerate, but maximal acceleration is not desirable. There seems to be an optimal time. What this optimal time is will surely depend upon each individual and on the subject matter. We still need a great deal of research to know what the optimal time would be.

Despite some premature and erroneous applications of his thinking to education, Piaget has had an over-all effect much more positive than negative. His findings about children's understanding of scientific and mathematical concepts are being used as guidelines for new curricula in these subjects. And his tests are being more and more widely used to evaluate educational outcomes. Perhaps the most significant and widespread positive effect that Piaget has had upon education is in the changed attitudes on the part of teachers who have been exposed to his thinking. After becoming acquainted with Piaget's work, teachers can never again see children in quite the same way as they had before. Once teachers begin to look at children from his perspective they can also appreciate his views with regard to the aims of education. He once said:

> The principal goal of education is to create men who are capable of doing new things, not simply of repeating what other generations have done—men who are creative, inventive and discoverers. The second goal of education is to form minds which can be critical, can verify, and not accept everything they are offered. The great danger today is of slogans, collective opinions, ready-made trends of thought. We have to be able to resist individually, to criticize, to distinguish between what is proven and what is not. So we need pupils who are active, who learn early to find out by themselves, partly by their own spontaneous activity and partly through materials we set up for them; we learn early to tell what is verifiable and what is simply the first idea to come to them.

Piaget's earliest book, entitled "The language and thought of the child,"
was published in 1926 (81). One section of it was devoted to the issue
of children's questions. Piaget pointed out that a knowledge of how
young children think is crucial to understanding and responding to their
queries. The following chapter extends Piaget's discussion and seeks
to provide practical suggestions for teachers and parents who are con-
fronted with the sometimes baffling questions posed by pre-school
children.

2
Children's Questions

"Are they going to shoot God next?" asked a 5-year-old boy when
he heard of the murder of Senator Robert F. Kennedy. Like so
many of us, this youngster was trying to comprehend and give
meaning to a frightening and irrational event. His attempt at
understanding, however, was expressed in the context of his own
limited experience and in a mode characteristic of child thought.
To the young child, God is simply an important person like a
President or Senator and is subject to that same immutable law—
no event without a purpose—which the child believes governs
all phenomena and admits of no accident or chance. In this lad's
view, the shooting of Senator Kennedy must have served some
grand purpose which might be further served by the shooting
of God. His question followed naturally from these premises.

This question, at once knowing and innocent, illustrates the
general problem facing today's parents. Thanks to TV, wide-
ranging travel, and the "information explosion," our children are
increasingly exposed to events and experiences for which they are
emotionally and intellectually unprepared. No less than adults,
children need to give meaning and organization to their experience
but are limited by the intellectual tools at their disposal. Children's

questions reflect their eagerness to cope intellectually with their world but in answering children's questions we need to take into account both this quest for understanding and their unique world view.

As adults, we are often handicapped because we assume that children make the distinctions which to us appear self-evident. We take for granted the distinction between physical and psychological causality, between events determined by natural law and those occasioned by human motivation. Accordingly, we automatically catalogue some questions as demanding a physical explanation (Why does the sun shine? Why does the rain fall?) and others as requiring a psychological explanation (Why did you break that? Why do you tease him?). Children, however, do not discriminate between these different types of causality and often ask about psychological causation in the form of questions which adults are accustomed to answering in physical terms. In responding to children's questions, then, we need to remember that even when a child seems to be inquiring about physical causality he is really interested in the psychological or moral determinants of the event.

The child's earliest questions usually begin around the age of 3, when for the first time he starts to use language to acquire information and not just to express his wants. Many of the earliest questions have to do with the labeling of objects. The child asks, "What is this?" and the parent replies, "A Volkswagen bus," or, "A butterfly." This is what Harvard psychologist Roger Brown has called "the perennial word game." Closely thereafter follow questions which are not so much questions as expressions of annoyance or frustration, such as the familiar "Why do I have to go to bed?" Such questions are perhaps best answered by putting the child's feelings into words and reiterating the rules of the game. "I know you don't want to go to sleep but daytime is for playing and nighttime is for sleeping."

The first fact-seeking as opposed to name-finding questions

usually begin toward the end of the fourth year, the start of the questioning age proper. Sometimes, when children discover that they can ask about more than names, they are dazzled by the possibility of knowing and begin asking questions at a breathless pace: "What makes you grow up? What makes you stop growing? Do old people grow down and become babies again? What are clouds made of? Where is the blimp going? Why do you put those things on your face? Why do you put those things in your hair? How come mommies have 'bumps' and daddies don't?"

Such a barrage reflects the child's discovery that there is so much to know and his wonder at so much mystery in the world. As one youngster expressed it, "Mommy, why is there such a lot of things in the world if no one knows all these things?" Here the child expresses not only his awe of all there is to be known in the world but also his belief that everything exists for the purpose of being labeled and understood.

In this connection, it is well to remember that to young children parents are all-wise, all-knowing, and all-powerful. The child assumes that every question can be answered and that parents have all the answers. The discovery that parents are fallible can sometimes come as a shock to the child, as it did to Edmund Gosse, the literary critic (48):

My mother always deferred to my father and in his absence spoke to me as if he were all-wise. I confused him in some sense with God; at all events I believed that my father knew everything and saw everything. One morning in my sixth year, my mother and I were alone in the morning room, when my father came in and announced some fact to us. I was standing on the rug gazing at him, and when he made his statement I remember turning quickly in embarrassment and looking into the fire. The shock to me was that of a thunderbolt, for what my father had said was not true. . . . Here was the appalling discovery, never suspected before, that my father was not as God, and did not know everything. The shock was not caused by my suspicion that he was not telling the truth as it appeared to him but the awful proof that he was not, as I had supposed, omniscient.

One of the earliest themes in a child's questioning has to do with origins. The beginnings of things, particularly of living things, are a great mystery to children, just as they were to the Greek philosophers. The origin of babies is of particular interest to children, especially to those who have seen their mothers pregnant. Typical of such questions is that of the young girl who asked, "Who was the mother when everybody was a baby?" And of the boy who, starting from his own experience in which only wives had babies, inquired: "Why does a lady have to be married to have a baby?" Perhaps most common of all is, "How does the baby get into mommy's stomach?"

In answering such questions, there is little merit in giving the child all the physiological details because they are almost certain to be misunderstood. A case in point is the child who, when told that while in his mother's stomach he was fed through the umbilical cord asked, "Then how come you like liver and I don't?" Parents, under the impression that they are being modern, may provide the child with anatomical and physiological facts that merely confuse rather than further the child's understanding.

In the case of questions about origins we perhaps need to take exception to the general rule of providing the child with factually correct information that is appropriate to his level of understanding. It does no harm, it seems to me, if the child believes that God created some men and women full-grown as an answer to the question of where babies come from when everyone was a baby. Nor does it do any irreparable damage if the child is not discouraged from believing that it is God who plants the seed in mommy's stomach (an answer which many children arrive at spontaneously). Such answers are in conformance with the child's belief that everything in the world—trees, lakes, rivers—is made by and for man. Reference to God is often preferable to the more explicit details provided by parents whose anxiety and discomfort about such questions often lead them to carry on at such lengths that the child comes to attach a significance to such matters which far exceeds their real importance. If the parent feels uncomfortable about invoking God in answering such questions he can always ask the child what he thinks and the child is likely himself to supply the theological explanation.

Closely related to questions about origins are those which have to do with death and which also begin to appear at about the fourth year. The young child has no notion that life ever ceases and assumes that animals and people live, or at least are conscious, forever. As one child remarked when he heard that his grandfather was to be buried next to his grandmother, "I guess it is so she will know that he is there." The first awareness of death as an end to life and consciousness may come as a shock to the child, who can be terrified by the idea. In such cases it is not unusual for the child to throw himself upon the bed and cry that he does not want to die nor want his parents to die.

In answering a child's questions about death it is perhaps as well to be factual without being explicit. One can say, for example, that "when someone dies we don't see or talk to them again." Or, if a child asks, "Why do we have to die?" one can answer, "To make room for other people, for all the new babies that are being born." Although it is tempting to explain death in physiological terms, in terms of the cessation of life processes, a child has little understanding of these processes and such explanations often serve only to confuse him. The young child is first and foremost concerned with the purpose which death serves and not with its physiological aspects.

Along with the theme of origins and death is another which appears at about the same time and is concerned with living things in general. Such questions as, "Why do leaves fall? Why do dogs walk on four legs? What do bees do?" stem from the child's implicit belief in the purposefulness of everything in the universe. Gifted storytellers have always known this and hence such stories as "How the elephant got its trunk" or "How the giraffe got its long neck." Such stories appeal to children because they answer the real import of their questions.

A general rule in responding to such questions is to begin the reply with a "to" rather than with a "because." In "Little Red Riding Hood," the wolf disguised as grandmother replies to Little Red Riding Hood's exclamations, "My what big eyes you have!" with "Better to see you with"; and "My what big ears you have!" with "Better to hear you with." We can take a leaf from that sly wolf's book and answer in the same way. Most phenomena and events do have a purpose, even if they were not created for that purpose as the child believes. Although it may take a little thought and imagination, the child's questions about nature can be answered in a manner which suits the child's intent and is factually correct. One can say, with intellectual integrity, that leaves fall "to cover the grass and flowers during the winter," and that the giraffe has a long neck "to reach fruit that grows high in the trees."

Toward the end of the question-asking age, ages 5 and 6, children begin to ask questions about the physical world, about amounts, number, space, and time. The animate world is the first to catch the child's attention because it is in motion and engages his curiosity. Once he begins to have some familiarity with the animate world he turns to the inanimate world, to the sun, moon, and stars, and to problems of quantification and classification. Such questions often reflect the transition to the elementary reasoning of the early school years.

Again, the danger here is that of giving the child an explanation which is too advanced for his reasoning abilities. A few years ago, for example, while driving with my son Paul, who was 5 years old at the time, he asked, "If we keep driving will we come to the end of the earth?" I started to reply that the earth was round and that no matter how far one traveled he would never reach the edge. I checked myself, however, realizing that there was no way to convey to a 5-year-old that the earth was round. The roundness of the earth is, or at least was up until the advent of space flight, a non-perceivable fact. It is a logical deduction from certain sorts of evidence such as the disappearance of ships on the horizon or the shape of the earth's shadow on the moon. The young child cannot engage in that sort of reasoning nor accept such proofs.

While groping for an answer, I recalled the reply of a child whom I asked whether it was better to travel by boat or by airplane. She answered, "If you go by water it is better to go by boat, and if you go by air it is better to go by plane." So to Paul I said, "Well, when you come to the end of the land there is water and when you come to the end of the water you arrive at some more land."

The questions of this period are frequently quite difficult to answer because they come from the child's exposure to the space age and the recent innovations in technology. Many of these questions are, however, often more complex than they seem because of what we adults read into them. One child, for example, asked his teacher, "What is the opposite of time?" Being in rapport with her children this teacher replied, "Having no time." She had recognized that, for the child, time is understood functionally with regard to having time to do things. From this point of view, the opposite of time is appropriately, "No time."

Still another teacher was asked "Why is N better than R." When she investigated she found that there were more N's on a worksheet and the child simply assumed that if there were more N's they were therefore better. Knowing this, she replied, "When there are more R's, R's are better and when there are more N's, N's are better." It is well, therefore, when confronted with such posers to explore the context of the question. This will, in turn, frequently provide a clue for providing the child with an answer nicely tuned to the intent of his question.

After the age of 6 or 7, the child's queries continue but become less numerous and increasingly approximate the form of adult questions. The content changes, too, and children begin to ask about historical personages, about distant places, and about the how of things. Such questions reflect the elementary school child's new abilities to deal with historical time and geographical space and to engage in sustained activity devoted to the pursuit of hobbies and playing games with rules.

A child's questions, then, mirror the development of his mind and express his intellectual curiosity and his wonder at the multiplicity of things. It is important that we answer the child's questions rather than dismiss them as a nuisance and a bother. The child's intellectual curiosity is a spark which can be easily smothered by adult derision and indifference. Particularly during those years from 4 to 6, the questioning age proper, when queries come with hailstone rapidity, do we need to attend to the child's remarks. Our aim should be to provide him with answers that are informative to him and intellectually respectable to ourselves. Whether or not we hit exactly the right note in our replies is perhaps less important than what our attempts to answer convey, namely, that we take the child seriously and that we respect his his eagerness to know.

The concept of time is part of the framework within which all experiences are fit. Young children, however, do not have as an elaborated concept of time as adults and they often interpret temporal events differently than we do. Past time, future time, and even duration are different for young children than for older children and adults. As the following chapter shows, time for the young child is not clearly distinguished from spatial and movement cues. In addition, the more complex concepts of clock, calendar, and historical time are attained only gradually during the elementary school years.

3

Of Time and the Child

On the evening of his father's birthday a four year old announced, "Daddy, you don't need any more birthdays, you are already all grown up." For this child, as for most pre-school children, getting taller is the same as getting older. In the view of young children, therefore, when a person attains his final height he also attains his final age. (Would that it were so!) How children overcome these early notions regarding age and other aspects of the complex concept of time is the subject of one of Piaget's books (Piaget, 1970) in which he reports many investigations of children's time conceptions including a study of what young people think about aging and age relations.

Piaget undertook these studies of children's time conceptions at the urging of Albert Einstein, whom Piaget met in 1931 at a small resort in Davos, Switzerland. The two met again some two decades later when Piaget spent a semester at the Center for Advanced Study in Princeton. Between the two meetings Piaget undertook a number of studies on children's ideas about time, and the recently translated book (originally published in 1946) is a compilation of that research and a distillation of Piaget's thinking regarding how the concept of time develops in children. While Piaget's studies and theorizing were primarily philosophical in intent, they have some very practical implications for parents and for educators.

In his investigations Piaget set out to show that children's ideas about time are neither entirely innate nor entirely learned but rather are gradually *constructed* by the child in the course of his interactions with the environment. In the young child, Piaget discovered, time is not clearly separated from notions of distance and velocity. That is to say, the pre-school child assesses time in terms of distance, distance in terms of speed, and speed in terms of time. As the child grows older and develops elementary reasoning powers, he arrives at an abstract or adult conception of time.

According to Piaget, an abstract concept of time is attained when the child combines his elementary notions of speed and of distance to arrive at the conception of a uniform motion that is independent of the variable motions and distances in which he is immediately involved and in which his immediate world abounds. Adults think of time in relation to the uniform movement of a watch mechanism, which is relatively the same for all watches and which remains constant whether we are walking, driving, or flying. It is because young children lack such a conception that they use distance and speed to assess time.

Some examples may help make concrete Piaget's views regarding the development of time conceptions in children. In one study, pre-school children were shown two small mechanical snails that ran upon a table. The snails were started at the same place and at the same moment but traveled at different speeds for different time intervals. In one version of the experiment, the "slow" snail was allowed to run for a longer time than the "fast" snail but not long enough to catch up with him. Young children had no trouble in saying which of the snails had stopped moving and which was still in motion. When both had stopped, however, and they were

asked, "Which snail stopped first?" they encountered more difficulty. Almost without exception, the pre-school children said that
the "slow" snail had stopped first (which was not the case) because it had not gone as far as the "fast" snail. These children, it
was clear, were assessing time spent traveling by means of the
distance traveled.

That children actually confuse time and distance and not just
words such as "longer" and "first," which we use in both the
spatial and temporal senses, was shown by another experiment.
The children were told that the "fast" snail (who traveled a longer
distance but stopped first) had stopped for lunch and they were
required to say whether the "slow" snail (who traveled a longer
time but a shorter distance) had stopped "before" or "after" the
"fast" snail stopped for lunch. Pre-school children said that the
"slow" snail had stopped before the "fast" snail stopped for lunch
because "it stopped in front of that one" (the "fast" snail). In
other words, the pre-school children thought of lunchtime as the
place where the "fast" snail stopped. In their view whether the
"slow" snail arrived before or after lunch depended upon his
position vis-à-vis the "lunch" space.

By the age of 7 or 8, however, most children can distinguish
between the time spent traveling and the distance traveled and
between fixed times (lunchtime, and so on) and fixed places (the
kitchen, and so on). When children of this age were presented
with problems similar to those described above, they said that
the "fast" snail stopped first and that the "slow" snail was "late"
for lunch. By the age of 7 and 8, then, children have a sense of the
existence of a general uniform time which is independent of the
speed or distance covered by particular moving objects.

The generality of these developmental findings was demonstrated by other experiments which gave, to the adult mind,
equally astonishing results. It is not possible to review all of the
studies here, but we will discuss one dealing with children's use of
time measures since it is particularly instructive. Young children

were shown a large hour glass with the lower half marked at the ¼, ½, and ¾ full levels. The children were asked to perform a task (transferring marbles from one jar to another) and to relate their work to the flow of the sand. After each child had established his own spontaneous rate of work, he was asked to work more quickly and to describe the movement of the sand. He was then asked to work more slowly and again to describe the concommitant movement of the sand. The young children were convinced that the sand moved more slowly when they were working slowly and more rapidly when they were working quickly.

To be sure, older children and adults are subject to the same illusion, namely, that time moves more quickly or more slowly depending upon the nature of our activity. The clock seems to move with excruciating slowness during a dull lecture but with amazing swiftness when we are on the ski slopes or out sailing. This psychological dimension to time is reflected in the updated old story, used to explain relativity, that when Raquel Welch sits on your lap an hour seems like a minute but when you sit against a hot stove, a minute seems like an hour.

Older children and adults, however, know that the experience of time moving more rapidly or more slowly with our activities is an illusion and that time really moves at a uniform rate. Young children cannot correct the time illusion because they lack the ability to construct an abstract concept of uniform motion. This ability usually becomes present in 7–8-year-old children. When children of this age participated in the experiment they said, "The sand always goes the same . . . it makes no difference whether you go quickly or slowly."

Many of the experiments performed by Piaget, such as those described above, dealt primarily with clock time. However, Piaget was also interested in seeing whether the same trends held for children's understanding of calendar time. Accordingly, he undertook several studies dealing with children's ideas about age and birth order which presupposes some understanding of calendar time. By and large the results were remarkably similar to those obtained in the studies dealing with clock time.

In the age and birth order studies children were asked whether they were older or younger than their brothers or sisters and "Who was born first." In the clock time studies the children knew which snail had stopped and which was in motion, but when both snails were still they could not say which one had stopped first. In the domain of age conceptions the same inconsistency obtains. The pre-school child knows whether he is older or younger than a particular sibling but not whether he was born before or after that child.

Two protocols follow that illustrate this phenomena.

Pam (4–6) does not know her birthday. She has a younger sister called Erica.

"How old is Erica?"
"Don't know."
"Is she a baby?"
"No, she can walk."
"Who is the older of you two?"
"Me."
"Why?"
"Because I'm the bigger one."
"When you are grownup, will one of you be older than the other?"
"Yes."
"Which one?"
"Don't know."
"Who was born first, Erica or you?"
"Don't know."
"Who is younger, Erica or you?"
"Erica."
"So which one was born first?"
"Don't know."

Jear (4–9).

"Have you any brothers?"
"Yes, Charles and Eric."

"Are they older or younger than you?"

"They are young" [1 and 3 years].

"Were you born before or after Eric?" [1 year].

"We were born at the same time. All three of us were born before the Escalade." [Geneva festival].

"Are they the same age?"

"No."

"Or the same age as you?"

"No."

"Who is the oldest of you three? . . . And the youngest?"

"Eric."

"Is your mother older than you?"

"She is young."

"And do you get a little older every year?"

"No, I stay young."

"Will you be the same age next year?"

"No, I'll have my birthday and I'm getting skates. I'll be 5½."

"Have you got a granny?"

"Yes, she's older than Mummy."

"Was she born before or after your mother?"

"Don't know."

"What do you think?"

"I don't know."

"And your grandfather—is he older than your father?"

"Oh yes."

"Why?"

"My Daddy is younger."

"Who was born first?"

"I don't know. My grandfather was old right away."

"Are you older than Eric?"

"Oh yes."

"Older than Charles?"

"Yes."

"Who is the oldest?"

"Me. I'll stay young and so will they."

"Who was the first to go to [nursery] school?"

"Me."

"And who will be the first to go to the big school?"

"Me."

"And who will be the first to be a man?"

"Don't know."

We can understand the difficulty encountered by these children, who knew whether they were older or younger than their brothers and sisters but not who was born first, if we recognize that for young children calendar time, like clock time, is a place. The child knows that he is in the "older" place or in the "younger" place but knowing this does not tell him how the places relate to one another in a temporal order. For pre-school children "older" and "younger" do not relate to a uniform time progression that holds for all individuals. It is only when children attain elementary reasoning powers at about the age of 7–8 that they can deduce from knowing who is older, who was born first.

A couple of examples at the older age levels follow.

Dour (7–5).

"How old are you?"
"7½."
"Have you any brothers or sisters?"
"No."
"Any friends?"
"Yes, Gerald."
"Is he older or younger than you?"
"A little older, he's 12 years old."
"How much older is he than you?"
"Five years."
"Was he born before or after you?"
"I don't know."
"But think about it, haven't you just told me his age? Was he born before or after you?"
"He didn't tell me."
"But is there no way of finding out whether he was born before or after you?"
"I could ask him."
"But couldn't you tell without asking?"
"No."
"When Gerald will be a father, will he be older or younger than you?"
"Older."
"By how much?"

"By five years."

"Are you getting old as quickly as each other?"

"Yes."

"When you will be an old man what will he be?"

"A grandfather."

"Will he be the same age as you?"

"No, I'll be five years less."

"And when you will be very, very old, will there still be the same difference?"

"Yes, always."

Gist (9) has a younger sister.

"She'll be 7 years old on 8 January."

"How many years younger than you?"

"Two years."

"When you will be a big lady, will she be the same age as you?"

"No, she'll always be younger than me."

"By how much?"

"Two years."

"Are you absolutely certain?"

"By 21 months." [Correct.]

"Why?"

"Because it will be the same as today."

"And when you are very old?"

"It will always be the same."

"Well then, tell me, which of you two was born first?"

"I don't know."

To demonstrate the generality of this tendency for young children to think of age as a place indicated by size, Piaget did some additional studies. In one of these investigations children were shown a picture of two trees. One of the trees was tall and thin while the other was short and thick. As the children were looking at the trees, they were asked to say which of the two trees was older and which was younger. The results were quite uniform, and almost without exception young children said that the tall tree was always older than the short tree. The results with the

young children were directly analogous to those obtained from
the snail experiment wherein the one that covered the most territory was thought to have traveled longest. Again by the age of
7–8 children overcame this confusion of time with place and size
and began to grasp it as a general uniform motion. Examples of
children at the two levels of conceptualization are given below.

Here are the protocols from two young children.

Roh (4–6).

"Is one of these two trees older than the other?"
"Oh yes, the tall one."
"Why?"
"Because it is tall."
"I think it may well be the other way round."
"I don't know but I would say it's the taller one."
"Can't a tiny tree ever be older than a big one?"
"Oh no, no, no!" [with an air of saying: you needn't mock me].

Zur (4–5).

"That one is 5½ and that one 4½."
"Why?"
"Because it's bigger."
"Can't one be older than someone and still be smaller?"
"Yes."
"In that case, mightn't the big tree be younger than the other one?"
"No."

Lea (4–6).

"The thick one is one year old and the tall one is two years old."
"Are you quite certain?"
"Yes."
"Can't one be bigger and yet be younger than someone else?"
"That never happens."

And here are protocols from youngsters at the "age of reason."

Gil (7–5).

"This one must be older, because it is bigger."

"How do you know?"

"By the size, but I could be wrong, because some big trees are young, trees don't all grow in the same way."

"Could they be the same age?"

"Yes, they could be, one might have grown taller while the other grew rounder, but one can't really tell because there are several things [to be considered]. There are several kinds of trees. One can never tell."

"Who can tell?"

"The man who planted them."

Dar (7–6).

"They may be the same age, because one is thick and the other one is tall."

"What do you think?"

"Perhaps the tall one is the older one, but that's just a guess: one would have to know when they were planted."

Bir (8 years).

"The big one may be older, but that's not certain because big trees can be old or young."

"So?"

"We have to know when they were planted."

Ed (9 years).

"One can't tell, because yew trees grow very slowly and lime trees very quickly."

These findings regarding the development of children's conceptions of aging and of birth order suggest that workable concepts of calendar time are attained at about the same age (usually age 7–8) that children attain workable conceptions of clock time. This is not surprising since both clock and calendar time presuppose a conception of uniform velocity which is arrived at once the child can think of time as that which remains the same when variable velocities and distances are considered as a ratio. It should be said, however, that while the child has an adequate practical conception of time at age 7–8, he still lacks a true sense of historical and future time both of which take further intellectual elaboration. Indeed it may not be until adolescence that young people can engage in meaningful long-range planning or arrive at a true historical perspective.

What Piaget discovered about young children's confusion of times with spaces may help to explain some of the dawdling that young children engage in around "suppertime," "bedtime," and so on. Children's reluctance to heed parental commands about such times may reflect the belief of pre-schoolers that "suppertime" and "bedtime" are places which do not arrive so long as one does not reach them. This could account for the observation that even those children who protest vigorously about coming to dinner or going to bed, give up their protests once they are seated at the table or settled in bed. Apparently, young children believe that it is only "suppertime" when you are at the table and that it is only "bedtime" when you are in bed. For young children, in a phrase, many fixed times are regarded as fixed places. Understanding this way of looking at things may help parents be more tolerant of pre-school children's proverbial "pokiness."

Piaget's findings have educational implications as well. Generally, time and distance or spatial concepts are taught much earlier than the ideas of speed and velocity. This reflects the widely held scientific view that concepts of time and distance are primary and fundamental whereas those of speed and velocity are secondary and derived. What Piaget has demonstrated, however, is that for the child, if not for the physicist, velocity is as primary and fundamental an intuition as either time or distance. Accordingly, Piaget's work suggests that the understanding of time, distance, and velocity concepts might well be enhanced if they were taught together rather than sequentially.

It should be said, perhaps, that teaching velocity concepts along with those of time and distance will not accelerate the child's mastery of these concepts but only make their mastery more solid and substantial. The confusion of time and space concepts is a natural stage in the development of these concepts that cannot be bypassed. And this, apparently, holds true for children all over the world. I felt heartened, for example, about my son's confusion of age with size when I heard about the remark of a four-year-old Russian boy for whom "nighttime" was clearly a bad place. When he was told that when it was daytime in Russia it was nighttime in America, the lad remarked, "Serves them right, those capitalists!"

As adults we often make assumptions about children which seem self-evident but which, on reflection, turn out to be incorrect. Some of these erroneous assumptions have to do with the ways in which children learn about themselves and about the world. In the following chapter several common assumptions about how children think and learn are shown to be misunderstandings of the actual way children go about acquiring information and dealing with their world.

4

Some Misunderstandings About How Children Learn

A young mother recently told me, with some pride, that she insists on her four-year-old daughter watching "Sesame Street" even when the child prefers to do something else. This mother is concerned about the intellectual development of her child and believes that making her daughter watch "Sesame Street" will help the youngster do better in school. This is not an isolated example; many parents today are pressuring their pre-school children to learn numbers, letters, shapes, and so on. Unfortunately, however, this parental concern for the child's intellectual development often seems to outweigh parental concern for the child's feelings, interests, and attitudes. What many parents fail to understand is that forcing a young child to learn specific content may produce an averse attitude to academic learning in general. Such a negative attitude will have more serious long-range effects on academic achievement than whether the child learns his letters, forms, and numbers today, tomorrow, or next week.

The foregoing example illustrates one of several common misunderstandings about the thinking and learning of young children that seem to be current today. In this chapter I want to briefly describe five such common misunderstandings. While I have chosen misunderstandings that hold particularly true for young children, many hold equally true for older children as well. Therefore, awareness of these misunderstandings may be helpful to adults dealing with young people at many different age levels.

CHILD AND ADULT THINKING AND FEELING

One of the most serious and pernicious misunderstandings about young children is that they are most like adults in their thinking and least like us in their feelings. In fact, just the reverse is true, and children are most like us in their feelings and least like us in their thinking. It is just this misunderstanding that prompted the mother mentioned earlier to demand that her daughter watch "Sesame Street." The same woman would not think of ordering her husband to watch a program she thought might "do him some good." Rather, she would recognize that commanding him to watch such a program would be the surest way to turn him against it. And yet, because she takes it for granted that children's feelings are different from adults', she tries to educate her child with a technique that she knows would never work with a grown-up.

As parents and teachers we are equally prone to regard children as being like us in their thinking. When, for example, a child uses a "dirty" word he has picked up from companions, parents often assume he understands the word in the adult sense and punish him accordingly. In fact, the use of such words can be an occasion for teaching children that "Some words make people feel good and some words make people feel bad, that is a word that makes people feel bad." Basically, children use such words not because they understand them so much as because of the reaction they produce in adults. Once they recognize that the reaction is not amusement they are more likely to be more circumspect in the future.

Adults are often misled about young children's thinking because little people are often so capable linguistically. A 4-year-old boy was wandering the halls in his father's office building and was asked by a friend whether he was looking for his father. "No, not really," he replied, "I'm looking for the candy machine." It would be easy to respond to such a lad as if he were at the adult level of thinking. And yet this same boy thinks that a pencil will get longer if it is pushed ahead of another one and believes that an amount of orange juice increases when it is poured from a low flat container into a tall narrow one. The child's language, however, conceals these limitations of his thinking.

LEARNING AND ACTIVITY

A second misunderstanding about young children is that they learn best while they are sitting still and listening. This misunderstanding arises because parents tend to generalize from their experience as adults. It is certainly true that as adults we often learn while listening quietly to a lecturer or while reading a book. But that does not mean that we are passive learners. Attentive listening and reading involve much activity, but it is mental not physical. Young children are not capable of mental activity or thinking in the same way that adults are. Young children have to learn through real actions performed on things whether these be blocks, dolls, or foodstuffs.

Consider a common nursery school activity such as making soup. In the course of making the soup children shell peas and peel carrots and potatoes. In the process they are learning the difference between peeled and unpeeled vegetables and between cooked and uncooked vegetables. Through discussion and observation, they learn how hot water softens some things (like vegetables) and hardens others (like eggs). They may also learn about colors and color changes as a result of cooking and about weights of materials before and after being cooked. Far from being simply play, making soup is, in fact, a mini-course about natural substances that teaches concept formation, language enrichment, and math facts. And, best of all, the activity has a consumable end product that everyone can enjoy.

Accordingly, when it is said that young children are "active" learners, this must be taken in a literal sense. It is the reason, for example, that Montessori said that "play is the child's work." In play, the child is practicing the various actions that will eventually be internalized as thought. Accordingly, however convenient it may be for grown-ups to think of children as learning while they are sitting still, what they learn in this way is likely to be learned by rote and to have little lasting value. In contrast, _what children acquire through active manipulation of the environment is nothing less than the ability to think._

RULE LEARNING

Still a third common misunderstanding about young children is the belief that they can learn and operate according to rules. Many parents have had the experience of telling young children over and over again not to hit their little brothers or sisters, or not to take apart their toys, or to say "thank you" when they are given something. Because young children have not yet internalized thought, they cannot internalize rules. Consequently, while the child understands the prohibition against hitting his brother and against breaking toys in particular instances, he is unable to generalize to new instances. The same is true for learning to say "thank you."

The young child's inability to learn externally imposed rules has special implications for the educational programs to which he is subjected. We have already noted that the young child learns best through playing with and manipulating materials in his environment. His inability to learn general verbal rules supports this observation and argues against formal education (involving verbal instruction, a curriculum, and fixed educational objectives) for this age group. Formal education, whether we speak of reading, arithmetic, or spelling presupposes the inculcation of rules and thus is inappropriate for the majority of pre-school children.

On the other hand, many activities, such as writing and printing letters, are appropriate educational enterprises for pre-school children and are an important preparation for later formal learning. Writing as preparation for reading makes good theoretical as well as pedagogical sense in view of the ideas offered earlier. We said that thinking is an internalization of action so that reading can be regarded, in part at least, as deriving from the internalization of writing actions. Obviously, reading involves much more than the ability to motorically reproduce letters, but motoric reproduction is a good example of an appropriate pre-reading activity for young children who are not yet ready for formal instruction in that skill.

VERTICAL ACCELERATION AND HORIZONTAL ELABORATION

Another widespread misunderstanding about children is that the *vertical acceleration* of mental abilities is more efficacious in cognitive growth than is *horizontal elaboration*. In fact just the opposite is likely to be the case. I once observed a group of 5 year olds who had been taught to read by dint of spending four or five hours a day at the task. The extraordinary thing about these children was that although they were able to read, they all whispered when they read. The first-grade children who had graduated from that class read well, but they whispered when they read too, and in even lower voices. It seemed that there was no fun in reading for them and that it had become something of a fearsome activity.

The point is that you always pay a price for what you do in life. Certainly children can be accelerated in particular skills if they are worked long and hard enough. But the price may be too steep in regard to what the child missed or the emotional problems that ensue in the process. Moreover, there is no clear-cut evidence that early acceleration in·any particular academic skill has long-lived benefits.

In contrast, it seems to me that both parents and teachers do not provide sufficient materials for the horizontal elaboration of abilities on a variety of different materials. What generally happens is that once a child learns, say, to recognize circles or squares, the adult wants him to go on to new things. While in fact, seeing all the possible circles and squares about him in the work-a-day world is a necessary way for establishing these concepts and for preparing the child to integrate such concepts to form a higher level concept such as "geometric forms." In general, a child who elaborates the skills he does have, such as the ability to order materials according to size, on a wide range of different materials (blocks, sticks, dolls, dogs, and so on), is likely to be better prepared for future learning than a child who has learned a great deal in a short time but who has not really had the opportunity to assimilate and practice what he has learned.

The situation is not unlike the student who has crammed for the test the night before as opposed to the student who has been studying regularly throughout the semester with the aid of additional readings. While the two students may not perform too differently on the exam, the student who has been elaborating his knowledge by studying regularly and broadly is likely to be better prepared for future courses than his roommate who makes cramming a regular practice. Parents who try to teach their young children special skills and content are, in effect, teaching a "cram course" and the results are likely to be as short-lived for the pre-school child as they are for the college student.

RAISING THE IQ

One other common misunderstanding about the learning of young children should be mentioned. This misunderstanding has to do with the belief that intelligence can be improved by instruction and that you can "raise your child's IQ" through teaching. To be sure, the IQ is very much affected by the environment, but most middle-class children have probably grown intellectually about as rapidly as their endowment permits. Further enrichment is not likely to have marked effects upon their intellectual ability. Children who have been intellectually deprived can, however, make significant gains in intellectual performance as a consequence of intellectual enrichment. The effects of environmental enrichment on intellectual growth is not unlike the effects of diet and vitamins upon physical growth. A child who has grown up with an adequate diet will not gain much from dietary supplements. But a child whose diet has been deficient in things like protein and vitamins can make remarkable physical gains as a result of being put on an adequate diet. In the same way, for intellectually well-nourished children, further intellectual enrichment is not likely to significantly increase their intellectual powers. But for intellectually undernourished children, intellectual nourishment can be very beneficial.

CONCLUSION

In this chapter I have described five common adult misunderstandings regarding the learning and thinking of young children. I have tried to show that, contrary to common belief, young children are most like us in their feelings and least like us in their thoughts; learn best when they are actively manipulating materials in their environment; do not learn according to rules; profit more from elaboration than acceleration of their skills and abilities; will show significant IQ gains as a result of environmental enrichment only if they come from intellectually impoverished backgrounds.

While the foregoing misunderstandings hold primarily for the young child, I have, nonetheless, encountered similar misunderstandings among parents and teachers who are dealing with older children and adolescents. In large measure, all of these misunderstandings derive from a contemporary overemphasis on intellectual growth to the exclusion of the personal-social side of development. Although I know that it sounds old fashioned to talk about the "whole child" and "tender loving care" (TLC), I strongly believe that many current problems in child rearing and education could be avoided if the adult's concern for a child's achievements as a student were balanced by an equally strong concern for his feelings of self-worth as a person.

Usually, when we think of mental growth, we tend to think of age-related increases in the amount of knowledge and mental ability acquired by the child. As the work of Piaget has shown, however, these increases in knowledge and ability are never haphazard and always move along particular paths and in particular directions. The present chapter details some of the developmental paths and directions prominent in the evolution of children's thinking.

5

How the Mind Grows:
Two Paths of Mental Development

The work of Jean Piaget has shown that the development of thought always moves from the egocentric to the sociocentric or from the highly personal and idiosyncratic ideas of young children to the socially validated and tested ideas held by older children and adults. Young children, for example, often think that aging stops once a person has reached adult stature or as one child put it, "You are grown up, you don't need any more birthdays." As the child grows older, and his fund of knowledge increases, he comes to understand that aging does not stop with the attainment of adult proportions. The child thus progresses from a very idiosyncratic conception of aging to one that has been socially validated. As revealed in Piaget's studies, this progression from egocentric to sociocentric modes of thinking proceeds along two different paths; with these paths of development this chapter is primarily concerned.

One of the paths taken by mental growth is *substitution* whereby the child replaces a less mature idea with a more mature one. In substitution, however, the new idea has no necessary link-up with the idea which it replaces. Young children often believe that the moon and the stars are made by men. Later this primitive idea is replaced by more scientific conceptions regarding the origin of celestial bodies. There is, however, no logical or causal connection between the idea of man-made moon and stars and the conception of these bodies as created according to the action of natural laws.

Two aspects of mental growth by substitution are worthy of special note. First, whenever we substitute a more mature idea for a less mature one, the earlier idea is not eradicated but remains a potential mode of thought. The college student who laughs at his superstitious younger brother for avoiding cracks in the pavement, nonetheless does not permit himself to think of the possibility of getting a good grade in chemistry for fear that even thinking about getting such a grade would destroy his chances. Likewise, the father who is quietly amused by his little daughter when she speaks to and feeds her toy animals and dolls, nevertheless secretly thanks his car for starting on a particularly cold and wintry morning. Accordingly, whenever mental growth proceeds by way of substitution, there is always the possibility that the displaced idea will re-emerge.

A second aspect of mental growth by substitution is that the child must be mentally ready for the new, more socially validated conception if it is really to become part of his thinking. Piaget tells a delightful story in this regard. In talking with a young lad of about seven or eight, he happened to ask if the boy knew how the lake of Geneva was formed. The response was a pleasant myth, apparently of the child's own creation. He said, "there was a giant who stood on the mountain holding a huge boulder above his head, and when he saw his enemy below he threw the boulder at him and this made a great hole in the ground. Then it rained and filled the hole full of water and that is how the lake was made."

Piaget said that it was indeed an interesting story, but asked if the boy would like to hear how the lake was really formed. The lad eagerly assented and Piaget proceeded to recount the geological explanation. "Long ago there were glaciers, or huge ice caps on all the mountains. Then the weather became warmer and these glaciers began to move down the mountains and cut huge holes at the bottom. As the weather became even warmer still, the ice melted and filled the holes with water. And that is how the lake of Geneva and other Swiss lakes were really formed." Piaget then asked the boy if he had understood; the lad said that he had and was able to repeat the essentials of Piaget's explanation.

Some months later, Piaget happened to meet the same young man and stopped to speak with him. Piaget asked whether the boy recalled their earlier discussion about the lake of Geneva and how it came to be formed. The boy answered that he remembered their talk very well. "In that case," said Piaget, "let us see whether you remember the story I told you about how the lake of Geneva was really formed." The boy replied, without a trace of malice or guile, "Well, there was a giant who stood on the mountain, holding. . . ." Substitution is, then, not automatic and requires that the child be psychologically ready to give up his old ideas and to accept new ones.

The second path of mental growth described by Piaget is that of integration, whereby less mature ideas are brought together to arrive at more complex and abstract conceptions. To illustrate, the young child tends to think of size in terms of either height *or* width. If he is asked to judge which of two blocks (both 2" × 6") is greater when one is on its side and the other on its end, he cannot do it. Within the space of a few moments he will judge the upended block as at first "bigger" because it is "higher" and then "smaller" because it is "thinner" than the other block. As the child's mental abilities develop, he integrates height *and* width and comes to think of "largeness" and "smallness" as involving both dimensions at once. The mature conception of size is thus built upon the child's earlier and less mature notions with respect to size.

In contrast to mental growth by substitution, which tends to be somewhat unstable, mental growth by integration is quite difficult to undo. Once a child has integrated both height and width into his concept of size he rarely, if ever, thinks of size in one-dimensional terms again. There are, however, some exceptions to this rule. Children with severe emotional disturbances do show some backsliding in concepts attained by integration but this may mean the concepts were never really solidly attained in the first place. Among the elderly also, there is some tendency to revert to more childlike modes of thinking and this may have to do with physiological deterioration. Outside of these possible exceptions, however, mental development by integration tends to be highly stable and irreversible.

As is true for growth by substitution, growth by integration presupposes a certain readiness to learn or to move forward. While it is possible to train young children to integrate height and width into a more complex conception of size, the effects of training will vary directly with the stage of the child's mental development. Only if the child has already begun on his own to coordinate the two dimensions will training in coordination be of value. Growth by integration is like growth by substitution in the one sense that both tend to follow a developmental timetable which is characteristic of the child and only partially modifiable by experience.

With these two paths of development in mind, we can now look in more detail at some of the concepts which evolve on the principle of substitution and others which evolve according to the principle of integration. After that, we can turn to the goal of substitution and integration, namely, sociocentric thought.

GROWTH BY SUBSTITUTION

By and large, the ideas which develop according to the principle of substitution appear to deal with biological, sociological, and psychological matters. To illustrate mental growth by substitution, then, we can look at how children acquire conceptions of moral judgment, consciousness, causality, and religious identity.

Piaget's studies of moral development provide a good illustration of how ideas evolve by substitution. To study children's moral judgments, Piaget used pairs of stories in which children were involved in misdeeds of various kinds. In one pair of stories, the first was about a boy who broke twelve cups while helping his mother set the table while the second was about a boy who broke one cup while trying to get some jam that he had been forbidden to have. Piaget read the paired stories to children at different age levels and asked them to judge which boy was more to blame.

The results Piaget obtained were straightforward. Young children (usually ages 5–7) routinely judged the boy who broke the twelve cups to have been most at fault. Among older children (usually 8–10) a rather different result was obtained. These youngsters argued that the boy going after the jam was the most to blame because his *intentions* were less honorable than those of the boy helping his mother set the table. Piaget obtained similar results when he presented children with a pair of stories involving the telling of falsehoods. In the first story of the pair, a boy came home from school and told his mother, to amuse her, that he had seen an elephant in the street. The boy in the second story told his mother, in order to deceive her, that he had received a better grade than he had actually been given by his teacher. When the stories were read to young children, they judged the falsehoods entirely on the basis of their extent of deviance from the truth, and without regard to the intentions of the children involved. Older children, for their part, argued that the boy who told the large falsehood to amuse his mother was less blameworthy than the lad who had told a small falsehood in order to deceive his mother.

In the growth of moral concepts, therefore, judgment of culpability based upon the intentions of the wrongdoer is substituted for the developmentally earlier judgment of culpability based solely upon the quantitative considerations. That this is a genuine substitution and not growth by integration is shown by the fact that adults still revert to judging actions on the quantitative basis rather than upon intentions, particularly when they deal with the transgressions of children. A child who breaks his mother's best lamp by accident is likely to be more severely punished than if he breaks an old cup on purpose. Likewise, a boy who accidently breaks his father's expensive stereo rig is likely to get a more intense reaction than if he willfully breaks an old, scratchy record. In short, as adults dealing with children, we often revert to our earlier moral conceptions and gear our reactions to the amount of material damage done by the child rather than to his intentions.

There is another domain wherein mental growth by substitution is quite common and that is in the domain of ideas about consciousness. Piaget reported that children's ideas about consciousness evolved in three stages. Among the youngest children (usually ages 4–5) everything that exists is also regarded as conscious. Stones can feel the prick of a pin, clouds can feel heat, grass feels hurt when it is pulled, and a boat feels the weight of its cargo and passengers. At the next stage (usually ages 6–7) a somewhat different concept of consciousness takes hold. Now children argue that only things which move are conscious. While youngsters at this stage deny that stones, walls, benches, and houses have feelings and thoughts, they continue to regard such things as the wind, bicycles, cars, and boats as being conscious of where they are going. Finally, at the third stage (usually ages 8–9), children arrive at the notion that only those things which move of their own accord are conscious. Put differently, among third-stage children the concept of self-direction and self-activation is substituted for the earlier notions that all or most physical things have conscious experience.

The substitutive nature of these ideas about consciousness is revealed in many well-known types of adult behavior. Although adults know that machines do not have feelings, they sometimes behave as if they did. One has only to watch men and women in front of a vending machine which has taken their money and given nothing in return. Under such circumstances it is not unusual for the adult to pound and kick the machine for all the world as if he intended to punish it for thwarting him; the adult behaves very much as if he did believe that the machine could feel.

Ideas about magic also evolve according to the principle of substitution. Piaget reports many instances of children's magical ideas wherein they believe that their own actions or thoughts could influence events otherwise outside their control. The following recollection by Mlle. Ve told by Flournoy is a very good example:

One of my most distant memories relates to my mother. She was very ill and had been in bed several weeks and a servant had told me she would die in a few days. I must have been about 4 or 5 years old. My most treasured possession was a little brown wooden horse, covered with "real hair" . . . A curious thought came into my head: I must give up my horse in order to make my mother better. It was more than I could do at once and cost me the greatest pain. I started by throwing the saddle and bridle into the fire, thinking that "when its very ugly, I shall be able to keep it." I can't remember exactly what happened. But I know that in the greatest distress I ended by smashing my horse to bits, and that on seeing my mother up, a few days later, I was convinced that it was my sacrifice that had mysteriously cured her and this conviction lasted for a long while. (77)

Piaget gave another example, the content of which suggests that it derives from his own experience:

One of us used to collect shells from the lake and the smallest kinds of snails. On his walks he would experience a number of feelings of participation showing the child's tendency both to see signs in everything and to confuse the sign with the cause of an event, the cause in this case being magical in nature. Thus, when he was seeking a particularly rare specimen, and on the way he found some other interesting specimen, he would decide from this whether or not he would find the specimen he was seeking. This was not based in the least on the similar habitat of the specimens but solely on occult ties; such as an unexpected discovery ought to lead to another discovery during the day. Or again, when from a distance he thought he saw the particular specimen, but on approaching found he was mistaken, he concluded that he would not find the specimen he particularly wanted that day. (77)

Here is one last example of magical thinking in childhood recalled by an adult:

If on my way to the dentist I passed by a particular street and the dentist then hurt me, I took care, the next time, to go a different way, so that he would hurt me less. (77)

Such magical ideas are gradually replaced as we grow older by the idea of chance events and by the understanding of the difference between psychological and physical causality, of the difference between events that can be produced by human thought and actions and those which are not so influenced. The earlier magical ideas are not eradicated, however, and remain dormant, ready to be revived. The body contortions gone through by some bowlers and golfers while their ball is en route is a reversion to the magical belief that our actions can magically influence events at a distance. Such thinking occurs in other instances as well; even though we as adults have substituted more advanced ideas for our more primitive notions of participation magic, we can, and frequently do, revert to magic or quasi-magical thoughts and actions.

A final example of mental growth by substitution can be observed in the evolution of children's conceptions of their religious identity. This development occurs in three stages that are roughly related to age. During the first stage, usually ages 4–7, children think of being a Protestant, Catholic, or Jewish as simply a matter of having a particular kind of name. Indeed, they confuse religious names with other general designations such as nationality. When a child of this age is asked whether all boys and girls in the world are Protestant, he is likely to reply, "No, because some are Russians and some are Eskimos." Likewise, children at this stage are prone to deny that they can be, say, an American and a Protestant at the same time because "You can't have two." Two names that is! For the young child being Protestant and American at the same time is equivalent to being both Henry Jones and Henry Smith at the same time. It is not fair and is against the rules to have more than one name.

At the second stage, usually ages 7–9, children acquire a different notion of religious identity. The crucial factor now becomes action. A Protestant is one who goes to a Protestant church and a Jew is one who goes to a synagogue. The generality of this view is shown by the fact that children of this stage say that a dog or a cat can be Protestant if he is permitted into the church but that he is not a Protestant if he is not allowed in the church. At this stage too, children recognize that a child can be both Protestant and American at the same time but for quite practical reasons, "You can live in America and go to church so you can be both."

Then at the third stage, usually ages 10–12, children attain an even more general conception of their religious identity. At this stage religious affiliation is thought of in terms of beliefs rather than in terms of actions or names. Children at this level define a Protestant as one who believes in Christ but not in the Pope and a Jew as someone who believes in the Old Testament but not in the New Testament. When asked whether a dog or a cat could be a Protestant, children at this stage reply "No, because they can't think about things like that, they are not very intelligent."

Ideas about religious identity thus evolve from an initial primitive notion of religion as a kind of name, to an intermediary notion of religion as a kind of action, to a final conception of religion as a set of particular beliefs. The earlier ideas about religious identity still persist, however, and are all too common in adult thinking. Religious prejudice probably stems, at least in part, from the tendency to identify religion with the actions of some of the people who profess that religion. Such actions then come to be regarded as the essence of the religion while the belief system which is its true essence is ignored.

In the realm of social and psychological ideas such as morality, consciousness, magic, and religion, therefore, we find that ideas evolve by substitution rather than by integration. That these ideas grow by substitution means that the earlier and more primitive ideas which preceded the more mature forms can always be returned to. As the above discussions have suggested, however, instability of the more advanced forms of these conceptions is probably a mixed blessing. Being able to think magically and naively may be helpful in the appreciation of art and in creative endeavors of all sorts. Yet reversion to more primitive modes of thought may also cause great personal and social upheavals. Reversion to earlier modes of thought is less characteristic of concepts about the physical, such as length, perspective, and speed which we will consider next.

GROWTH BY INTEGRATION

Most of the ideas which evolve according to the principle of integration have something logical or quantitive about them. The idea of "length" is a case in point. Among pre-school children, the longest of two sticks is the one which extends beyond the other one. While this is a rough and ready test which usually works well enough it does not work when the two sticks (say A and B) are of the same length but are unevenly aligned. In this situation, A extends beyond B on the right while B extends beyond A on the left. When young children (usually ages 4–5) are confronted with this problem they behave much as they do on the size problem described earlier. That is to say, if they look to the right then they judge A to be longer than B and if they look to the left, then they judge B to be longer than A. Furthermore, the same child will make both judgments within the space of a few moments, as one youngster put it "It [stick A] is longer and it is shorter, I'll take one of each!"

At about the ages of 7–8, however, children do not have any problem assessing the length of two equally long sticks even when these are unequally aligned for they can now integrate their two previously contradictory judgments. Now they recognize that no matter how A and B are aligned, the extent to which A goes beyond B on the right will always be equal to the extent to which B extends beyond A on the left. Once children discover that these differences are always equal to one another they deduce that the two sticks are of equal length. The more mature conception of length thus evolves through the child's coordination of two disparate length judgments into a more general judgment based on the conception of length as always involving not just one, but two directions at the same time.

Another example of mental growth by integration comes from Piaget's work on the evolution of measurement. Piaget studied children's conceptions of measurement by having them build a block tower on one table to the same height as another tower (the model) located on another table. The task was made difficult by the fact that the child had to build his tower on a lower table than the one that was holding the model and by the fact that a screen was placed between the two tables. The child could, however, move freely between the two tables and there were many sticks and paper strips that he could use as measuring instruments.

Three more or less distinct stages emerged in children's solution to this problem. At the first stage (usually ages 4–5), children tended to use their bodies as measuring instruments and either tried to hold their hands at the right level or took some body part, their nose or chin, as an orienting point in moving from table to table. In building their towers, however, the children at the first stage forgot about the tables being different heights and tried to build both towers to the same absolute height from the floor rather than to the same relative height from the tables. At the second stage (usually 5–6), children began to use independent measures such as sticks and paper strips to transport the height of the tower from the model to the second table. These children, however, would only use a stick or paper strip which was exactly the height of the model tower. Finally, at the third stage (usually ages 6–7), the idea of unit measures were interposed and children employed sticks and paper strips of varying lengths. They made remarks such as "This tower is 2½ sticks high."

In this evolution of the notion of measuring, we can see the progressive integration of the conception of measuring instrument. The notion of a portable measurement is present at the first stage, while the notion of a portable measure that is independent of the body appears at the second stage. Then, at the third stage, these earlier notions are incorporated with the idea that there can be portability *within* the measuring instrument itself (the idea of a unit) so that the same element can be used more than once in measuring something. The idea of the portability within a measuring device permits children to talk about the tower as being twice or three times as high as their measuring stick.

Mental growth by means of integration can also be seen in the development of the idea of perspective. To study the evolution of this conception, Piaget employed a three-dimensional plaster model of three mountains different in color, height, and size, and further distinguished in that one had snow painted on its peak, the second a wooden cross, and the third a little house. Pictures of the three mountains were taken from the level of a child's gaze and from many different compass directions. Children who participated in the study were encouraged to walk around the table and to view the configuration from every possible angle. A small doll was also available which could be placed anywhere in relation to the mountains.

In one test with these materials, the doll was placed at one point on the table and facing the mountains while the child was seated at a different point around the table. The child was then given some twenty photographs of the mountains from different directions and was asked to choose the one which corresponded to what was seen by the doll. The results were quite consistent and showed a regular progression with increasing age. Young children (usually ages 5–6) chose the picture of the mountains which conformed to the view they themselves were looking at. Children at this stage could not take the doll's perspective into account at all. At a somewhat more advanced stage level, (usually 6–7) children chose a picture other than the one corresponding to their own viewpoint, but which had no relation to the viewpoint of the doll! While these children recognized that the doll had a different perspective than they did, they appeared unable to figure out what perspective that was. Only towards the ages of 8–9, did children correctly select the picture of the mountains that corresponded with the vista before the doll. Among the older children, then, there was an integration of perspectives, with the older child apparently able mentally to put himself in many different positions and imagine how the mountains would look from those positions.

A final example of mental growth by integration can be taken from Piaget's work on children's conception of speed. This work was undertaken at the suggestion of Einstein, whom Piaget met at a Swiss resort in 1926. Einstein was curious about the way in which children arrived at the notion of speed, an idea crucial to his theory of relativity. Among the many studies Piaget conducted on this theme was one involving, as material, two concentric tracks (concentric circles drawn on a large sheet of paper and spread out on a large table). A toy car was placed on each circle at the same moment of arc; both cars were started at the same time and moved around the tracks so that they both arrived back at the starting point at the same time. The children who had witnessed the "race" were then asked whether the two cars had traveled at the same rate of speed.

Again, a regular development roughly related to age was observed. Children (usually ages 6–7) said that if the two cars started at the same time and stopped at the same time then they must have traveled at the same speed. In short, among these youngsters, speed was evaluated entirely in terms of *time* taken, and the distance traveled was ignored. Among somewhat older children, (usually ages 7–8) distance began to be taken into account in their evaluation of speed. While these youngsters sought to coordinate time spent traveling as well as distance traveled, they did not succeed particularly well. When they had the circumference of the circles in mind, they said that the two cars traveled at different speeds. On the other hand, when they considered the fact that the cars started and finished at the same time they judged that the two had traveled at the same speed. It was only among the oldest children (usually ages 8–9) that an integrated conception of speed, incorporating both time and distance, appeared. Examples of such integration were evident in responses such as the following, "The car on the outer circle traveled faster because it is a longer route and they both started and stopped at the same time."

Many other examples of concepts which develop by means of progressive integration could be provided but perhaps those given above will suffice to illuminate this mode of mental development. In all instances of integration, higher level conceptions are not simply substituted for those at an earlier level. On the contrary, at each successive stage of development, the ideas of the previous level become the integral building blocks of the higher order conceptions of the next stage.

THE DIRECTION OF MENTAL GROWTH

We began with the statement that mental growth moves in a particular direction, namely, from an egocentric to a sociocentric orientation towards reality. In the previous section, we explored the two paths by which the mind moves towards sociocentric thinking without discussing the nature of sociocentric thought itself. This section will describe in a little more detail the nature of sociocentric thought which appears to be the goal of mental development. Put differently, so far we have considered the means by which mental evolution occurs and now we need to look more closely at the ends towards which those means are directed.

In Piaget's view, whether children's ideas evolve by integration or by substitution, their direction is always the same, namely, towards ever greater objectivity, reciprocity, and relativity, the three touchstones of sociocentric thought. That mental growth does move in these directions can be documented with some of the material previously used to describe mental growth by substitution and integration.

Consider, for example, the young child's belief that physical objects are endowed with consciousness and that mental events have physical properties (pre-school youngsters believe that thinking is done with the mouth and that dreams are made of wind). As children grow older they come to distinguish between what is psychic and what is physical and to recognize the properties peculiar to each type of phenomena. Likewise, as children mature they also begin to discover illusions, find that things are not always what they seem, and come to realize that their senses can be deceiving. All of these attainments point to a progressively more objective mode of thought in the sense that children become increasingly able to distinguish between the public world of objects and the private world of thoughts and feelings.

Children's thinking also develops in the direction of greater reciprocity to the extent that they become increasingly able to see the world from the standpoint of others. This development was nicely evidenced in Piaget's perspective study described earlier. We can see a comparable development in other domains as well. Young children often have trouble grasping the idea that their brothers and sisters can have brothers and sisters. If asked, a young boy will readily acknowledge that he has a brother but will vehemently deny that his brother has a brother. As the child matures and becomes capable of putting himself in his brother's position, he discovers that *being* a brother implies *having* a brother, evidence that he has attained reciprocity of thought.

The final direction taken by mental evolution is towards greater relativity, a good example of which is Piaget's work on the child's conception of speed. The same developmental direction can be observed in the evolution of the child's understanding of such relational conceptions as "above," "below," and "on top of". Among young children such relations are thought of absolutely so that if a brick is "on top of a box" they say that the box cannot at the same time be on top of the ground. With increasing age, children gradually discover that "above," "below," and "on top of" correspond to relations between things rather than to properties of things. The late arrival of relative thinking in children helps to account for the fact that prepositions are among the last categories of words to appear in the child's speaking vocabulary.

In summary then, children's thinking grows both by substitution and integration, and in the direction of ever-increasing objectivity, reciprocity, and relativity.

Piaget's use of the term egocentrism has nothing negative in its connotation referring only to the lack of differentiation characteristic of any particular stage of development. In this sense, egocentric behavior is of considerable value because it helps to tie the cognitive types of behavior peculiar to a particular age period to social attitudes and personality. In this chapter I have tried to illustrate the egocentric behavior of each major period of development with particular emphasis upon the egocentrism of middle childhood and adolescence. Much of the material, particularly that on the assumptive realities *and* cognitive conceit *of school-age children and the* imaginary audience *and the* personal fable *of adolescents is speculative, in the sense that it is based as much on my clinical experience with young people as it is on research data.*

6

Egocentrism in Children and Adolescents

Within Piaget's theory of intellectual growth, the concept of egocentrism generally refers to a lack of differentiation in some area of subject-object interaction (87). At each stage of mental development, this lack of differentiation takes a new form and is manifested in a new set of behaviors. The transition from one form of egocentrism to another takes place in a dialectic fashion such that the mental structures which free the child from a lower form of egocentrism are the same structures which ensnare him in a higher form of egocentrism. From the developmental point of view, therefore, egocentrism can be regarded as a negative by-product of any emergent mental system in the sense that it corresponds to the fresh cognitive problems engendered by that system.

Although in recent years Piaget has focused his attention more on the positive than on the negative products of mental structures, egocentrism continues to be of interest because of its relation to the affective aspects of child thought and behavior. Indeed, it is possible that the study of egocentrism may provide a bridge between the study of cognitive structure on the one hand and the exploration of personality dynamics on the other (12; 49). This chapter describes personality phenomena attributable to egocentrism in childhood and adolescence, after a brief review of the earlier forms egocentrism takes in the course of cognitive growth.

FORMS OF EGOCENTRISM IN INFANCY AND EARLY CHILDHOOD

In presenting the childhood forms of egocentrism, it is useful to treat each of Piaget's major stages as if it were primarily concerned with resolving one major cognitive task, and to describe the ego- centrism of a particular stage with reference to this task. It must be stressed, however, that while the cognitive task characteristic of a particular stage seems to attract the major share of the child's mental energies, it is not the only cognitive problem with which he is attempting to cope. In mental development there are major battles and minor skirmishes, and if the latter are ignored here it is for purposes of economy of presentation rather than because they are considered insignificant.

Sensory-motor egocentrism (0-2 years). The major cognitive task of infancy might be regarded as *the conquest of the object.* In the early months of life, the infant deals with objects as if their exist- ence were dependent upon their being present in immediate per- ception (83; 11). The egocentrism of this stage corresponds, there- fore, to a lack of differentiation between the object and the sense impressions occasioned by it. Towards the end of the first year, however, the infant begins to seek the object even when it is hidden, thus showing that he can now differentiate between the object and the "experience of the object." This breakdown of egocentrism is brought about by mental representation of the absent object, the earliest manifestation of the symbolic function which develops gradually during the second year of life and whose activities dominate the next stage of mental growth. It is characteristic of the dialectic of mental growth that the capacity to represent the object internally also enables the infant to cognize the object as externally existent.

Pre-operational egocentrism (2–6 years). During the pre-school period, the child's major cognitive task can be regarded as *the conquest of the symbol.* During the pre-school period the symbolic function becomes fully active, as evidenced by the rapid growth in the acquisition and utilization of language, by the appearance of symbolic play, and by the first reports of dreams. Yet this new capacity for representation, which loosed the infant from his egocentrism with respect to objects, now ensnares the pre-school child in a new egocentrism with respect to symbols. At the beginning of this period the child fails to differentiate between words and their referents (81) and between his self-created play and dream symbols and reality (64; 79). Children at this stage believe that the name inheres in the thing and that an object cannot have more than one name (16; 19; 20).

The egocentrism of this period is particularly evident in children's linguistic behavior. When explaining a piece of apparatus to another child, for example, the youngster at this stage uses many indefinite terms and leaves out important information (81). This is sometimes explained by saying that the child fails to take the other person's point of view; it can also be explained by saying that the child assumes words carry much more information than they actually do, because he believes that even the indefinite "thing" somehow conveys the properties of the object it is used to represent. In short, the egocentrism of this period consists in a lack of clear differentiation between symbols and their referents.

Towards the end of the pre-operational period, the differentiation between symbols and their referents is gradually brought about by the emergence of concrete operations (internalized actions which are roughly comparable in their activity to the elementary operations of arithmetic). One consequence of concrete operational thought is that it enables the child to deal with two elements, properties, or relations at the same time. A child who has attained concrete operations can, for example, take account of both the height and width of a glass of colored liquid and recognize that, when the liquid is poured into a differently shaped container, the changes in height and width of the liquid compensate one another so that the total quantity of liquid is conserved (17; 81). This ability to hold two dimensions in mind at the same time, also enables the child to hold both symbol and referent in mind simultaneously and thus distinguish between them. Concrete operations are, therefore, instrumental in overcoming the egocentrism of the pre-operational stage.

EGOCENTRISM IN CHILDHOOD

With the emergence of concrete operations, the major cognitive task of the school-age child becomes that of mastering classes, relations, and quantities. While the pre-school child forms global notions of classes, relations, and quantities, such notions are imprecise and cannot be combined. The child with concrete operations, on the other hand, can nest classes, seriate relations, and conserve quantities. In addition, concrete operations enable the school-age child to perform elementary syllogistic reasoning and to formulate hypotheses and explanations about concrete matters. This system of concrete operations, however, which lifts the school-age child to new heights of thought, nonetheless lowers him to new depths of egocentrism.

Operations are essentially mental tools whose products, series, class heirarchies, conservations, etc. are not directly derived from experience. At this stage, however, the child regards these mental products as being on a par with perceptual phenomena. His egocentrism now derives from his inability to differentiate clearly between what he thinks and what he perceives. Some examples may help to clarify the form which egocentrism takes during the concrete operational stage.

In a study reported by Peel (74), children and adolescents were read a passage about Stonehenge and then asked questions about it. One of the questions had to do with whether Stonehenge was a place for religious worship or a fort. The children (ages 7–10) answered the question with flat statements, as if they were stating a fact. When they were given evidence that contradicted their statement, they rationalized the evidence to make it conform with their initial position. Adolescents, on the other hand, phrased their replies in probabilistic terms and supported their judgments with material gleaned from the passage.

Similar differences between children and adolescents have been found by Weir (110).

In his studies Weir used a simple probability learning task. Subjects, ranging in age from 4 to 17, were confronted with a box containing three knobs and a pay-off chute. The knobs were programmed so that one of them would pay off (in candy or tokens) 66 per cent of the time, another was programmed to pay off 33 per cent of the time and a third knob paid off zero per cent of the time. The task was to find the maximal pay-off strategy in the system and the maximizing solution was simply to keep pushing the knob that paid off 66 per cent of the time.

Results showed that pre-operational children maximized early (when it comes to candy young children learn quickly!). Adolescents had somewhat more trouble. They invented a wide range of hypotheses regarding the patterns and sequences of knob pressing to attain maximization. After trying and rejecting these hypotheses they eventually discovered that one knob was more likely to pay off than others and finally reverted to pressing the 66 per cent knob all of the time. Elementary school children, however, had considerable difficulty with the problem. They often adopted a "win-stick" and "lose-shift" strategy in which they persisted despite all the evidence that this was not a maximizing procedure. These children were likely to blame the machine rather than their strategy for their difficulty. Other investigators (22) report related findings.

This period of concrete operational egocentrism (ages 7–11) described by Piaget coincides with the *latency* period described by psychoanalysis during which the "family romance" between children and their parents is at minimal intensity. The remainder of this section will attempt to show how a consideration of some of the cognitive formations that derive from the child's egocentrism can complement and amplify the interpretations of latency behavior that have been provided by dynamic psychology and psychiatry.

Egocentrism, we have argued, refers to a lack of differentiation in some sphere of subject-object interaction. In the case of the latency-age child this lack of differentiation derives directly from his new found ability—thanks to concrete operations—to reason from assumptions and hypotheses. In the course of such reasoning the child often fails to distinguish between his hypotheses and assumptions on the one hand and empirical evidence on the other. *It is this lack of differentiation between assumption and fact that constitutes the egocentrism of the concrete operational period.*

The failure to distinguish between hypotheses and reality means, in effect, that the child often treats hypotheses as if they were facts and facts as if they were hypotheses. That is to say, ordinarily we test hypotheses against evidence and if the evidence contradicts the hypotheses we reject it and try another. Children, in contrast, often reject or reinterpret facts to fit the hypotheses. As a consequence such youngsters often operate according to what might be called *assumptive realities,* assumptions about reality that children make on the basis of limited information and which they will not alter in the face of new and contradictory evidence. Although assumptive realities resemble delusions, in the sense that both involve a failure to distinguish between thought and reality, assumptive realities derive, at least originally, from new cognitive abilities and lack the systematization and narcissism of true delusions. Moreover the assumptive behavior engaged in by children is often entered into in the spirit of "fun" or "play" which suggests that at some level of consciousness, the child is aware that he is operating according to a convenient fiction.

Perhaps the most pervasive assumptive realities of latency have their origin in the child's ability to detect flaws in reasoning and errors in supposed statements of fact. Concrete operations insure that the child will discover that his parents are not after all omniscient. This discovery was sensitively described (48) by Edmund Gosse in a passage quoted on page 28. Growing out of this discovery, inevitably made by all children, are two complementary assumptive realities that pervade the latency period. One of these is that adults are, to put it gently, not very bright. Again Gosse insightfully records the formation of this cognition.

The theory that my father was omniscient or infallible was now dead and buried. He probably knew very little; in this case he had not known a fact of such importance that if you did not know that, it could hardly matter what you knew.

The complementary assumptive reality, also suggested by this passage derives from the child's discovery that he, in some instances at least, knows more than the parents. In effect, the child assumes, as Gosse suggests, that if the adult is wrong in one thing then he must be wrong in nearly everything. Moreover, he also assumes that he himself, since he is right in one thing, must be correct in most things. This assumption is abetted by the fact that the child is often unaware of the origin of his knowledge and believes that he comes by it himself (78). We might call this complex of assumptive realities, involving the conception of the adult as none too bright and the child as clever, cognitive conceit. Although cognitive conceit is not a very overt psychic formation in children, it is an underlying orientation which is easily brought to the fore and helps to account, in part at least, for many different facets of latency behavior. Let us look now at some latency phenomena from the standpoint of cognitive conceit.*

Consider first the Peter Pan fantasy, the wish to remain a child that derives from the antipathy many latency-age children feel towards the prospect of growing up. To be sure children are ambivalent and still want many of the prerogatives of older children and grownups. Yet, since adults are not very bright, and are easily outwitted, as Peter Pan showed in his use of the alarm clock to best Captain Hook, the latency-age child has real qualms about growing up. That is to say, the latency-age child may suspect that he will become stupid as he matures and be reluctant to give up his cognitive conceit. His perception of adults as hairy and smelly does not increase his enthusiasm in this regard. The dynamic reasons for the child's wish to remain a child cannot be denied, but cognitive conceit may well be an equally potent factor in the Peter Pan fantasy.

In addition to the Peter Pan fantasy, children's literature abounds in evidence of the cognitive conceit of children. Whether it is "Emile and the Detectives" or "Tom Sawyer" or "A High Wind in Jamaica" or "Alice in Wonderland" in each story adults are outwitted and made to look like fools by children. Indeed I would not be surprised if young people regard Winnie the Pooh (that bear of little brain) as the essence of adult bumbling while they themselves identify with the superbly cool and clever Christopher Robin. Children enjoy such fiction at least in part because it reinforces their cognitive conceit with respect to adults.

The well-known foundling fantasy (67) could be interpreted as still another manifestation of cognitive conceit. In its most

---

* In some children circumstances turn cognitive conceit into its opposite "cognitive ineptitude" and such children persist in the belief that others know everything and that they know nothing.

usual form, the foundling fantasy involves the belief that the child has been adopted and that his real parents are in fact wealthy and of royal descent. Clearly this fantasy derives from a sensed discrepancy on the part of the child in the comparison between his parents and himself. The area in which this sensed discrepancy is most likely to occur (as the quotation from Gosse suggests) is in the realm of mental ability and knowledge. Again I do not want to deny the dynamic significance of the foundling fantasy but only wish to insist upon taking into account its probable cognitive origin.

A similar case could be made for children's jokes which have been so ably described by Wolfenstein (117). A typical joke of this age period is of the following variety:

A mother loses her child named "Heine". She asks a policeman, "Have you seen my Heine?" to which the policeman replies "No but I sure would like to!"

or, another variant:

A woman owns a dog named "Free Show." While the woman is taking a bath, the dog gets out of the house. The woman discovers this and runs out of the house naked shouting "Free Show, Free Show."

One would, I think, be hard put to deny the hostile and sexual aspects of these stories. Note, however, that the joke also depends upon the gullibility and stupidity of the adult, namely, that the mother in the first story would not know the meaning of "Heine" or that the woman in the second story would be stupid enough to run out into the street naked shouting "Free Show." Such jokes recapture the situation in which the parent is discovered not to be omniscient and in which the child knows more than the parent. Accordingly, such jokes also derive some of their impact from the reinforcement they provide for the child's cognitive conceit.

Still other evidence for the pervasiveness of cognitive conceit in children comes from the parodies of adult manners and morals which are an integral component of child language and lore. Children make fun of much that adults regard as serious and even sacred. For example

> Jesus lover of my soul
> Lead me to the sugar bowl
> If the sugar bowl is empty
> Lead me to my mother's pantry

Even before the formal abdication of the Duke of Windsor, English children were singing

> Hark the Herald angels sing
> Mrs. Simpson's swiped our King

Last fall, a six year old came home chanting

> Jingle bells, Wallace smells
> and Humphrey ran away
> Oh what fun it is to run
> In a Nixon Chevrolet

Such parodies reflect, among other things, the child's amused attitude at the sorts of things grown up people regard as serious and important.

Likewise, a good deal of juvenile sophistry also reflects cognitive conceit. The strategy is to hoist the adult on his own petard. For example, an eight year old boy came to the dinner table with his hands dripping wet. When his mother asked why he had not wiped his hands he replied, "But you told me not to wipe my hands on the clean towels." His mother threw up her hands and replied, "I said not to wipe your *dirty* hands on the towels." Children delight in such sophistries because they reaffirm cognitive conceit and because they provide good practice material for their new reasoning abilities. While juvenile sophistry is clearly a passive aggressive maneuver, its dependence upon cognitive structure and the satisfaction it provides for cognitive needs should not be ignored.

A more far-reaching consequence of cognitive conceit can be observed in children's moral behavior. While it is true that by the age of six or seven children have internalized rules and know what is right and wrong, they nonetheless continue throughout most of latency to take what does not belong to them and to deviate from the truth. A possible reason for this discrepancy between what the child knows and what he does is that he perceives the rules as coming from adults. While the child has respect for adult authority (the power to punish) he has little respect for adult intelligence. He thus sees no reason, other than fear of punishment, to obey rules adults have laid down. Accordingly, convinced as he is of his own intellectual superiority, the child takes the rules as a challenge to his own cleverness and attempts to break them without getting caught. For the child, breaking rules is not primarily a moral matter but much more a matter of proving his cleverness by outwitting adults.

With regard to moral behavior, then, we might speak of an *external conscience* operative during the elementary school years. It is external in the sense that the child views the rules and the reasons for obeying them as residing outside rather than within himself. Jiminey Cricket, for example, is Pinocchio's external conscience and Pinocchio's cavalier relationship to Jiminey nicely reflects the child's attitudes towards a conscience imposed by adults. It is only towards the end of childhood and the onset of adolescence, when young people formulate their own rules, that these rules begin to internally regulate behavior. The asceticism, the physical regimes of adolescents as well as their rigidly maintained group mores, demonstrate how binding are those rules which the young person formulates himself or accepts on the basis of personal commitment. At adolescence, then, a true conscience begins to be formed whereas during childhood conscience is still external to the child's personal values and beliefs.

As a final example, I would like to show how cognitive conceit operates in one major form of latency behavior, namely, children's games. Concrete operations make it possible for children to play games with rules, a type of play not known in pre-school children.

When latency-age children play games with rules they play with one aim in mind, namely to win! This is particularly true when they are playing a child's game with an adult, but it is also true, to a lesser extent, when children play amongst themselves.

Now the desire to win could be said to derive, in part at any rate, from cognitive conceit, the child's belief in his own cleverness and his need to prove it. Obviously competitiveness has other dynamics as well but the need to win can also reflect a desire to reassert the child's conception of himself as superior in knowledge and in ability. This is obvious in the way the children often boast when they win. The assumptive reality nature of cognitive conceit becomes manifest when the child loses. In this event, the child will often overtly or covertly find reasons why he lost and why he will win in the future. Often the reasons are at best gratuitous and *ad hoc* but serve nonetheless to maintain the assumption of intellectual superiority.

An assumptive reality related to cognitive conceit is the belief that adults are benevolent and well-intentioned. The child usually has some evidence to support this assumption but he also tends to deny or distort evidence to the contrary. The assumptive reality of the "good parent" may also help to account for the difficulty one finds in getting disturbed (as well as normal) children to say anything negative about their parents in a therapeutic situation. This is true even when it is clear, from other information, that the child has plenty to be unhappy about.

Here is a clinical example provided by Woltman (118) in which the attempts to maintain the assumptive reality of parental "goodness" are exaggerated.

One eight year old boy showed a great deal of preoccupation with the figure of what he called "a good man." First he referred to a piece of clay as a house and said that a good man lived in the house selling vegetables; then he changed the story and said that the house was full of candy and that all the candy belonged to a man inside the house. Finally, he made a clay face of a man which he covered completely with bits of clay. He said, "The man is good because his whole face is covered with candy." The boy came from a broken home which the father had deserted. His preoccupation with the good man obviously was an attempt to create an ideal image of the father figure and the wish to have the father come back. It also turned out that this boy, who could not accept the harsh reality of the irresponsible father, had to convince himself over and over again that there was such a thing as a "good father."

Clearly there is, among other things, denial operating here but denial might be defined as the tendency to cling to a hypothesis or assumption which is contradicted by the facts and to re-interpret the data to fit the hypothesis.

The child's conviction of the benevolence of parents and adults provides a healthy balance to cognitive conceit. A conviction regarding adult good intentions tempers and mellows the child's eagerness to outwit the adult and to make him appear foolish. If it were not for this assumptive reality with regard to grownups, the latency-age child would be much more difficult to live with than is usually the case.

Assumptive realities can also be more temporary and arise in particular situations. This frequently occurs when the child does something he knows to be wrong. Although the child may be aware that he has committed a wrong he may also make some assumption about his behavior that excuses or exonerates his act so that he feels genuinely innocent. When he denies the action on the basis of this assumptive reality he is more than likely to infuriate the adult. Many toe-to-toe shouting matches between parent and child follow upon the child's denial of guilt and the parent's adamant demand that the child confess his misdeed. At such times the parent fails to appreciate that for the child an assumptive reality is the *truth*.

It might be noted in passing that some rigidities that workers like Wertheimer (112) have noted in the thinking of school chil-dren may result from assumptive realities. In math, for example, children often learn a rule and assume that this applies to all figures or problems. At least some intellectual difficulties encountered by latency-age children may, in part at least, be explained by this tendency to take a rule or conviction as a self-evident reality which must be applied to all and sundry situations. It might be, for example, that some so-called "learning blocks" are exaggerations of a "normal" cognitive formation which has become exaggerated and exacerbated due to emotional problems.

The assumptive realities which derive from the egocentrism of the latency-age child also helps to account for the unique character of play, fantasy, and imagination during this period. Although children have given up the fairy tale fantasy and are geared to finding out about the real world, they often approach this reality in an assumptive way. Davidson and Fay (13) nicely illustrate how assumptive realities emerge in the play of latency-age children and the tenacity with which these children cling to assumptions about reality despite the arguments and evidence offered by adults to dissuade them:

> Many of the interests of seven to eleven year old children, although strongly tied to reality can be seen to be deeply rooted in fantasy. For instance, Paul, eight, would periodically spend days digging in the yard to find buried treasure—"jewels" and "olden day things." He dug up several pieces of china which he carefully washed and tried to fit together, convinced that they were fragments of ancient pottery and probably of great value.

Whether young people are digging for treasure, or building a fort, or planning a money-making project, they often persist despite the cautions and evidences to the contrary given by adults. An assumptive reality seems operative in such situations.

It should be said, too, that the egocentrism of this period probably also plays a part in the latency-age child's love of mystery, adventure, and magic. Assumptive realities presuppose a particular view of the world in which facts can be made to do your bidding and hence have something flexible and uncertain but controllable about them. Children like stories of mystery, adventure, and magic because these stories also presuppose a world in which new and unexpected events repeatedly occur but are always susceptible to mastery. The success of the Nancy Drew as well as the Hardy Boys series is ample testimony that girls as well as boys perceive the world in this way.

Before closing it is perhaps well to make clear that while assumptive realities are believed in and acted upon by the child he also operates at a more concrete practical level of reality. Just as primitive man prayed for rain but also irrigated his fields (94), so do children believe in their intellectual superiority while they frequently behave as if adults were wiser and more knowledgeable. Put differently, at the practical level, the child often accepts the adult's greater knowledge and ability while he continues to deny it in the plane of cognition. The same holds true for other assumptive realities. At the practical level, for example, a child may know that his father is mean and that he had better keep out of his way, while on the cognitive plane he maintains the assumption of parental benevolence.

It is only in adolescence, with the advent of formal operations, that these two planes of action and thought are brought into coordination. With formal operations, the young person can conceptualize his own thought and discover the arbitrariness of his hypothesis. He discovers, too, the rules for testing hypotheses against facts and hence is now able to deal with facts and hypotheses in an experimental fashion. This leads to the recognition that many of his hypotheses are wrong and gives him a new respect for data and a diminished confidence in his own ability. He then begins to be self-critical so that cognitive conceit is gradually given up. The passing of cognitive conceit is hastened as the adolescent attempts adult tasks (work) and begins to measure himself by adult standards.

In concluding this general discussion of egocentrism and latency behavior, two general points should be reiterated. The first has to do with the permanence of those mental formations attributable to concrete operations.

As in the case of most developmental phenomena, formations that appear at one level of development do not disappear at the following stages and may manifest themselves at each succeeding stage in the life cycle. This appears to hold true for the assumptive realities in general, and for the cognitive conceit and external conscience in particular, that emerge during the concrete operational period.

Evidence of adult behavior governed by assumptive realities in general is easy to come by. Indeed, the old saying, "love is blind" captures very well the fact that under some circumstances an individual may adopt an hypothesis and cling to it regardless of factual evidence to the contrary. Likewise, the romantic image of love and marriage held by so many young women in our society, despite all of the everyday evidence which gainsays this image, is a good example of how even young adults can believe in and behave according to assumptive realities.

With regard to cognitive conceit, we are all familiar with the young scholar who attacks a major figure, such as Freud or Piaget, on some minor point and then proceeds to dismiss the whole body of the master's work. At the same time, having found the real or imagined error, the young scholar is convinced of his own intellectual superiority. This is cognitive conceit at the adult level repeated with a parentlike figure. Behavior regulated by external conscience is also easy to discern among adults. Men away from home at a convention will sometimes do things which they would never do at home. In a different or a foreign setting, the instrumentalities of the external conscience (neighbors, employers, friends, marital partners) are absent and, as is true for children, one of the satisfactions of misbehavior in this context is the thought of having outwitted the inhibiting external forces. This is often expressed as "If the folks back home could only see me now."

The second point has to do with the status of the mental formations and the interpretations offered above. In order not to be misunderstood, I have tried throughout the discussion to indicate that I believe the egocentrism interpretation of latency behavior is a necessary complement to and *not* a substitute for dynamic interpretations. In their use of multiple models both Freud and Piaget have made it very clear that at this stage in our understanding we need many different models to give a comprehensive account of human thought and action. Hopefully, and this is the spirit in which the above discussion has been offered, interpretations of the same phenomena from the stand- .point of many different models will prepare the way for a truly comprehensive psychological theory that is at once cognitive *and* dynamic.

ADOLESCENT EGOCENTRISM

From the strictly cognitive point of view, as opposed to the psychoanalytic point of view (6; 38) or the ego psychological point of view (36), the major task of early adolescence can be regarded as having to do with *the conquest of thought.* Formal operations not only permit the young person to construct all the possibilities in a system and construct contrary-to-fact propositions (56); they also enable him to conceptualize his own thought, to take his mental constructions as objects and reason about them. Only at about the ages of 11–12, for example, do children spontaneously introduce concepts of belief, intelligence, and faith into their definitions of their religious denomination (15, 19, 20). Once more, however, this new mental system which frees the young person from the egocentrism of childhood entangles him in a new form of egocentrism characteristic of adolescence.

Formal operational thought not only enables the adolescent to conceptualize his thought, it also permits him to conceptualize the thought of other people; this capacity, however, is the crux of adolescent egocentrism. This egocentrism emerges because, while the adolescent can now cognize the thoughts of others, he fails to differentiate between the objects towards which the thoughts of others are directed and those which are the focus of his own concern. The young adolescent, because of the physiological metamorphosis he is undergoing, is primarily concerned with himself. Accordingly, since he fails to differentiate between what others are thinking about and his own mental pre-occupations, he assumes that other people are as obsessed with his behavior and appearance as he is himself. *This belief that others are preoccupied with his appearance and behavior constitutes the egocentrism of the adolescent.*

One consequence of adolescent egocentrism is that, in actual or impending social situations, the young person anticipates the reactions of other people to himself. These anticipations, however, are based on the premise that others are as admiring or as critical of him as he is of himself. In a sense, then, the adolescent is continually constructing, or reacting to, *an imaginary audience.* It is an audience because the adolescent believes that he will be the focus of attention, and it is imaginary because, in actual social situations, this is not usually the case (unless he contrives to make it so). The construction of imaginary audiences would seem to account, in part at least, for a wide variety of typical adolescent behaviors and experiences.

The imaginary audience, for example, probably plays a role in the self-consciousness which is so characteristic of early adolescence. When the young person is feeling critical of himself, he anticipates that the audience—of which he is necessarily a part—will be critical too. And, since the audience is his own construction and privy to his own knowledge of himself, it knows just what to look for in the way of cosmetic and behavioral sensitivities. The adolescent's wish for privacy and his reluctance to reveal himself may, to some extent, be a reaction to the feeling of being under the constant critical scrutiny of other people. The notion of an imaginary audience also helps to explain the observation that the affect which most concerns adolescents is not guilt but, rather, shame, i.e., the reaction to an audience (68).

While the adolescent is often self-critical, he is frequently self-admiring too. At such times, the audience takes on the same affective coloration. A good deal of adolescent boorishness, loudness, and faddish dress is probably provoked, partially in any case, by a failure to differentiate between what the young person believes to be attractive and what others admire. It is for this reason that the young person frequently fails to understand why adults disapprove of the way he dresses and behaves. The same sort of egocentrism is often seen in behavior directed towards the opposite sex. The boy who stands in front of the mirror for two hours combing his hair is probably imagining the reactions he will produce in the girls, and the girl applying her makeup is probably imagining the admiring glances that will come her way. When these young people actually meet, each is more concerned with being the observed than with being the observer. Gatherings of young adolescents are unique in the sense that each young person is simultaneously an actor to himself and an audience to others.

One of the most common admiring audience constructions, in the adolescent, is the anticipation of how others will react to his own death. A certain bittersweet pleasure is derived from anticipating the belated recognition of his good qualities. As often happens with such universal fantasies, this one has been realized in fiction in the passage from *Tom Sawyer* where Tom sneaks back to his home, after having run away with Joe and Huck, to discover that he and his friends are thought to have been drowned:

But this memory was too much for the old lady, and she broke entirely down. Tom was snuffling, now, himself—and more in pity of himself than anybody else. He could hear Mary crying and putting in a kindly word for him from time to time. He began to have a nobler opinion of himself than ever before. Still, he was sufficiently touched by his aunt's grief to long to rush out from under the bed and overwhelm her with joy—and the theatrical gorgeousness of the thing appealed strongly to his nature too—but he resisted and lay still.

Corresponding to the imaginary audience is another mental construction which is its complement. While the adolescent fails to differentiate the concerns of his own thought from those of others, he at the same time overdifferentiates his feelings. Perhaps because he believes he is of importance to so many people, the imaginary audience, he comes to regard himself, and particularly his feelings, as something special and unique. Only he can suffer with such agonized intensity or experience such exquisite rapture. How many parents have been confronted with the typically adolescent phrase, "But you don't know how it feels. . . ." The emotional torments undergone by Salinger's Holden Caulfield exemplify the adolescent's belief in the uniqueness of his own emotional experience. At a somewhat different level, this belief in personal uniqueness becomes a conviction that he will not die, that death will happen to others but not to him. This complex of beliefs in the uniqueness of his feelings and of his immortality might be called a *personal fable*, a story which he tells himself and which is not true.

Evidences of the personal fable are particularly prominent in adolescent diaries. Such diaries are often written for posterity in the conviction that the young person's experiences, crushes, frustrations are of universal significance. Another kind of evidence for the personal fable during this period is the tendency to confide in a personal God. The search for privacy and the belief in personal uniqueness leads to the establishment of an I-Thou relationship with God as a personal confidant to whom one no longer looks for gifts but rather for guidance and support (33).

The concepts of an imaginary audience and a personal fable have proved useful, at least to the writer, in the understanding and treatment of troubled adolescents. The imaginary audience, for example, seems often to play a role in middle-class delinquency (23). As a case in point, one young man took $1,000 from a golf tournament purse, hid the money and then promptly revealed himself. It turned out that much of the motivation for this act was derived from the anticipated response of "the audience" to the bravado of his action. In a similar vein, many young girls become pregnant partly because their personal fable convinces them that pregnancy will happen to others but never to them and so they need not take precautions. Such examples could be multiplied but suffice to illustrate how adolescent egocentrism, as manifested in the imaginary audience and in the personal fable, can help provide a rationale for some adolescent behavior. These concepts can, moreover, be utilized in the treatment of adolescent offenders. It is often helpful to these young people if they can learn to differentiate between the real and the imaginary audience, which often boils down to a discrimination between the real and the imaginary parents.

After the appearance of formal operational thought, no new mental systems develop and the mental structures of adolescence must serve for the rest of the life-span. The egocentrism of early adolescence nonetheless tends to diminish by the age of 15 or 16, the age at which formal operations become firmly established. What appears to happen is that the imaginary audience, which is primarily an anticipatory audience, is progressively modified in the direction of the reactions of the real audience. In a way, the imaginary audience can be regarded as an hypothesis, or better as a series of hypotheses, which the young person tests against reality. As a consequence of this testing, he gradually comes to recognize the difference between his own preoccupations and the interests and concerns of others.

The personal fable, on the other hand, is probably overcome (although probably never in its entirety) by the gradual establishment of what Erikson (36) has called intimacy. Once the young person sees himself in a more realistic light as a function of having adjusted his imaginary audience to the real one, he can establish true rather than self-interested interpersonal relations. Once relations of mutuality are established and confidences are shared, the young person discovers that others have feelings similar to his own and have suffered and been enraptured in the same way.

Adolescent egocentrism is thus overcome by a two fold transformation. On the cognitive plane it is overcome by the gradual differentiation between his own preoccupations and the thoughts of others, while on the plane of affectivity it is overcome by a gradual integration of the feelings of others with his own emotions.

In sum, the cognitive structures peculiar to a particular level of development can be related to the affective experience and behavior characteristic of that stage. A consideration of egocentrism, then, would seem to be a useful starting point for any attempt to reconcile cognitive structure and the dynamics of personality.

This chapter continues the discussion begun in the previous one and concerns the relation of cognitive structures to thought and behavior. What I have tried to demonstrate is that many of the phenomena typical of a given age behavior can be accounted for, in part at least, by the cognitive attainments of this age period. Again, the analysis of thought and behavior in cognitive terms does not contradict the dynamic or psychoanalytic interpretations, but rather complements them.

7

Cognitive Structure and Experience in Children and Adolescents

Every affective experience whether it be a simple sensation, a general feeling or a complex emotion presupposes some form of cognitive structuring. For example, the recognition of the location of a simple sensation presupposes a general body schema. Similarly, the recognition of a general feeling as distinct demands a comparison with previous states, which at the very least engages judgmental and memory structures. The same holds true for emotions; the ability to recognize and label one's emotions requires the capacity to discriminate amongst the many possible emotions, and this in turn must engage cognitive structures.

From the developmental point of view, i.e., from the point of view which sees mental structures as manifesting a progressive evolution, we should therefore, expect to find changes in experience coincident with changes in cognitive structure. Put rather more directly, if the child lacks some of the cognitive structures he will have as an adult, he must of necessity lack some of the affective experiences he will encounter when he is mature. On a purely descriptive level this appears to be true. Prejudice, for example, rarely appears until adolescence nor does the formation of cliques based on social class lines. It is also rare for a young child to bear a long-lasting grudge toward another young person. Depressive states are also rarely seen in pre-adolescents. Let us consider then the relation of cognitive structure to experience first in children and then in adolescents.

COGNITIVE STRUCTURE AND EXPERIENCE
IN CHILDREN

The age of six to seven has long been regarded as the "age of reason" and Piaget's work on children's thinking (80) has shown that this label was well-chosen. It is only at about elementary school age that children manifest the ability to move from premise to conclusion in their arguments, to nest smaller class concepts within larger class concepts (boys and girls equal the class of children), and to perform elementary arithmetical operations such as addition and subtraction. Moreover, as a consequence of concrete operations children gradually come to appreciate, among other things, clock, calendar, and historical time; Euclidian, geographical, and celestial space; and the distinction between physical and psychological causality.

For our purposes, however, the latency-age child's attainments in the field of interpersonal communication and relations are of primary concern. Among these attainments, three are of particular note. First, the child at this stage can take another person's point of view and engage in true communication, with give and take about a particular subject. Second, the child at this level is capable of comparing what he hears and sees with what he knows, and is, therefore, able to make judgments regarding truth and falsehood and regarding reality and appearance. Third, the latency-age child is now able not only to reason from premise to conclusion but also from rule to particular instance—he can operate according to rules.

The ability to take another person's point of view and to engage in true communication makes possible the child's assimilation to the peer culture. Assimilation to this peer culture is facilitated by the existence of a large body of language and lore (which has been abundantly described by such writers as Opie and Opie [73] and others) that provides the child with modes of peer interaction such as jokes, jeers, taunts, superstition, quasi beliefs, ritual, and so on. Adults, in effect, never teach children how to relate to peers and since these modes of interaction are not innate they must be acquired. The language and lore of childhood fulfills this function. Much of this language and lore is in the form of simple couplets such as

> Roses are red
> Violets are blue
> Onions smell
> And so do you

which resemble the syllogism and provide the child with material upon which to practice his budding reasoning abilities.

Coupled with this assimilation to the peer culture is a new estrangement from some forms of fantasy material attributable to the child's ability to compare what he knows with what he hears and sees. Among other things his new understanding of the difference between the real and the apparent brings about the deduction that there is no Santa Claus, and no such things as fairies, giants, and the like. The elementary school child may still enjoy such fictions but he makes it known that he is well aware that they are not real and are merely make believe.

Finally, the child's new ability to behave according to rules makes it possible for him to engage in organized play and to profit from formal instruction. With respect to play behavior, the child of elementary school age gets interested in every game from tic tac toe to chess. While initially he may have trouble learning and following the rules, the significant accomplishment of the period is his new recognition that the game must be played according to certain regulations. The ability to profit from formal instruction rests upon the same accomplishment. All formal education involves the transmission of rules whether these are the rules of phonics, grammar, or arithmetic. Concrete operational thought is a necessary prerequisite to formal education because it makes possible the comprehension of rules upon which all formal education is based.

These are but a few of the many new attainments of the concrete operational period. Perhaps these examples, will nonetheless suffice to illustrate the extent to which the system of concrete operations brings the elementary school child closer to the intellectual level of adolescents and adults. Let us now look at the contribution of cognitive structures to adolescent experience.

COGNITIVE STRUCTURE AND EXPERIENCE IN ADOLESCENCE

This section traces some of the experiences, which make their first appearance in adolescence, to the new cognitive structures which come to fruition at about the time of puberty. I do not wish to imply that these new structures *cause* the experiences in question but only to suggest that they are a necessary if not a sufficient condition for their occurrence. Indeed, the majority of adolescent experiences can only be fully understood within the context both of the new mental capacities which mark the advent of this age period and in the context of the new affective transformations which have been described by others (38, 36, 6). If I here ignore the psychodynamics of adolescence it is for the purpose of emphasizing the role of cognitive structure and not to imply that motivational factors are unimportant.

Our knowledge about the cognitive structure of adolescents is due, in large measure, to the work of Piaget and Inhelder (56). In their work on adolescent thinking, they have pointed out some of the ways that the thought of the adolescent differs from that of the child. The adolescent is, in the first place, capable of combinatorial logic and can deal with problems in which many factors operate at the same time. For example, consider the problem of arranging four differently colored poker chips into all possible combinations. There are 16 possible combinations in all. If the colors are red, blue, yellow and green the combinations would be: R; B; Y; G; RB; RY; RG; BY; BG; YG; RBY; RBG; BYG; RYG; RBYG; and none. Most adolescents can easily form all of these combinations; children cannot, and it is in this sense that the combinatorial reasoning of the adolescent goes beyond the more elementary syllogistic reasoning of the child.

A second feature which sets the thought of the adolescent off from that of the child, is his ability to utilize a second symbol system, i.e., a set of symbols for symbols. It is not without reason, for example, that algebra is never taught to elementary school children. The capacity to symbolize symbols makes the adolescent's thought much more flexible than that of the child. Words carry much more meaning because they now can take on double meanings, they can mean both things and other symbols. It is for this reason that children seldom understand metaphor, double entendre, and cartoons (97). It also explains why adolescents are able to produce many more concepts to verbal stimuli than are children (25). For our purposes, the most significant result of this aspect of adolescent thought is that it enables the adolescent to take his own thought as an object which is to say that he can now introspect and reflect upon his own mental and personality traits.

Still a third characteristic of adolescent thinking is the capacity to construct ideals, or contrary-to-fact situations. The adolescent can accept a contrary-to-fact premise and proceed with the argument as if the premise were correct. Once again, the capacity to deal with the possible as well as the actual liberates the adolescent's thought so that he can now deal with many problem situations in which the child is stymied. Most importantly, for our purposes, the capacity to deal with the possible means that the future is now as much of a reality as the present and is a reality which can and must be dealt with.

In addition to expanding the adolescent's adaptive potentials, these aspects of adolescent thinking also pave the way for new experiences and reactions unknown to childhood. It is to these experiences, for which the new cognitive structures of adolescence are necessary prerequisites, that we now need to consider.

The capacity to deal with combinatorial logic and to consider all possible factors in a given problem solving situation, lays the groundwork for some characteristic adolescent reactions. One consequence of the capacity for combinatorial logic is that, particularly in social situations, the adolescent now sees a host of alternatives and decision-making becomes a problem. He now sees, to illustrate, many alternatives to parental directives and is loath to accept the parental alternatives without question. He wants to know not only where a parent stands but also why, and is ready to debate the virtues of the parental alternative over that chosen by himself and his peers. Indeed, the adolescent's quarrels with parental decisions are part of his own indecisiveness. While he is having trouble making decisions for himself, at the same time he does not want others making decisions for him. Paradoxically, but understandably, the adolescent's indecisiveness also frequently throws him into a new dependence, particularly on his peers, but also on his parents. The adolescent demands that his parents take a stand if only so he can rebel against it.

Without denying the validity or importance of the dynamic factors, which lie beneath the adolescent's difficulties with his parents, the cognitive aspects of the struggle must be recognized. Were the adolescent not capable of grasping alternatives to parental directives and were he not in turmoil over making his own decisions, at least some of the storm and stress of this period would never appear or at least would appear in quite a different form. In primitive cultures, for example, where the more advanced mental structures may not be attained, there may be little storm and stress. In short, the presence of structures which enable the adolescent to construct multiple alternatives, sets the stage for characteristic conflicts between young people and their parents as well as for the increased dependence upon the peer group for final decision-making.

Another structural feature of adolescent thought with repercussions for adolescent experience, is the capacity to think about thinking, to introspect. For the first time, the adolescent can take himself as an object, evaluate himself from the perspective of other people with respect to personality, intelligence and appearance. The adolescent's self-consciousness about himself is simply a manifestation of this new capacity for introspection. Now that the adolescent can, so to speak, look at himself from the outside he becomes concerned about the reactions of others to himself. Many adolescents undertake a regime of physical or intellectual exercise because in examining themselves they find a discrepancy between what they are and what they wish to be, between the real and the ideal self. For the child, this discrepancy is seldom conscious but in adolescence, the capacity to introspect and examine the self from the standpoint of others brings it home in full force. It is for this reason, perhaps, that a child with a physical handicap (such as a deformed arm) who has been a happy optimistic child experiences his first real depression in adolescence.

This introspection has another consequence that might well be mentioned. The adolescent becomes secretive about his thoughts. He recognizes now that his thought is private and, more importantly, that he can say things which are diametrically opposed to his thoughts. When a child fabricates, he tends to believe the fabrication so that once it is constructed he defends it as the truth. This is not the case with the adolescent, who knows very well that what he is saying and what he is thinking are quite different and who doesn't believe his fabrications although he can make them sound entirely convincing. The adolescent thus begins creating the social disguises, so common in adults and so rare in children, behind which the young person conceals thoughts and wishes that are quite at variance with his verbal assertions. At one extreme these disguises are tact and politeness while at the other extreme they are deceit and exploitation. The potential for both are present as soon as the young person can say one thing and think another and be aware that he is doing so.

The capacity to construct ideals and to reason about contrary-to-fact propositions also plays a considerable role in adolescent experience and behavior. For one thing, the young person can conceive of ideal families, religions, and societies and when he compares these with his own family, religion, and society he often finds the latter wanting. Much of adolescent rebellion against adult society derives, in part at least, from this new capacity to construct ideal situations. These ideals, however, are almost entirely intellectual and the young person has little conception of how they might be made into realities and even less interest in working toward their fulfillment. The very same adolescent who professes his concern for the poor spends his money on clothes and records, not on charity. The very fact that ideals can be conceived, he believes, means that they can be effortlessly realized without any sacrifice on his part.

It is for this reason that young people feel that adults have compromised and sold out, that while adults profess justice, integrity, obedience to the law, they hypocritically fail to put these ideals into practice. In effect, the adolescent not only constructs ideal families, religions, and societies, he also constructs ideal persons. The short-lived adolescent crush is a case in point. It is short-lived just because no human person can match the ideal created in adolescent thought. The adolescent, moreover, tends to lack compassion for human failings both with respect to himself and to others. But while he is down on adults for ethical hypocrisy, he flails himself for personal shortcomings such as the control of masturbation, the making of social blunders, and academic or athletic failures. Perhaps it is because the adolescent is relatively uninvolved with serious issues of justice, integrity, and obedience to the law, that he feels so superior to adults in these regards.

These exaggerations of adolescence come gradually to an end as the young person is forced to adapt to the realities of adult life. As he begins to engage in productive work, he reassesses the adult world as well as his own limitations and becomes more accepting of both.

Although Piaget does not consider himself as primarily an educator, his work has had its greatest impact upon education and educators. Piaget is most widely read and talked about in education courses and at professional meetings of educators, but his work has not had as great an impact on psychology or philosophy. Oddly enough, however, Piaget's major essays on learning, which would be most relevant to education, have still to be translated and are not widely known. This chapter discusses Piaget's conception of learning as well as the implications of his psychology for the philosophy of education and the practice of teaching.

8

Piaget and Education

The past decade has borne witness to a phenomenal growth of interest in Piaget's work and thought. While this interest is widespread among psychologists, psychiatrists, pediatricians, sociologists, and philosophers, it is particularly prominent among educators. As a consequence, books and articles dealing with Piaget's work and directed toward educators are appearing in ever increasing numbers (e.g., 7, 40, 42, 75).

Before proceeding a few cautionary remarks are in order. Piaget is not an educator, nor is he principally concerned with problems of education. In its primary intent, his work has been philosophical, and designed to provide a theory of knowledge and of knowing based upon empirical evidence. Philosophies of knowledge, however, have always had considerable impact upon educational theory and practice. This was as true for the philosophies of Plato and Aristotle as it was for those of Descartes, Locke, and more recently the Vienna Circle, but in each case educators have had to draw their own implications with respect to educational theory, the processes of learning, and methods of instruction.

The same holds true for Piaget's work. He has provided a new and empirically based conceptual framework and schema from which to view educational problems. What we see from that framework or within those concepts, however, is very much determined by our own predilections, attitudes, and biases. It is necessary to state this at the outset because this chapter reflects my interpretation of the implications of Piaget's work for education. Put differently, if there are any ideas of value they most assuredly are attributable to Piaget while the commonplaces must remain my own responsibility.

THE PHILOSOPHY OF EDUCATION

Every philosophy of education presupposes, in addition to a set of values and a theory of instruction, a particular image of the child which dominates the other components. When, for example, Calvinistic theology postulated that the child was imbued with original sin, the corresponding educational values and teaching practices were oriented accordingly. Puritan education aimed at developing self-control and discipline with the use of fear, threat, and punishment as motivational aids. Centuries later, when Freud described childhood as the period of neurotic and psychotic formations, a different educational philosophy arose which aimed at freeing the child from inhibitions and repressions, and the educational mode was permissiveness and freedom from constraint.

Piaget's impact upon educational philosophy will probably derive from the unique image of the child that his work projects. Once that image is clearly formulated, the educational philosophy which the image suggests will be easy to adumbrate. To uncover this image we need to recall briefly Piaget's unique methodology and his discoveries regarding the development of children's thinking.

Like other investigators in the child area, Piaget has used observation and testing in his investigations of children's thinking. Unlike other investigators, however, he also employed an analytic tool that might be called *empathic inference.* Starting from his observations of child behavior, or from the child's test responses, Piaget proceeded then to infer how the child *must have experienced the world in order to behave as he did.* To illustrate, Piaget (82) observed that his infant son Laurent, who was crying vigorously at the sight of his bottle, showed no distress and ceased crying when the bottle disappeared from view. Piaget empathically inferred from this datum that Laurent had no awareness of the fact that objects continue to exist when they do not impinge upon his senses.

It was with the aid of empathic inference, and a multitude of ingenious experiments that Piaget made his most important discoveries about children's thinking. In a very real sense Piaget discovered what amounts to the "dark side" of the child's mind, namely, those beliefs and concepts foreign to the adult intellect and which were hitherto both unknown and unsuspected. To illustrate, Piaget discovered that young children believe that the sun and moon follow them when they walk, that dreams come in through the window at night, and that everything that moves is alive. In other domains he found that young children believe that number, length, amount, and area change with a change in their appearance.

Now the image of the child suggested by these discoveries is that of a person who, relative to adults, is a *cognitive alien.* That is to say, the child, like the person from a foreign country, thinks differently and, figuratively at any rate, speaks a different language. It is useful to contrast this image of the child with that promulgated by Freud. For Freud (39) the child was, relative to adults, an *emotional alien.* In Freud's view the child was, at least potentially, polymorphous perverse and incestuously enamoured of the parent of the opposite sex. On the other hand, however,

Freud imbued the child with cognitive capacities in infancy which were in many ways comparable to those of the adult.

To compare these two images of the child more succinctly we might say that, for Freud, the child is similar to adults in his thinking but different from them in his feelings which for Piaget just the reverse holds true. In Piaget's work the child is similar to adults in his feelings but different from them in his thoughts.

There are several rather general principles of education implicit in Piaget's image of the child as an intellectual alien in the adult world. First of all, it implies that the foremost problem of education is *communication*. According to the Piaget image, the child's mind is not an empty slate. Quite the contrary, the child has a host of ideas about the physical and natural world, but these ideas differ from those of adults and are expressed in a different linguistic mode. The first prerequisite, then, for educating children, is developing effective modes of communication with them. That is to say we must learn to comprehend what children are saying and to respond in the same mode of discourse.

A second implication is that the child is always unlearning and relearning as well as acquiring entirely new knowledge. The child comes to school with his own ideas about space, time, causality, quantity, and number. His ideas in these areas are, however, incomplete in comparison with those of adults. The concept of education must, therefore, be broadened to encompass aiding children in the modification of their existing knowledge in addition to helping them to learn new material.

Still a third implication for educational philosophy implicit in the view of the child as a cognitive alien is that the child is by nature a knowing creature. If the child has ideas about the world which he has not been taught (because they are foreign to adults) and which he has not inherited (because they change with age) then he must have acquired these notions through his spontaneous interactions with the environment. This means that the child is trying to construct a world view on his own and is limited only by his abilities and experience. Education need not, then, concern itself with instilling a zest for knowledge within the child since the desire to know is part of his makeup. Rather, education needs to insure that it does not dull this eagerness to know by overly rigid curricula that disrupt the child's own rhythm and pace of learning.

The image of the child held at any particular point in history must reflect and be reflected by events in the society as a whole. This was certainly true in Calvin's day as well as Freud's. Accordingly, one test of the validity and viability of Piaget's image of the child is the extent to which the cognitive alienation that Piaget posits for the child, holds for the larger society as well.

It is probably fair to say that a major characteristic of contemporary modern societies is the breakdown of interpersonal communication. While there have always been failures to communicate between labor and management, the difficulties are greatly increased today as businesses have grown enormously large and chains of command correspondingly longer. The same holds true for government where the "credibility gap" is but another name for the breakdown in communication that seems endemic today. Easily the most dramatic indications of the communication problems in modern society are the evidences of the "generation gap" and the campus revolts. Even in the university, the citadel of reasoned communication, the gaps in understanding between students and faculty, between faculty and administration, and between students and administration are everywhere evident. If communication is difficult in the university, what must it be like in other domains?

Likewise, it is probably not too far-fetched to interpret some of the current movements in the theater and in literature as attempts to redress the balance and to re-establish communication even if this has to be at the most primitive body level. The current emphasis upon sensitivity training in business and in education is still another evidence of the recognition that something needs to be done to get people to understand one another. In all of these activities, a common element is an attempt to penetrate the impersonalization and dehumanization of a highly technological and automated society. People want to be recognized as individuals rather than numbers or statistics, and such recognition must come from interpersonal communication.

Piaget's image of the child as cognitively but not affectively alien to adults is thus entirely in keeping with a dominant problem of our time. Specialization, the meteoric increase in available knowledge, and the proliferation of media has intellectually alienated us from all but small groups of people. Our commonality rests in our emotional reactions, and artists and writers work increasingly on our most basic ones to produce some consensus of understanding. It is probably fair to say that cognitive alienation is becoming a symptom of our times, and Piaget's image of the child as cognitively alien from adults reflects, in part at least, a phenomenon of our society at large.

THE PROCESS OF LEARNING

In his essays on learning (84, 85) Piaget makes a distinction between learning in the strict sense (modifications of behavior and thought as a result of experience) and learning in the broad sense (modifications of behavior and thought which result from experience *and* from processes of equilibriation or complex feedback activities between maturation and experience). For our purposes we will consider only his discussion of learning in the narrow sense because learning in the broad sense covers the whole of human development.

Within the realm of learning in the strict sense Piaget again distinguishes between two different modes of experience that result in behavior modification. One mode occurs when things act upon us which Piaget calls physical (P) experience. Another occurs as a result of our actions upon things which Piaget labels logico-mathematical (LM) experience. Piaget attaches considerable importance to this distinction and it is the focus of much of his discussion of learning. Indeed, the major implications of Piaget's work for the process of learning derive from the differences between P and LM experiences.

In the first place, P learning involves the discovery of the qualities and properties of things. Shape, color, and form are results of energies emanating from things and acting upon us. Such experiences are, moreover, arbitrary in the sense that they are devoid of logical necessity. There is no logical reason for cherries to be red, sweet, and juicy; they simply are that way. In addition, the modifications of behavior and thought which result from physical experience are for the most part extrinsically motivated. A child learns that candy is sweet and that certain berries are sour by tasting them; properties of the objects or their consequences facilitate learning.

LM experience on the other hand involves learning about the properties and relations which belong not to things but rather to our actions upon things. Concepts such as "right" and "left," "causality," "quantity," and "number" all derive from our actions upon things.* LM experiences have a logical necessity not present in physical experience. When a child discovers that number is conserved—remains unchanged across a transformation in its appearance—he asserts that this will hold true across all trans-formations. Conservation is based on deductive reasoning (24), and hence the conclusion is generalized as a logical necessity. Finally, LM experiences are intrinsically motivated in that the discovery of, say, conservation is self-satisfying. The discovery or realization of logical truth does not need to be rewarded in

*The concept of "action upon things" must be broadly construed to include not only motor manipulation but also perceptual exploration and judgment. It is the abstraction from motor and perceptual actions that is the basis of LM learning.

any physical way because the exercise of reason is pleasurable in of itself. We shall return to this motivational issue later and deal with it in more detail.

Piaget's distinction between P and LM learning is not unlike the distinction between associative and insightful learning made by Gestalt psychologists (65, 63). Insightful learning also involves the action of the subject upon things (the reorganization of the field) and is self-rewarding (the "aha" experience). For the Gestalt psychologists, however, the laws of organization are not derived from the subject's actions upon things but are rather inherent in the organism. For the Gestalt psychologist (111, 112) the task is to get the subject to utilize the principles and laws of organization appropriately. For Piaget, in contrast, principles of organization and relations are not inherent in the organism but must be learned or abstracted from his actions upon things.

In Piaget's view, all learning can be shown to manifest a logical form which brings us to a last and all important distinction between P and LM learning. The logic manifested in P learning is of a more primitive and less complete form than that manifested by LM learning. When a subject learns (by association) a list of words, he has in fact organized a series which might be described as A before B before $C > D > E$ and so on. This is a primitive seriation because the subject cannot, without relearning, reverse the series. When, however, a child learns to seriate a set of size-graded blocks, the capacity to seriate them from smallest to largest implies the capacity to seriate the objects in the opposite direction. The difference in the two modifications is that the child learned the seriation as a consequence of his own actions whereas in the case of the word list, the order was imposed by the activity of the experimenter.

The practical implications of Piaget's distinction between physical and logico-mathematical experience and learning can be limited to a discussion of the LM mode of experience since we are all familiar with P learning from elementary texts in psychology and education. Certain aspects of LM learning are of particular relevance to education.

ASPECTS OF LM LEARNING

There are several important features of LM learning that are in some ways unique in comparison with P learning. These aspects have to do with: a) the relation of LM learning to maturation and development; b) the unique content of LM learning; c) the effects of LM learning upon the child's perception of the world and d) the relation of LM learning to motivation and reinforcement.

Learning and Development. If P learning is regarded as primarily an associative process then such a process can clearly be observed at and possibly even prior to birth (101). Changes in this process as the child grows older would lie, from this point of view, in the area of increased rapidity or efficiency of functioning. In recent years, however, even investigators concerned with P learning have suggested that there may be changes in the learning process itself as the child grows older (114). Investigators have attributed such changes to neurophysiological growth (53), to learning to learn (51), to verbal mediation (61), and to cumulative learning (41).

These approaches differ from Piaget's view in that they try to attribute changes in the learning process to the learning process in question. Harlow's (51) notion of "learning sets," for example, ascribes the ability to discriminate to practice in discrimination. Likewise the "verbal mediation" suggested by the Kendlers (61) and the hierarchies described by Gagné (41) presuppose associative learning processes; any new learning process derived from associative processes is of necessity "associative" in nature and hence not really "new." Even though there may not be any really new processes which emerge with age there is the possibility that P learning may be influenced by developmental changes in LM learning.

LM learning, in contrast, involves induction and deduction rather than association; the modes of induction and deduction change with age and development. These changes can be described in terms of the number of variables or factors that the child can integrate or deal with at any given age level for, while the basic logical operations are present in rudimentary form even in infancy, their coordination and hierarchical integration changes with age.

During the first two years of life, the infant can learn about objects by comparing them in a rather global and undifferentiated fashion. A stranger's face, for example, is discriminated on the basis of its global configuration rather than upon a specific characteristic. During early childhood (2–7 years), children begin to single out various dimensions and qualities but deal with them one at a time without integration. Number is thought of in terms of the length or the density of a collection but the child does not think of number as involving the coordination of these two dimensions. During middle and late childhood, the elementary school years, the child begins to coordinate and integrate two variables or dimensions at the same time. He understands that a friend can be a boy and a child at the same time and that the amount of liquid in a container depends upon both the container's height and its width. It is only in adolescence, however, that children can learn and make discoveries by taking many different variables into account simultaneously; the adolescent can discover all the sixteen possible combinations of five chemical agents and reagents that will color water a particular color and make it clear again (56).

The changes in learning ability described above clearly express in somewhat different form the mechanisms available to the child at Piaget's sensory-motor, pre-operational, concrete operational, and formal operational stages. Piaget's task is to explain how these stages and their corresponding learning processes come about. It is at this point that the distinction between learning in the broad sense and learning in the narrow sense becomes all important. We have been talking about changes in LM learning —learning through the abstraction of our actions upon things, which is a form of learning from experience alone. To explain these changes in learning in the narrow sense, Piaget invokes the concept of learning in the broad sense, namely, learning that involves the complex feedback activity of maturation *and* experience; he calls this process equilibration.

By invoking the notion of learning in the broad sense, Piaget has avoided the difficulty encountered by those who attempt to explain age changes in P learning. Piaget has recognized that it is not possible to get a new process out of the continuous utilization of an old one, without invoking another higher order process. It is equilibration between maturation and experience that determines the changes in the LM learning process and not the mere functioning of that process itself. Consequently, the changes in LM learning that come about with age are not simply more of the same (as in P learning), but rather are qualitatively distinct processes.

For Piaget, then, learning in the broad sense of the modification of behavior as the result of the *equilibration* of maturation and experience determines the nature of learning in the narrow sense of a modification of behavior due to experience *alone*. Or, since learning in the broad sense corresponds to what we usually mean by development, and learning in the narrow sense refers to what we usually mean by learning, we might simply say that for Piaget, development determines learning.

Content and LM Learning. Whenever we talk about the content of learning we generally have in mind a body of knowledge or facts which might be called P content. To learn geography, for example, is to learn some facts about the political and physical features of the earth. LM content must also be learned but is more general in nature and serves to organize the more discrete factual information. Such contents have to do with our ideas of space, time, causality, and number that serve in the organization and relation of all particular facts. In school, for example, the teacher assumes that the child knows such categories as "same" and different," and such spatial relations as "right" and "left" and "top" and "bottom." She uses words like "more" and "less" as well as "because" without thinking to explain them. These LM concepts are, however, not innate and must themselves be learned.

An essential difference between P contents and LM contents is that the P contents a child has learned are relatively unaltered by his progressive mental growth whereas the LM contents are radically transformed. A child may learn his birthdate when he is six or seven and that P content, or date, is retained without alteration throughout his life. In contrast a child may first learn about "left" and "right" when he is four or five but the meaning of these terms will continue to evolve until he reaches the age of 11 or 12 (16; 78). LM learning changes with age and the products or contents of that learning can be expected to change as well.

To make concrete the change in LM contents that occurs as a consequence of growth in LM learning processes, consider the development of the child's conception of "right" and "left" mentioned earlier. The infant has a concept of "right" and "left" in the sense that he can orient to sound or sights coming from particular directions. His sense of direction is, however, part of a total bodily orientation and is not yet differentiated from the objects or stimulation which produce the orientation reaction. At the pre-school level, the child can label his "right" and "left" hands but he does not recognize their relational character. When an adult stands opposite him he says the adult's "right" and "left" hands are directly opposite his own. During the elementary school period the child can take another person's point of view and designate that person's "right" and "left" hands correctly even when the person is opposite him. It is, however, only toward adolescence that young people understand that one and the same element can, at the same time, be on the right of one thing and on the left of another.

This example of how LM contents are transformed in accordance with changes in LM learning illustrates another important difference between LM contents and P contents. The child has P content or he does not—either he knows that Independence Day is celebrated on the 4th of July or he does not. With LM contents, however, the situation is different. As the example given above demonstrates, even the infant has a global conception of "right" and "left." What is important about LM contents is that the child has a *different* conception of right and left at successive age levels. LM contents can, then, never be evaluated as present or absent or as right or wrong. In evaluating LM contents all we can say is that the infant's concept of right and left is *different* from that of the young child whose conception is *different* from that of the elementary school child whose conception is *different* from that of the adolescent and the adult.

Piaget describes two mechanisms * by which LM contents evolve. One of these mechanisms is *integration* and the other is *substitution*. Most quantitative and relational conceptions such as "number" and "right" and "left" evolve by integration. In the evolving conception of right and left, for example, the earlier absolutistic notions are incorporated in, and made part of, the later more relational conception. The same holds true for number. The young child's idea of number as a single dimension is later integrated into a conception of number as two dimensions in combination.

Substitution, in contrast, is much more common among concepts that deal with causality and the living world. Although most of us, as we grow older, substitute an abstract conception of life for the animistic views we held in childhood, backsliding is frequent. Whenever we kick a car because it fails to start or curse

* These mechanisms are described in detail in Chapter 5.

a television set for fading at the wrong moment, we have reverted to animistic thinking. When the content of a given concept changes by means of substitution, therefore, there is always the possibility of reversion to the earlier level of conceptualization and understanding.

Piaget's description of LM contents as changing with age either by integration or substitution as a consequence of changes in LM learning has important consequences for education. In the pedagogical literature two emphases have alternated down through the ages. One of these was the emphasis upon teaching facts and more facts while the other emphasis was upon training children in certain logical thought processes (formal discipline). The implication in Piaget's work is that this emphasis upon content *or* process is, at least with respect to LM learning, a false dichotomy. In LM learning, content cannot be taught without affecting process and vice versa. If a child is taught about "right" and "left," he is also being taught to abstract from his own actions and hence the process of LM learning is affected as well.

From an educational standpoint, therefore, Piaget's work suggests that much more attention ought to be paid to LM contents, to the basic concepts within which experience is arranged and organized. The value of instruction in these domains is twofold. First, training of LM contents will affect both process *and* content so that the instruction will have broader impact. Secondly, since LM contents serve as the framework for P learning, the learning of P contents might be facilitated as well.

LM Learning and the Child's Perception of the World. A very important characteristic of LM learning has to do with its effects upon the subject's views of the world about him. In general P learning tends to be analytic in that it enables us to better differentiate among various features in the environment. LM learning is, on the contrary, synthetic in the sense that it helps us to organize events into larger wholes. Such organization is possible because LM learning derives from our actions upon things—which actions are infinite in their variety—and not directly from the things themselves. Accordingly, while P learning takes us closer to things by making us more aware of their properties, LM learning takes us farther from things by stressing their relations to other things. Put rather more simply we might say that P learning changes *what* we see whereas LM learning changes *how* we see what we do.

A few examples of the effects of LM learning on perception may help to make the foregoing ideas more concrete. Whenever a stimulus is more or less unstructured it provides an opportunity for us to act and impose an organization upon it, that is to say, to utilize LM learning. The well-known Rorschach inkblots provide such an unstructured stimulus. When subjects look at the blots they are completely unaware of their own activity in organizing the material. That they are organizing the material is, however, clear from the fact that one subject will see a "bear" where another will see a "tree" or "threatening clouds." What is significant about responses to the Rorschach is that: a) the subject organizes the stimulus and b) he is unaware of having done so and assumes that the "bear" or "tree" is present in the blot.

Roughly the same holds true for cognitive organizations mediated by LM learning. When the child discovers that a row of pennies contains the same number as are present in a pile, he acts as if the equality were present in the pennies themselves and as if he had nothing at all to do with finding their equality. As in the case of the Rorschach response, the child organizes the stimulus but is aware only of the result and not of the act of organization. In contrast to the Rorschach response, however, the child's response to conservation problems (apparent but not real changes in properties, qualities, and relations) does not reflect individual or personal organizations but rather the mental operations characteristic of all "normal" children of about that age.

This difference between the Rorschach type of response and

the conservation type of response is all important. It is easy to recognize the subjectivity of the Rorschach response because individuals vary so much in the kinds of responses they give. Conservation responses, on the contrary, are so uniform, indeed so universal, beyond a certain age that their subjectivity had been overlooked until Piaget discovered it. This discovery means that much in the world about us which we regard as "out there" is really, in part at least, a product of our own mental actions. We are not aware of our part because all adults externalize the products of their mental actions in the same fashion and hence view the world in the same way. To detect such universal externalizations one has to study their development in the child.

An important educational implication in the discovery of the partial subjectivity of apparently objective knowledge is that just as children differ from adults in their thinking so too do they literally as well as figuratively *see* the world differently than do adults. The adult, moreover, is frequently unaware of this difference (for the same reason a subject is unaware of his part in producing the Rorschach response). Because he externalizes the products of his own mental activity and takes the world as independent of thought he often fails to comprehend how the child can view it differently. Children's infamous "why" questions are a case in point. When a child asks "why is the light green?" he does not want a physical explanation dealing with the wave lengths of light. On the contrary, he wants to know the purpose of the green light, namely, to allow the cars to go.

This difference (frequently unacknowledged) in viewpoints between children and adults is particularly pernicious in education. Most good teachers intuitively recognize the unique world view of the child and gear their instruction and verbalizations accordingly. Those who do not, fail to understand the child at crucial moments in the educational process and they in turn may not always make themselves understood. It seems reasonable to expect that teacher education should include instruction as to how children at different age levels view the world and how this view differs from that of adults.

LM Learning and Motivation. In recent years increasing attention has been paid by psychologists and educators to the self-rewarding quality of many types of learning and behavior. The existence of "competence" motivation (113) and of curiosity drives (2) are such obvious features of human behavior it is a wonder it took psychology so long to recognize them. While the positing of these types of motivation greatly broadens the forces propelling P types of learning, they are still of little relevance to the logico-mathematical learning described by Piaget because even the "intrinsic" motivations described by White and Berlyne are seen as something separate from and as acting upon the learning process itself. Curiosity and competence motivation lead to the "stamping in" or to the "stamping out" of behavior but are separate from the stamping process itself.

In the case of LM learning, however, any distinction between the process of learning and its motivation is false and artificial. For Piaget, the motivation of the LM learning process is inherent in the process itself and can be discerned only when that process is looked at from a particular point of view. Piaget's position can be made a little less abstract by an analogy. Ordinarily we do not ask "Why does the heart beat?" or "Why does the stomach digest food?" because "why" is usually employed in the psychological or intentional sense. Since the heart and the stomach have no separate ego, to ask why they behave as they do in the intentional sense is absurd. If, however, we ask for the physical or physiological reasons for their activities the question is not absurd and can be given a reasonable answer.

This analogy was not selected at random because for Piaget the mind is an organ of the body whose fundamental processes (assimilation, accommodation, and equilibriation) are common to all organs. The mind functions as it does because of these processes and because of the way it is constructed. When we ask "why" a child learns conservation, then, we have to look at the mind from the standpoint of its structure and function. It is only in terms of mental structures and functions that the "why" question about conservation can be answered. The infant does not consciously set out to discover the conservation of the object nor is he driven to it by hunger or thirst. Likewise, the concrete operational child does not consciously set out to discover the conservation of number, of mass, weight, and volume, of length, area, time, and speed. The child's discovery of these various conservations is as natural a product of the mind's structures and functions as are the products of the heart's beating or the stomach's digestion. Indeed, the apparently universal attainment of many of these conservations (46) attests to the status of these attainments as products of structures and processes common to most children. From the Piaget perspective, then, the question as to why the child attains conservation has to be answered in a particular way. The answer cannot include reference to motives, intentions, or rewards, but must describe the structures and processes which govern the functioning of the mind. Current computer simulations of human intelligence (72; 96) take just this approach to the "explanation" of human cognition.

For education this view of mental functioning means that some of the most important ideas the child acquires, those which structure his experience in general, are not taught but are spontaneously (unintentionally) acquired. In addition, it means that learning is going on *all of the time*. Learning in Piaget's broad sense is coextensive with life processes and the child learns every moment of his waking life. The child who sits watching a fly move along the sill is learning something. Likewise, the youngster who creates chaos in the classroom may not be learning the curriculum but he is learning how to create chaos. And the child who sits quietly doing nothing is learning how to withdraw from the world without antagonizing it. Learning then is an ongoing activity for every child.

This point cannot be overemphasized. Too often we take a rather narrow view of learning and assume the child is learning only when he is acquiring what we want him to learn; a "slow learner" is one who does not acquire the curriculum at a "normal" rate. But it is a big mistake to identify learning ability with curriculum acquisition. The slow learner is fast to learn that he is slow. He learns quickly how to mask his deficiencies either by memory (so that he appears to be reading) or by defensive maneuvers such as becoming the class clown or bully. What the child learns about himself may, in the long run, be more important to his educational progress than what he learns from the curriculum. In summary, then, perhaps the most important implication of Piaget's views regarding motivation and learning is that we need to conceive of learning more broadly and to recognize that it is an ongoing life process. Once we acknowledge that children are learning something, all of the time—even if it is not what we set out to teach them—then we have considerably broadened our options for reaching children and for directing their mental growth.

THE PRACTICE OF TEACHING

Effective teaching is still more of an art than it is a science. This does not mean that teaching cannot be taught; but the acceptance of teaching as art means that it cannot be reduced to sound knowledge of subject matter or to skill in handling curriculum or audio-visual materials. The successful teacher needs, in addition to technical skill and certain fundamental personality traits, an orientation toward teaching and toward children that will guide her in the effective and appropriate use of her technical skills. Although Piaget has not spoken to the problem of teaching directly, his work does suggest an orientation that might be of value to those who are not born teachers but who have become teachers or have had teaching thrust upon them. This orientation involves the three principles of communication, valuation, and dedication.

Communication. It has already been suggested that an important implication of this image was that effective education presupposes meaningful communication between teacher and pupil. Later, in the discussion of LM learning, it was pointed out that externalization (the process by which we take our own mental productions as given in the environment) is an important hindrance to effective communication between adults and children. The teacher who knows about the differences between adult and child world views is likely to communicate and educate more successfully than one not so prepared. Communication with children then requires that the teacher be trained in the vagaries and vicissitudes of children's thinking and that she be willing to discourse at that level.

Equally important is the understanding of the child's non-verbal communications. The way in which a child sits and moves, the tone of his voice, and his nervous habits are as much communications as his verbal productions. The teacher must be sensitive to all levels of communication if she wishes truly to understand and relate to her charges. Training in the non-verbal as well as the verbal communications of children is particularly important in working with children who come from different socio-economic backgrounds. Each ethnic and socio-economic group has its own non-verbal signals which must be read if true communication is to occur. Here again, the implication of Piaget's work is that teachers be trained in understanding the child's verbal as well as non-verbal productions as a prerequisite to effective instruction.

Valuation. Education and applied psychology have long tended to be test oriented. One characteristic of tests is that they presuppose "right" and "wrong" answers. So long as we are dealing with P type learning, this kind of dichotomy makes sense. Columbus did discover America in 1492 and 1493 just as two and two make four and not six. When we come to LM learning, however, the issue is not so clear. As pointed out earlier, the child has a progression of concepts of space, time, causality, and quantity which differ from one another in their completeness and adequacy.

In the case of LM concepts, therefore, it would be misleading to say that the four year old who conceives of "right" and "left" as attributes has a "wrong" conception of these terms for we, as adults, use such terms in a variety of senses, some of which are coincident with the way in which the child uses them. Although "right" and "left" are usually employed in the relative sense they are also used in the absolute sense when we speak of our "right arm" or our "left arm." The child's use of "right" and "left" as absolute designations is thus not wrong, it is merely limited. To describe less differentiated concepts as "wrong" thus ignores the fact that such usages are "right" even for adults in particular circumstances.

Accordingly, when we deal with LM type concepts we must not *evaluate* them as right or wrong but rather *value* them as genuine expressions of the child's budding mental abilities. When we deal with spatial, temporal, causal, or quantitative concepts, we need to explore the kinds of meanings children give to such terms. Such exploration reveals the level and reference frame of the child's understanding and makes clear the next step needed to broaden this understanding. More importantly, such exploration avoids the inhibiting suggestion that the child's incomplete (but partially correct) understanding of such terms is "wrong." A teacher who sees a child's productions as having value, as meaning something, avoids putting the child on the track of always seeking "right" answers. More importantly, perhaps, her orientation conveys to the child a sense of her attempt to understand him and her respect for his intellectual productions.

Dedication. The ability to communicate adequately with children and to value their responses will have little impact if the teacher lacks dedication to certain values. Implicit in the Piaget conception of education is the premise that the teacher must be dedicated to growth, to her personal growth as well as to the growth of her pupils. Education is, after all, adults and children interacting, and personal, social, and intellectual growth is what the interaction is all about.

A dedication to growth means, in the first place, that learning is living and that no matter what the child is doing, he is learning something. The teacher dedicated to growth will attempt to surmise what even her "worst" pupils are learning and will try to counteract the negative self-images, the feelings of failure and inadequacy that accompany poor academic achievement. (This is not to say that a teacher must be a psychotherapist—far from it. The emotionally disturbed child has no place in the classroom if he so distracts the students or so preoccupies the teacher as to disrupt the educational process.)

A teacher dedicated to growth must also be dedicated to her own personal growth. She must be willing to try new things, to evaluate their effectiveness objectively, and to discard and modify as the situation warrants. As the teacher matures in her own life, as she marries, has children, and sees them mature, her attitudes toward her students will also change. What the teacher learns as a wife and mother are invaluable in her role as teacher if she is willing to use her experience in this way.

Example is still the most effective tutor. The teacher who is curious to learn, who is willing to be innovative, to evaluate and be critical, and to try again will instill similar values in her young charges. A teacher cannot really expect her pupils to be creative, objective, and critical if she is not. Children do model

themselves after the teacher's behavior (52); teacher resourceful-
ness, dictatorialness, and punitiveness had significant effects upon
such pupil behavior as involvement, achievement, and con-
creteness.

Teacher dedication can be manifested in an infinite variety of
ways, and sets no limits on the teacher's individuality and uniqueness of expression. Likewise, a true dedication to growth involves
a commitment to helping every child find his own abilities in his
own way and in his own time. In addition it involves the recognition that growth, like life in general, involves conflict, constant
change, and no end of problems. The teacher who reflects, in her
own behavior, a dedication to growth and the courage to live is a
teacher in the best and most comprehensive sense of that word.

Over the past decade, interest and work in the area of early childhood have made it the growth stock among educational disciplines. In the design of early childhood programs, two names, Piaget and Montessori, are repeatedly heard. Although these two workers came from different backgrounds and had quite different orientations toward children, they have nonetheless arrived at some common beliefs about the nature and nurture of mental growth. The next chapter compares and contrasts the orientation and ideas of these two giants of early childhood education.

9

Piaget and Montessori

In recent years there has been a renaissance of American interest in the work of Jean Piaget and Maria Montessori. Although the reasons for this rebirth of interest are many and varied, two reasons appear beyond dispute. First of all, both Piaget and Montessori have observed hitherto unexpected and unknown facets of child thought and behavior. Second, and in this lies their impact, both of these innovators have derived the general laws and principles regarding child thought and behavior which were implicit in their observations. In the case of Piaget, these observations led to a new philosophy of knowledge while in the case of Montessori, they led to a new philosophy of education.

Unfortunately, it is not possible, in a presentation such as this one, to do any sort of justice to the contributions of these two innovators. Under the circumstances, all that I would like to do is to describe, and to illustrate with research data, three original ideas about child thought and behavior which Piaget and Montessori arrived at independently but share in common. Before turning to those ideas, however, it seems appropriate, by way of introduction, to note some of the parallels and divergences in the Piagetian and Montessorian approaches to child study.

PARALLELS AND DIVERGENCES

Among the many parallels between the work of Piaget and Montessori, one of the most pervasive is the predominantly biological orientation which they take toward the thought and behavior of the child. This is not surprising in view of their backgrounds. Piaget, for example, was publishing papers in biology while still in his teens and took his doctorate in biology at the University of Lausanne. Likewise, Montessori was trained as a physician (she was the first woman in Italy to receive a medical degree) and engaged in and published medical research (102). This shared biological orientation is important because both these workers see mental growth as an extension of biological growth and as governed by the same principles and laws.

In addition to, and perhaps because of, this shared biological orientation, both Piaget and Montessori emphasize the normative aspects of child behavior and development as opposed to the aspects of individual difference. Piaget, for example, has been concerned with identifying those mental structures which, if they hold true for the individual, also hold true for the species. Likewise, Montessori has been concerned with those needs and abilities that are common to all children such as the "sensitive periods" and the "explosions" into exploration. This is not to say that Piaget and Montessori in any way deny or minimize the importance of individual differences; far from it. What they do argue is that an understanding of normal development is a necessary starting point for a full understanding of differences between individuals.

The last parallel in the approaches of Piaget and Montessori is more personal. Both of these workers manifest what might be called a *genius for empathy with the child*. When reading Piaget or Montessori, one often has the uncanny feeling that they are somehow able to get inside the child and know exactly what he is thinking and feeling and why he is doing what he is doing at any given moment. It is this genius for empathy with the child which, or so it seems to me, gives their observations and insights —even without the buttressing of systematic research—the solid ring of truth.

Despite these parallels, Piaget and Montessori also diverge in significant ways in their approaches to the child. For Piaget, the study of the child is really a means to an end rather than an end in itself. He is not so much concerned with children *qua* children as he is with using the study of the child to answer questions about the nature and origin of knowledge. Please do not misunderstand; Piaget is in no way callous toward the child and has given not a little of his considerable energies and administrative talents to national and international endeavors on the part of children. He has not, however, concerned himself with child-rearing practices, nor—at least until recently and only with reluctance—has he dealt with educational issues (88). Piaget sees his contribution primarily in the area of logic and epistemology and only secondarily in the area of child psychology and education.

Montessori, on the other hand, was from the very outset of her career directly concerned with the welfare of the child. Much of her long and productive life was devoted to the training of teachers, the education of parents, and the liberation of the child from a pedagogy which she believed was as detrimental to his mental growth as poor diet was to his physical growth. Montessori, then, was dedicated to improving the lot of the child in very concrete ways.

The other major divergences between these two innovators stem more or less directly from this central difference in approach. Piaget is primarily concerned with theory while Montessori's commitment was to practice. Moreover, Piaget sees his work as being in opposition to "arm chair" epistemology and views himself as the "man in the middle," between empiricists and nativists. Montessori, in contrast, saw herself in opposition to traditional pedagogy, which she regarded as medieval in its total disregard for the rights and needs of the child.

CONVERGING IDEAS

Let us focus upon Montessori's ideas rather than her methods, for that is where the convergence of Piaget and Montessori is greatest and where the available research is most relevant. Definitive research with respect to the effectiveness of Montessori's methods seems yet to be completed.

Nature and Nurture. It would be easy, but unfair and incorrect, to contrast Piaget and Montessori with those who seem to take a strong nurture position with respect to mental development. Even if we start with extreme environmentalists (107, 8), it would be a misrepresentation to say that they deny the role of nature in development. The real issue is not one of either nature or nurture but rather one of the character of their interaction. One of the innovations of Piaget and Montessori lies, then, not so much in their championing of the role of nature as in the original way in which they have conceived the character of nature-nurture interaction.

Both Piaget and Montessori see mental growth as an extension of physical growth, and it is in the elaboration of this idea that they have made their unique contributions to the problem of nature-nurture interaction. Their position means, in the first place, that the environment provides nourishment for the growth of mental structures just as it does for the growth of physical organs. It means in addition, and this has been stressed particularly by Montessori, that some forms of environmental nourishment are more beneficial than others for sustaining mental growth just as some foods are more beneficial than others for sustaining physical growth. The "prepared environment" in the Montessori school is designed to provide the best possible nourishment for mental growth.

The relation between nature and nurture in mental growth is, however, not as one-sided as that. Not only does the child utilize environmental stimuli to nourish his own growth, but growth must adapt and modify itself in accordance with the particular environment within which it take place. Of the many possible languages a child might learn, he learns the one to which he is exposed. The same holds true for his concepts and percepts which are, in part at least, determined by the social and physical milieu in which he grows up. Both Piaget and Montessori recognize and take account of this directive role which the environment plays in the determination of mental content. Indeed, the beauty of the Montessori materials (such as sandpaper letters, number rods, form and weight inset boards) lies in the fact that they simultaneously provide the child with nourishment for the growth of mental capacities and with relevant educational content. In short, for both Piaget and Montessori, nature interacts in a dual way with nurture. As far as mental capacities are concerned, the environment serves as nourishment for the growth of mental structures or abilities whose pattern of development follows a course which is laid down in the genes. Insofar as the content of thought is concerned, nurture plays a more directive role and determines the particular language, concepts, percepts, and values that the child will acquire.

What evidence do we have for this conception of the dual character of nature-nurture interaction? That the environment is a provider of nourishment for an inner-directed pattern of structural development, there is considerable evidence from Piaget-related research. For example, children of different nationalities— British, Arab, Indian, and Somali—were given a battery of Piaget-type number and quantity tasks. Regardless of nationality and language, these children gave the same responses as Piaget had attained with Swiss children (8). It has been found more recently (50) that there is little difference between Chinese and American children with respect to the age at which they manifested concrete reasoning. These cross-cultural findings suggest that children can utilize whatever stimuli are available in their immediate environs to foster their mental growth just as children all over the world can utilize quite different diets to realize their physical growth.

At the same time, there is also considerable evidence that environmental stimulation directs the content of thought. In a cross-cultural study (66) for example, there were differences even at the six-year-old level in response to the question "What are you?" Most white American children thought of themselves primarily as "a boy" or as "a girl" while South African Bantu youngsters usually described themselves in terms of race. Furthermore, Lebanese children frequently responded to the question in kinship terms and gave responses such as "the nephew of Ali." This study amply illustrates the role of the physical and social environment in shaping the child's self-concept.

For both Piaget and Montessori, then, nature-nurture interaction has a dual character. In the case of mental capacities, nature plays the directive role and nurture is subservient, while just the reverse is true with respect to the content of thought. It is in their emphasis upon the dual character of nature-nurture interaction that Piaget and Montessori have made their signal contribution to this age-old problem.

Capacity and Learning. Within experimental psychology, the child is generally viewed as a naive organism. That is to say, a child is one who is lacking in experience although his capacity to learn is no different from that of the adult. If differences between children and adults exist, then they reside in the fact that adults have had more opportunity and time to profit from experience than have children. For both Piaget and Montessori, however, the child is a *young* organism, which means that his needs and capacities are quite different from those of the adult. This issue can be put more directly by saying that for the experimental psychologist capacity is determined by learning, whereas for the developmental psychologist learning is determined by capacity or development.

To make this point concrete, let me use a crude but useful analogy. Over the past ten years, we have seen several "generations" of computers. The early computers were relatively slow and quite limited in the amount of information which they could store. The most recent computers, on the other hand, are extremely fast and have enormous memories. Even the earliest computers, however, could handle some of the programs that the high-speed computers can. On the other hand, no matter how many programs were run on the early computers, their capacity was not altered but remained fixed by the limits of their hardware. To be sure, by ingenious programing, these early computers were able to do some extraordinary things, but their limitations in terms of hardware persisted.

The several generations of computers can be likened to the several stages in the development of intelligence. Just as the hardware of the computer determines its memory and speed, so the mental structures at any given level of development determine the limits of the child's learning. Likewise, just as the number of programs run on a computer leaves its speed and memory unaltered, so does the number of problems a child has solved or the number of concepts attained not change his problem-solving or concept-learning capacities. Furthermore, just as we can, with elaborate programing, get the computer to do things it was not intended to do, so we can with specialized training get children to learn things which seem beyond their ken. Such training does not, however, change their capacity to learn any more than an ingenious computer program alters the speed or memory of the computer. This is what Piaget and Montessori have in mind by the notion that capacity determines learning and not the reverse.

This idea is frequently misunderstood by many advocates of Piaget and Montessori. Indeed much of the acceptance of Piaget and Montessori in America today seems to be based on the promise which their ideas hold out for accelerating growth. Nothing, however, could be further from their own beliefs and intentions. Piaget was recently quoted as saying, "It's probably possible to accelerate, but maximal acceleration is not desirable. What seems to be an optimal time . . . will surely depend on each individual and on the subject matter" (58). In the same vein, Montessori wrote, "We must not, therefore, set ourselves the educational problem of seeking means whereby to organize the internal personality of the child and develop his characteristics: the sole problem is that of offering the child the necessary nourishment" (70).

The view that capacity determines what will be learned has been supported in a negative way by the failure of many experiments designed to train children on Piaget-type reasoning tasks (50, 99, 115, 116). In addition, however, there is also evidence of a positive sort which substantiates the role of capacity in the determination of what is learned. One study, for example, demonstrated that while six-, seven-, and eight-year-old children could all improve their perceptual performance as a result of training, it was also true that the oldest children made the most improvement with the least training (29). A more recent study has shown (34) that there are some perceptual concepts—such as setting or background—which kindergarten children cannot attain but which are easily acquired by second-grade youngsters. In the same vein, it has also been demonstrated that there are marked differences in the conceptual strategies * employed by children and adolescents and that these strategies limit the kinds of concepts which elementary-school children can attain (22, 25, 26). Similar findings have been reported elsewhere (110, 74).

There is, then, evidence that capacity does determine what is learned and how it is learned. Such findings do not deny that children "learn to learn" or that at any age they can learn tech-

---

* In a problem-solving task, for example, once a child sets up an hypothesis, he continues to maintain it even when the information he receives clearly indicates that it is wrong. The adolescent, on the other hand, immediately gives up an hypothesis that is contradicted by the data and proceeds to try out a different one.

niques which enable them to use their abilities more effectively. All that such studies argue is that development sets limits as to what can be learned at any particular point in the child's life. These studies are in keeping with the positions of Piaget and Montessori. As we have seen, neither of these innovators advocates the acceleration of mental growth. What they do emphasize is the necessity of providing the child with the settings and stimuli which will free any given child to realize his capacities at his own time and pace.

Cognitive Needs and Repetitive Behavior. One of the features of cognitive growth which Piaget and Montessori observed and to which they both attached considerable importance, is the frequently repetitive character of behaviors associated with emerging mental abilities. Piaget and Montessori are almost unique in this regard since within both psychology and education repetitive behavior is often described pejoratively as "rote learning" or "perseveration." Indeed, the popular view is that repetition is bad and should be avoided in our dealings with children.

What both Piaget and Montessori have recognized, however, is the very great role which repetitive behavior plays in mental growth. In his classic work on the origins of intelligence in infants, Piaget (80) illustrates in remarkable detail the role which primary, secondary, and tertiary circular reactions play in the construction of intellectual schemas. Likewise at a later age, Piaget (81) has pointed out the adaptive significance of children's repetitive "Why?" questions. Such questions, which often seem stupid or annoying to adults, are in fact the manifestation of the child's efforts at differentiating between psychological and physical causality, i.e., between intentional or motivated events and events which are a consequence of natural law.

Montessori has likewise recognized the inner significance of repetitive behavior in what she calls the "polarization of attention." Here is a striking example:

I watched the child intently without disturbing her at first, and begin to count how many times she repeated the exercise; then, seeing that she was continuing for a long time, I picked up the little arm chair in which she was seated and placed chair and child upon the table; the little creature hastily caught up her case of insets, laid it across the arms of the chair and gathering the cylinders into her lap, set to work again. Then I called upon the children to sing; they sang, but the little girl continued undisturbed, repeating her exercise even after the short song had come to an end. I counted forty-four repetitions; when at last she ceased, it was quite independently of any surrounding stimuli which might have distracted her, and she looked around with a satisfied air, almost as if awakening from a refreshing nap. (70)

The role of repetitive behavior in intellectual development is not extraordinary when we view mental growth as analogous to physical growth. Repetitive behavior is the bench mark of maturing physical abilities. The infant who is learning to walk constantly pulls himself into an erect position. Later as a toddler he begins pulling and dropping everything within reach. Such behavior does not derive from an innate perversity or drive to-toward destruction but rather out of a need to practice the ability to hold and to let go. What the child is doing in such situations is practicing or perfecting emerging motor abilities. Mental abilities are realized in the same way. In the course of being constituted, intellectual abilities seek to exercise themselves on whatever stimuli are available. The four-year-old who is constantly comparing the size of his portions with those of his siblings is not being selfish or paranoid. On the contrary, he is spontaneously exercising his capacity to make quantitative comparisons. The Montessori child who repeatedly buttons and unbuttons or replaces insets into their proper holes is likewise exercising emerging mental abilities. Piaget and Montessori see such repetitive behaviors as having tremendous value for the child and as essential to the full realization of the child's intelligence.

Although there is not a great deal of research evidence relevant to the role of repetition in mental growth, some findings from one of our studies point in this direction. In this study (35), we showed kindergarten-, first-, second-, and third-grade children a card with eighteen pictures pasted upon it in the shape of a triangle. The children's task was simply to name every picture on the card. The kindergarten children named the pictures according to the triangular pattern in which the pictures were pasted. That is to say, they began at the apex and worked around the three sides of the triangle. This same triangular pattern of exploration was employed by third-grade children and to some extent by second-grade children. First-grade children and some second-grade youngsters, however, did a peculiar thing. *They read the pictures across the triangle from top to bottom and from left to right.*

Why did the first-grade children read the pictures in this clearly inefficient way? The answer, it seems to me, lies in the fact that these children were in the process of learning the top to bottom and left to right swing which is essential in reading English. Because they had not entirely mastered this swing, they spontaneously practiced it even where it was inappropriate. Viewed in this way, their behavior was far from being stupid, and the same can be said for older slow-reading children who read the pictures in the same manner as the first-graders.

These findings thus support the arguments of Piaget and Montessori regarding the adaptive significance of repetitive behavior in children. Repetitive behavior in the child is frequently the outward manifestation of an emerging cognitive ability and the need to realize that ability through action. It was the genius of Piaget and Montessori which saw, in such repetitive behaviors as sucking and putting insets into holes, not stupidity, but rather, intelligence unfolding.

Within psychology, intelligence has been primarily the province of the practitioner, the individual involved in assessing human potential for educational or clinical purposes. As a result, intelligence is most often thought of in terms of a test score or an IQ which reflects an individual's brightness relative to others of the same age and circumstances. There is, however, another more qualitative conception of intelligence which has guided the work of Jean Piaget. In the present chapter the psychometric and developmental approaches are compared and contrasted. Three practical implications of Piaget's conception of intelligence are also discussed.

10

Two Approaches to Intelligence

The rapid growth of interest in the work and theory of Jean Piaget, has made imperative the consideration of his conceptions with those widely used in psychology. The need is particularly great with respect to the concept of *intelligence* which is employed both by Piaget as a developmental psychologist and by psychologists and educators whose orientation is the psychometric assessment of individual differences. The Piagetian and psychometric conceptions of intelligence are in some ways conceptually similar and in some ways conceptually different; both approaches relate to practical issues in the modification of intelligence.

CONCEPTUAL SIMILARITIES

There are many parallels and affinities between the psychometric or mental test approach to the problem of intelligence and the developmental approach as represented by Piaget. This is not surprising in view of the fact that Piaget began his career as a

139

developmental psychologist by working in Binet's laboratory where he sought to standardize some of Burt's (10) reasoning tests on Parisian children. Indeed, Piaget's "method clinique" is a combination of mental test and psychiatric interview procedures which consists in the use of a standardized situation as a starting point for a flexible interrogation. The affinities, however, between the two approaches to intelligence run more deeply than that; both accept genetic and maturational determination in intelligence, the use of non-experimental methodologies, and the conception of intelligence as being essentially rational.

Implicit and often explicit in both the psychometric and Piagetian positions is the assumption that mental ability is, in part at least, genetically determined. With respect to the psychometric position, it assumes that at least some of the variance in intelligence test performance is attributable to variance in genetic endowment (9, 59). Piaget (89) also acknowledges the importance of genetic factors for intellectual ability but qualifies this by pointing out that what may be genetic in one generation may not always have been so and could be the partial result of prior environmental influences. So, for Piaget, as for the biologist Waddington (105) there is a certain relativity with respect to what is attributed to genetic endowment.

One consequence of their joint acceptance of the partial genetic determination of intellectual ability, is that both psychometricians and Piaget recognize the importance of maturation in human development. Both recognize that there is a slight tendency for early precocity to be associated with slower mental growth at later ages and perhaps with a lower average intelligence level at maturity.

In addition to their shared genetic or maturational emphasis, the Piagetian and psychometric approaches to intelligence have still another common feature: their failure, for the most part, to use the experimental method in the strict sense of that term. Most of the studies which attempt to get at the determinants of test intelligence are correlational in nature. By and large such studies attempt to relate the tests scores of parents and their children, of twins, or of adopted children and their parents, or of the same children tested at different points in time, and so on. Only in rare instances (98) is an attempt made to modify intelligence by active intervention and with the utilization of a control group which does not receive the experimental treatment. While experimental work on human intelligence might well be desirable, such research often raises serious moral and ethical questions.

Piaget has not employed the experimental method because it was not appropriate for the problems he wished to study. These problems required a natural history type of enquiry wherein relevant phenomena had to be carefully observed and classified. In his studies Piaget has, nonetheless, revealed a wide range of hitherto unknown and unsuspected facts about children's thinking, which have in America now become the starting points for a great deal of experimental investigation.

There is a third and final commonality in the mental test and Piagetian viewpoint resides in what these two positions regard as the nature or essence of intelligence. While there is considerable variability among psychometricians in this regard, many agree in general with the position taken by Jensen (59). Jensen argues that the "g" factor which is present in all tests of mental ability appears in its purest forms on tests of generalization and abstraction. Spearman (100) called these activities the eduction of relations (A is greater than B; B is greater than C so A is in what relation to C?) and of correlates (Complete the series A AB ABC ____). While intelligence tests contain measures of many different types of mental abilities, including language and perceptual skills, the psychometric approach holds that the most central feature of human intelligence is its rationality or as Wechsler (108) put it:

"Intelligence is the aggregate or global capacity of the individual to act purposefully, to think rationally and to deal effectively with his environment."

For Piaget, too, reasoning, or logical processes, are the essence of intelligence. Piaget, however, is more specific in his description of these reasoning capacities, and defines them in terms of mental operations which have the properties of mathematical groupings in general and the property of reversibility in particular. An operational grouping is present when in the course of any mental activity one can always get back to the starting point. For example, if the class of boys and the class of girls is mentally combined to form the class of children it is always possible to recapture the sub-class by subtraction, that is to say, the class of children minus the class of boys equals the class of girls. Verbal material learned by heart is, however, not rationally organized, for no matter how well a passage is learned, it is impossible, without additional effort, to say it backwards. If an operational system were involved, having learned the passage forward would automatically imply the ability to say it backwards. In Piaget's view, neither perception nor language are truly rational since neither one shows complete reversibility. So while perception and language play an important part in intellectual activity, they do not epitomize that activity.

The psychometric and Piagetian approaches to intelligence thus agree on its genetic determination, at least in part; on the use of non-experimental methodology; and upon the essentially rational nature of mental ability. After this look at their commonalities, it is perhaps time to look at their differences.

CONCEPTUAL DIFFERENCES

Despite the commonalities noted above, the psychometric and developmental approaches to intelligence also differ in certain respects. These differences, however, derive from the ways in the psychometricians and Piaget approach and view intelligence and not from any fundamental disagreements regarding the nature of intelligence itself. In other words, the differences are that the two approaches are interested in assessing and describing the same facets of intelligent behavior from different perspectives. The differences center about: a) the type of genetic causality invoked; b) the description of mental growth provided and c) the contributions of nature and nurture assessed.

Each approach emphasizes a somewhat different mode of genetic determination or causality; to clarify them, we must recall some of the basic features of evolutionary theory upon which all modern conceptions of intelligence are based.

Within the Darwinian conception of evolution there are two major phenomena that have to be taken into account: within species variability and natural selection. For any given species of animal or plant one can observe a range of variations in such features as color, shape, and size. This within species variability, we know today, is due to the chance pairings of parental genes and gene complexes which occur because each parent contributes only half of its genetic complement to its offspring. Variations within a given species at a given time are, therefore, primarily due to chance factors, namely, the random genetic assortments provided by the parent generation. One determinant of variability among animals and plants is simply chance.

In the psychometric conception of intelligence, this random type of variation is just what is presupposed. Test intelligence, it is assumed, is randomly distributed in a given population at a given time and such distributions should resemble the bell-shaped curve of the normal probability function. Measurement of human abilities does in fact reveal a tendency for such measurements to fall into normal distributions. In addition "regression towards the mean" (children of exceptionally bright or dull parents tend to be less bright and less dull than their parents) is also characteristic of randomly determined genetic traits.

Obviously this description of genetic determination is extremely over-simplified and we know that a test score is determined by many different factors not all of which are genetic, such as environmental and error of measurement variance. With the exception, perhaps, of the selective mating variable, however, such factors can again be assumed to operate randomly, so that one might say that the chance distribution of observed test scores is the product of many underlying chance distributions. That the psychometric approach presupposes a random distribution is also shown by the fact that the criterion of a true change in intellectual ability is the demonstration that such a change could *not* be attributed to chance factors.

That variability within a species is in part determined by chance gene and gene complex assortments has been amply demonstrated. There are, however, other forms of organismic variability which cannot be attributed to chance. Natural selection, the other component of evolution, is never random but always moves in the direction of improved adaptation to the milieu. To illustrate, over the past hundred years there has been a gradual predominance of dark over light colored moths in the industrial sections of England. Kittlewell (62) demonstrated the survival value of dark coloration by showing that light moths placed on soot darkened bark were more readily eaten by insectivorous birds than were similarly placed dark moths. When variations across generations are considered, the variations are not random but rather show a clear-cut direction.

Neither is the course of individual development random. In the case of individual growth, however, the direction of progress is determined by biochemical mechanisms which are only now being elucidated. As Waddington (106) points out, animals consist of a limited variety of cells, and organ differentiation as the egg matures depends upon the action of chemical agents which Speman (4) called *organizers* with definite loci, called *organization centers*, in the cell material.

When Piaget speaks of the genetic determination of intelligence, he means the non-random action of biochemical organizers and organization centers. This is the kind of determination that he has in mind when he argues that the *sequence* in which the child attains the successive components of a concept or in which he acquires systems of mental operations, are invariant. In the formation of body organs the order of differentiation is fixed because each new phase of differentiation produces the organizer for the next stage; in Piaget's view this has its analogue in the growth of cognitive structures, because the earlier cognitive structures are prerequisite to the elaboration of the later ones. For Piaget, then, genetic determination means that there are factors which give development a definite, non-random direction.

In observing that the Piagetian and psychometric approaches to intelligence postulate different forms of genetic determinism, one must bear in mind that these two positions are not contradictory. The mental test approach to intelligence is concerned with inter-individual differences in ability and these are, insofar as we know, largely randomly determined. Piaget, in contrast, is concerned with the intra-individual changes occurring in the course of development and these, to the best of our knowledge, are not random but rather have a direction given them by specific organizing mechanisms.

Let us look now at a somewhat different issue, the chronology of mental growth. Here again we find a difference in perspective. In psychometric terms, the course of mental growth is plotted as a curve which measures the amount of intelligence at some criterion age that can be predicted at any preceding age. As Bloom (5) has pointed out, when age seventeen is taken at the criterion age, some 50 per cent of the total IQ at that age can be predicted at age four, and an additional 30 per cent can be predicted from ages four to eight. Based on correlational data of this sort, curves of mental growth appear to rise rapidly in early childhood and taper off to a plateau in late adolescence. Such curves, it must be noted, say nothing as to the *amount* or *quality* of knowledge at given age levels. It is not that the child of four has half the knowledge or mental capacity he will ever have but rather from what he has at age four we can predict with 50 per cent accuracy the relative level of mental functioning he will have at age seventeen.

From the psychometric perspective, therefore, intellectual growth is largely a statistical concept derived from correlations of test scores obtained at different age levels for the same individuals. Such curves can be interpreted as reflecting the rate of mental growth but say nothing about the nature of what is developing. Indeed, if intelligence is defined in the narrow sense of the abilities to generalize and abstract, then qualitative differences in these abilities will be obscured by the curve of mental growth which suggests merely a quantitative increase in mental ability with increasing age.

Looked at from the standpoint of Piagetian psychology, however, mental growth means the formation of new mental structures and consequently the emergence of new mental abilities. The child, to illustrate, cannot deal with propositional logic (43) or with metaphor (97). Adolescents, in contrast, have no trouble with either. In the Piagetian view, therefore, mental growth is not a quantitative but rather a qualitative affair and presupposes significant differences between the thinking of children and adolescents as well as between pre-school and school age children.

These qualitative differences are, in fact, built into the items of mental tests but are obscured by the assignment of point scores to successes and failures. On the Wechsler Intelligence Scale for Children (109) various of the sub-tests recognize qualitatively different responses only by assigning them additional points. A child, to illustrate, who says that a peach and a plum are alike because "they both have pits" is given a single point whereas a child who says "they are both fruit" is given two points. On other sub-tests, such as the arithmetic sub-test, there is no point differential for success on problems which patently require different levels of mental ability. To illustrate, correct answers to the following two problems are both given only a single point:

If I cut an apple in half, how many pieces will I have?

Smith and Brown start a card game with $27 each. They agree that at the end of each deal the loser shall pay the winner one third of what he (the loser) then has in his possession. Smith wins the first three deals. How much does Brown have at the beginning of the fourth deal?

Clearly, the items on any given sub-test can tap quite different mental processes but these qualitative differences are ignored by assigning equivalent point scores to the various items regardless of the mental processes involved.

This is not to say that Piaget is right and that the mental test approach is wrong. The quantitative evaluation of mental growth is necessary and has considerable practical value in predicting school success. The qualitative approach is also of value, particularly when diagnosis of learning difficulties and educational remediation are in question. Which approach to mental growth one adopts will depend upon the purposes of the investigation. The only danger in the quantitative approach is to assume that, because sub-tests include items of the same general type and are scored with equal numerical weights, that they therefore assess only quantitative differences in the ability in question.

Still a third way in which the psychometric and Piagetian views of intelligence differ has to do with the manner in which they treat the contributions of nature and nurture to intellectual ability. For the psychometric approach this contribution is treated substantively, with regard to the amount of variance in intellectual ability that can be attributed to nature and nurture respectively. Piaget, on the contrary, treats these contributions functionally with respect to the regulative role played by the environment or inner forces for any given mental activity.

The psychometric approach is substantive (and static) in the sense that it regards intelligence as capable of being measured and holds that such measures can be used to assess the extent to which nature and nurture contribute to intellectual ability. We are indebted to writers such as Burt (9) and Jensen (59) for making clear the many and complex determinants into which test performance can be analyzed. Without wishing to minimize these other determinants, let us consider only how the psychometric approach arrives at the contribution of the heredity and environmental factors.

As Jensen makes clear, heritability is the proportion of variability among observed or phenotypic intelligence (test scores) that can be attributed genotypic variations. Estimates of heritability are obtained from correlational data for subjects with known kinship relations: parents and children, siblings, and identical twins. The contribution of the environment to variability in intelligence test scores is estimated from that variability which cannot be attributed to any other factors. It is, in fact, the residual variance, that which is left after all the other factors contributing to intelligence test performance have been accounted for. For the psychometrician, then, nature and nurture are regarded as substantive and static and their contributions are assessed quantitatively with the aid of statistical procedures.

Piaget has quite a different conception of the contributions of nature and nurture. In Piaget's view, these contributions must be conceived functionally and dynamically with respect to their regulatory control over various mental activities. A similar conception has been proposed by David Rapaport (95) who, in a different context, wrote of "the relative autonomy of the ego." He argued that certain mental processes, such as perception, are most responsive to the environment and so tend to guarantee a partial independence of the mind from the domination of instinctual drives. Other processes, such as fantasy, are most responsive to internal forces and these in turn guarantee a limited independence of the mind from the domination of the environment. The presence and activity of both types of processes thus insures that the mind is enslaved neither by the environment nor by drives but retains a "relative autonomy" from both.

This view helps to introduce Piaget's, for it (91) is roughly similar. He argues that intelligence is an extension of biological adaptation which, in lieu of the instinctive adaptations in animals, permits relatively autonomous adaptations bearing the stamp both of our genetic endowment, and of our physical and social experience. On the plane of intelligence what we inherit are the processes of assimilation (processes responsive to inner promptings) and of accommodation (processes responsive to environmental intrusions). Assimilative processes guarantee that intelligence will not be limited to passively copying reality; accommodative processes insure that intelligence will not construct representations of reality which have no correspondence with the real world. To solidify this functional conception of the contributions of nature and nurture to intelligence, let us consider several different mental abilities which are differently regulated by internal and external forces.

Imitation (79) is clearly an accommodative process in the sense that it is most responsive to environmental influence and is relatively independent of inner forces. The vocal mimic, for example, is expert to the extent that he can capture the pitch, timbre, and inflections of his model's voice and to the extent to which he can suppress those aspects of his own speech which differ from the model's.

Symbolic play, in contrast, is largely assimilative in that it is most responsive to inner needs and is relatively independent of environmental influence. The child who uses a stick alternatively as a gun, as an airplane, and as a boat, has responded to the object largely in terms of his own inner needs and with a relative disregard of its real properties.

Reason—the process of intelligence—manifests an equilibrium

between assimilative and accommodative activities and is thus relatively autonomous of both inner *and* outer forces. To illustrate, suppose we deduce, from the premise that Helen is taller than Jane and that Jane is taller than Mary, that Helen is the taller of three girls. We have in so doing attained a new bit of knowledge, an adaptation, but without altering the elements involved (assimilation without transformation of the objects) and without modifying the reasoning processes (accommodation without alteration of mental structures). Reason, or intelligence, is thus the only system of mental processes which guarantees that the mind and the environment will each retain their integrity in the course of their interaction.

Accordingly, for Piaget as for Rapaport, the question is not how much nature and nurture contribute to mental ability, but rather the *extent to which various mental processes are relatively autonomous from environmental and instinctual influence.* Such a conception is functional and dynamic, rather than substantive and static, because it deals with the regulatory activity of nature and nurture upon various mental processes. Those processes which show the greatest independence from environmental *and* internal regulation, the rational processes, are the most advanced of all human abilities. It is for this reason that Piaget reserves for them alone the term intelligence.

In summary, the psychometric and Piagetian approaches to intelligence differ with respect to: a) the type of genetic causality which they presuppose; b) their conceptions of the course of mental growth and finally, c) the manner in which they conceive the contributions of nature and nurture to intellectual ability. Again, the differences between the two positions arise from differences in perspective and emphasis and are not contradictory but rather complementary. Both approaches to the conceptualization of human intelligence provide useful starting points for the assessment and interpretation of human mental abilities.

PRACTICAL ISSUES

Let us look at three practical issues related to the modification, stimulation, and assessment of intellectual abilities. Some of the attacks upon these issues involve some misinterpretation of the Piagetian position. First, Piaget's insistence upon the qualitative differences between the modes of thinking at different age levels has been wrongly taken to suggest the need for pre-school instruction in order to move children into the concrete operational stage more quickly. Second, Piaget's emphasis upon the non-chance or self-directed nature of mental development has mistakenly been taken as justification for the use of methods such as "discovery learning" which supposedly stimulate the child's intrinsic motivations to learn. Finally, Piaget's use of the term intelligence to describe what his tasks assess has led to some premature efforts to psychometrize his materials. Let us, then, try to clarify the implications of Piaget's conception of intelligence for pre-school instruction, motivation and mental growth, and for the assessment of intelligence.

Pre-School Instruction. There appears to be increasing pressure today in popular and academic literature to begin academic instruction in the early childhood, i.e., at 3 to 5 years. (Bruner's famous hypothesis to the effect that "We begin with the hypothesis that any subject can be taught effectively in some intellectually honest form to any child at any stage of development," [8] as well as the work of others [54, 5, 71, 37, 98] have all been used in the advocacy of pre-school instruction.) Piaget and Montessori, as well as other workers, have been invoked in this connection as well. The argument is essentially that the pre-school period is critical for intellectual growth and that if we leave this period devoted to fun and games, we are lowering the individual's ultimate level of intellectual attainment. Parental anxiety and pressure about the matter has been so aroused that legislation has been passed or is pending in states such as New York, Massachusetts, and California for the provision of free pre-school education for all children whose parents wish it.

What is the evidence that pre-school instruction has lasting effects upon mental growth and development? The answer is, in brief, that there is none. To prove the point one needs longitudinal data on adults who did not have pre-school instruction but who were equal in every other regard to children receiving such instruction. With the exception of the Montessori schools, however, the pre-school instruction programs have not been in existence long enough to provide any evidence on the endurance of their effects. Indeed, most of the work on the effects of nursery school education (44, 60), has shown that any positive effects soon wear off. It is interesting that no one, to my knowledge, has done a long term follow up on adult Montessori graduates. Have they done better in life than children from comparable backgrounds not so trained? In any case, it is this longitudinal data, which is not yet available, that is crucial to the proposition at hand.

Studies of mental growth such as those of Bloom (5) suggest that half of the individual's intellectual potential is realized by age four, but this does not necessarily mean that the pre-school period is all-important for intellectual growth and that interventions during this period will have lasting effects. Let us look at Bloom's facts a somewhat different way. He writes "Both types of data suggest that in terms of intelligence measured at age 17, about 50% of the development takes place between conception and age 4, about 30% between ages 4 and 8, and about 20% between ages 8 and seventeen." An equally plausible implication of this statement contradicts the value of pre-school instruction. If the child has only 50 per cent of his intellectual ability at age 4 but 80 per cent at age 8, it might be better to delay his education three years so that he can profit more fully from instruction. With 80 per cent of his ability he is likely to learn more quickly and efficiently and is not as likely to learn in ways that he will need to unlearn later. Without stretching the facts, it is possible to interpret the Bloom statement as implying that instruction should *not* be introduced into the pre-school program.

Not only is there no clear-cut longitudinal data to support the claims of the lastingness of pre-school instruction, there is evidence in the opposite direction. Several workers (60, 90) suggest a negative correlation between early physical maturation and later intellectual attainments which in turn suggests the hypothesis that *the longer we delay formal instruction, up to certain limits, the greater the period of plasticity and the higher the ultimate level of achievement.* There is at least as much evidence and theory in support of this hypothesis as there is in favor of the early instruction proposition. Certainly, from the Piagetian perspective there are "optimal periods" for the growth of particular mental structures which cannot be rushed.

I am not arguing against the benefits of pre-school experience for children. Pre-school instruction may well be of value for those disadvantaged youngsters who do not benefit from what has been called the "hidden curriculum of the middle class home" (103). But there is no evidence for the *long term effects* of either instruction or enrichment with advantaged or disadvantaged children. Nursery school experience may, and most assuredly does, have immediate as well as long-range value for children to the extent that it helps them to appreciate and enjoy their immediate world to the full and to develop new social skills. Even if nursery school does no more than lighten the burdens of childhood for even a brief period each day it is worthwhile. The contributions of the nursery school, no less than that of the vacation, do not have to be long-lived to be of value.

There is yet another side to this issue of pre-school instruction. This is the consideration that the emphasis on pre-school education has obscured the fact that it is in reality the elementary school years that are crucial to intellectual growth. It is during these years that the child learns the basic tool subjects, acquires his conception of himself as a student and develops his attitudes toward formal education. In this connection it might be well to quote a less publicized finding of Bloom's study, "We may conclude from our results on general achievement, reading comprehension and vocabulary development, that by age 9 (grade 3) at least 50% of the general achievement pattern at age 18 (grade 12) has been developed whereas at least 75% of the pattern has been developed by age 13 (grade 7)."

With respect to the intellectual operations of concern to Piaget, similar trends appear to hold true. While children all over the world and across wide ranges of cultural and socio-economic conditions appear to attain concrete operations at about the age of 6 or 7 (46), the attainment and use of formal operations in adolescence, in contrast, appears to be much more subject to socioculturally determined factors such as sex roles and symbolic proficiency (19, 26, 47). Apparently, therefore, for the average child environmental variation during the elementary school period is much more significant than during the pre-school period for later intellectual attainments of the Piagetian variety. In short, there is not much justification for making the pre-school bear the blame for our failures in elementary education. The years from six to twelve are still the crucial ones with respect to later academic achievement.

Intrinsic Motivation. There has recently been an increasing recognition (3, 55, 113), that certain mental activities can be self-rewarding and do not have to be externally reinforced. European writers such as Piaget (88) and Montessori (70) recognized the existence of this "intrinsic motivation" long ago and Montessori in particular gave incomparable descriptions of children who suddenly discover they can read and proceed to read everything in sight. Piaget (92) too has argued that needs and interests are simply another aspect of all cognitive activities.

In their efforts to capitalize upon this intrinsic motivation, however, educators seem to have missed the point of what Montessori and Piaget had in mind. To maximize intrinsic motivation and to accelerate mental growth we have recently had an emphasis upon "learning by discovery" and upon "interesting reading materials" and so on. These approaches miss the point because they assume that intrinsic motivation can be built into materials and procedures which will in turn maximize mental growth. But as Piaget and Montessori pointed out (see p. 112) intrinsic motivation resides in the child and not in methods and procedures. It is the child who must, at any given point in time, choose the method of learning and the materials that are reinforcing *to him*. Without the opportunity for student choice and the provision of large blocks of time, during which the child can become totally engrossed in an activity, the values of intrinsic motivation will not be realized.

But by the time most children have reached the third or fourth grade a good deal of their intrinsic motivation for learning has been stifled. This is because spontaneous interest follows neither the curriculum nor the clock but rather the timetable of the child's own growth schedule. We can all remember occasions when we were so totally engrossed in an activity that we forgot time, food, and rest. At such times we are at our creative and productive best and afterwards the feeling of exhaustion is coupled with a deep sense of accomplishment. In the school, however, we do not permit children to become totally involved in an activity but rather shuttle them from activity to activity on the hour or half hour. The result is what might be called *intellectually burned children*. Just as the burned child shuns the fire so the intellectually burned child shies away from total intellectual involvement.

What are the dynamics of this condition? In clinical practice we often see children (and adults) who are unwilling to form any emotional attachments. In the history of such children one always finds a series of broken relationships due to a wide variety of causes including the death of parents or the forced separation from them. Such children have learned that every time they have reached out and became emotionally involved, rejection, hurt, and misery were the result. Consequently they prefer not to get involved anymore because the pain and anguish of still another broken relationship is just too high a price to pay for an emotional attachment. The intellectually burned child is in somewhat the same position. He refuses to become totally involved in intellectual activities because the repeated frustration of being interrupted in the middle is just too much to bear.

Accordingly, the educational practice which would best foster intrinsically motivated children in the Piagetian and Montessori sense would be the provision of "interest areas" where children could go on their own and for long periods of time. Only when the child can choose an activity and persist at it until he is satiated can we speak of truly intrinsically motivated behavior. Where such interest areas and time provisions have been made, as in the World of Inquiry School in Rochester, New York, the results are impressive indeed.

Mental Tests. With the interest in Piaget's work has grown a corresponding interest in psychometrizing the tasks which he has introduced. Attempts are currently under way to build scales and intelligence tests with the Piagetian tasks. The idea is attractive because the Piagetian tasks are so much richer than traditional test items in the behavioral data they provide. But the psychometric and Piagetian perspectives with respect to intelligence differ in important ways and tend to complement one another in others. The question is, therefore, What is to be gained by the psychometrizing the Piagetian tasks and equally important, what might be lost?

Before attempting to answer this question, it is important to recall the different origins of the mental test and the Piagetian tasks. Intelligence tests and intelligence testing grew out of pressing educational, clinical, and research needs which became evident at the beginning of this century (45). From the very first, therefore, mental tests were practical tools whose use could be justified on the basis of the fact that they worked and did the job they were supposed to do. Piaget's tasks, in contrast, were designed to test his hypotheses regarding how the child attains certain concepts. In the case of the Piagetian tasks, therefore, their justification lay in whether or not they revealed developmental trends in the kinds of concepts about which Piaget was concerned.

It is important to keep in mind this difference of origins of mental tests and Piagetian tasks when considering the applicability of Piagetian tasks to practical ends. We can put the question more directly and ask whether Piagetian tasks, converted to a standardized and reliable scale, would serve us better than our existing intelligence, achievement or clinical tests. Let us then consider, in turn, the applicability of a Piagetian scale in the assessment of general intelligence, of academic achievement, and of clinical syndromes.

The major use of general intelligence tests such as the Binet (104) or the Wechsler Scales (108, 109) is to rank individuals of the same age as to their relative brightness. Even though Piaget and psychometricians conceive intelligence as essentially rational, psychometricians conceive intelligence more broadly than Piaget. Most general intelligence tests contain measures of language ability, of rote memory, and of perceptual motor coordination as well as of reasoning ability. Traditional intelligence tests thus sample a much wider range of human abilities than do the Piagetian tasks which assess primarily reasoning ability. So, while there is no question that a scale of Piagetian tasks could be used to differentiate among individuals, it is questionable whether such a scale would be as useful as one which provides a broader profile of individual performance.

Tests of educational achievement are generally geared to the curricula which are taught in the schools. By and large they assess, with some fidelity, the child's progress in academic subjects. The

Piagetian tasks, in contrast, assess those concepts that the child has learned more or less on his own and without the benefit of direct instruction. A child's performance on a battery of Piagetian tests would, therefore, be of little practical value to teachers and school administrators at the present time. Even if she were given the results of the child's performance on Piagetian tasks, the teacher would not know what to do with the information. A great deal of curriculum and other work needs to be done before a child's performance on Piagetian tasks will have practical relevance for teachers and parents concerned with the child's academic achievement.

Most clinical diagnosis in psychiatry and clinical psychology is based on a Freudian model and employs Freudian concepts. Clinicians are accustomed to interpreting both objective and projective tests in terms of Freudian conceptions of personality. The clinician, like the teacher, is simply not prepared to use the information given by the Piagetian tests because it is based on an entirely different model and framework. This is not to say that Piagetian tests cannot be used in the clinic, for both Inhelder (57) and E. J. Anthony (1) have shown how valuable the tests can be for the clinician. Both Inhelder and Anthony, however, had to translate clinical problems into cognitive conceptions consonant with the Piagetian scheme of things. Not many clinicians are prepared to do that.

Accordingly, I cannot see, at the present time at least, much point in substituting a scale of Piagetian tasks for intelligence, achievement, or clinical tests that are already in use. A great deal of theoretical and empirical work needs to be done before the information provided by Piagetian tasks will be relevant to laymen, educators, and clinicians. That is to say, until educators and clinicians come to see their problems in cognitive developmental terms, a subject's performance on a scale of Piagetian tasks will have little practical value for them. And, if a test has no practical value, it will not be used.

In summary, then, the Piagetian conception of intelligence provides no real support for those who advocate formal pre-school instruction, or for those who suggest that methods and materials in and of themselves will arouse intrinsic motivation or for those who wish to psychometrize Piagetian tasks for practical educational or clinical purposes. In the long run, we will benefit most from Piaget's contribution if we accept him on his own terms and if we do not attempt to make his ideas conform to our own preconceived positions.

Piaget is best known for his work on children's thinking. He has, however, also done considerable research on the development of perception in children. This work has received little attention both because it has yet to be translated into English and because the work deals primarily with illusions. A major thrust of my own research efforts has been to build upon Piaget's research and theory in the area of perception and to deal with its application to practical educational problems. Some of the implications of Piaget's work on perception for reading and for remedial education are described in this chapter.

11

Reading, Logic, and Perception: An Approach to Reading Instruction

Within psychology, the perceptual aspects of reading are most frequently dealt with as problems in stimulus-response learning. This stimulus-response orientation to the perceptual aspects of reading is not, however, unique to psychologists and appears to underlie the major methods of reading instruction employed in the schools. Both the "look-say" and the "phonic" methods of reading instruction seem to assume that the perceptual task in reading is that of discrimination and association. But there is a somewhat different version of the role of perception in reading —a version which derives from the developmental theory of perception propounded by Piaget (86). It should perhaps be said at this point, that Piaget himself has not been concerned with the problem of reading and that the interpretation of reading which is presented here is not necessarily the way in which he would approach the problem were he to attack it.

THE PIAGET THEORY OF PERCEPTUAL GROWTH

Although Jean Piaget is perhaps best known for his work on conceptual development, he has also elaborated a general theory of perceptual growth (86, 93). While Piaget's qualitative theory of perceptual development would seem to have relevance for a wide range of perceptual phenomena, he and his colleagues have limited their research almost entirely to the quantitative aspects of his theory since these can be tested in the study of geometric illusions. The research and teaching procedures described in the present paper derive from an attempt to explore systematically some implications of the qualitative aspects of Piaget's theory of perceptual growth for the perception of meaningful materials.

The qualitative aspect of the theory can be briefly summarized. According to Piaget (93), the perception of the young child is *centered* in the sense that it is caught and held by the dominant aspects of the visual field. In each particular case, the dominant aspects of the field are determined by Gestalt-like features such as continuity, proximity, and closure which Piaget speaks of as *field effects*. With increasing age, however, and the development of perceptual activities (internalized actions), the child's perception becomes increasingly *decentered* in the sense that it is progressively freed from its earlier domination by field effects. This theory can be put more succinctly by saying that, for Piaget, perception in the young child is primarily determined by peripheral sensory processes whereas in the older child and in the adult, central nervous processes come to play the leading role.

This brief sketch of the theory needs to be amplified somewhat to show its direct relevance to the research described below. First of all, for Piaget, perceptual activities are not all of a kind and include such diverse processes as exploration, reorganization, schematization, transport, and anticipation (set). Furthermore, while all of these diverse activities are probably present from the start of life in some form, they do not apparently all develop at the same rate. That is to say, the same child may be more decentered with respect to exploration or transport than he may be with respect to reorganization or schematization. Finally, the degree to which a child is able to decenter in any given situation is always a joint function of the level of maturity of the particular perceptual activity and the strength of the field effects presented by the configuration. In short, decentration is never a once-and-for-all phenomenon but rather is always relative to the particular characteristics of the subject/object interaction.

While this sketch of Piaget's theory is necessarily schematic and incomplete, it suffices as a rationale for the research on the various perceptual activities which is described below. The theme which dominates this research is that all perceptual processes can be seen as embodying a kind of logic.

Perceptual Reorganization. Perceptual reorganization has to do with the ability to mentally rearrange a stimulus pattern or array without acting physically upon it. A simple example of such reorganization is the unscrambling of scrambled words. The reader can, for example, identify the color word present in the scrambled letters *lube* by visually rearranging the letters. A similar process is involved in figure-ground reversal where, depending upon the visual arrangement of the elements, different forms are seen.

To assess the development of perceptual reorganization, we have devised a set of ambiguous pictures (21, 32) which in theory require perceptual reorganization in order to perceive all the possible figures in the drawings (see Figure 1). When these pictures were shown to children at different age levels, it was found that the ability to detect the hidden figures improved regularly with age. The results were thus in keeping with Piaget's theory which predicts that perceptual activities should improve with age (maturation) as well as with experience.

In order to make concrete the way in which logic is involved in perceptual reorganization, consider the "duck in the tree" depicted in Figure 1. Let C = the contour line common to the duck and to the tree. Further, let W stand for the white area in the shape of a duck and B stand for the black area in the shape of a tree. Now the organizing activity which permits recognition of

Figure 1

the duck can be expressed as follows: $C + W =$ Figure (duck) and $B - C =$ Ground. Contrariwise, the reorganization which leads to the recognition of the tree might be expressed: $B + C =$ Figure (tree) and $W - C =$ Ground. The reason that these activities are not entirely identical with the operations of logic and intelligence rests in the fact that a possible logical combination, namely, Figure $- B$ (or W) $= C$ is not at the same time a possible perception. A contour line can be conceived as independent of the surrounding areas but it cannot be *perceived* in isolation. Even with this reservation, however, it is clear that perceptual reorganization can be regarded as involving a kind of logic.

Perceptual Schematization. Perceptual schematization has to do with the ability to organize parts and wholes in such a way that both retain their unique identities without at the same time losing their independence. To assess this activity, we have devised a set of seven drawing (Figure 2) in which whole figures are made of parts with independent meanings. When these drawings were presented to children at different age levels (30), the nursery school children saw only the parts, the kindergarten and first grade children saw only the wholes, and the children in the second grade and beyond saw the wholes and parts in combination; they said, "a man made out of fruit."

On the logical plane, the relations between parts and wholes are frequently determined by logical multiplication. Logical multiplication occurs whenever we form a new class out of two classes which overlap in membership. The class "American Protestants" can, to illustrate, be thought of as the logical product of the multiplication of the class of Americans by the class of Protestants. Graphically portrayed, the logical product would correspond to the area shared in common by two overlapping circles when these circles represent the classes being multiplied. The ability to logically multiply classes such as Protestant and American does not emerge until middle childhood (20).

Figure 2

Looked at from the standpoint of logic the ability to visually coordinate parts and wholes would also seem to involve a kind of logical multiplication. That is to say, to recognize that a given figure is a "man made out of fruit" the child must recognize that one and the same round form can represent *both* an apple and a head; that one and the same pear shape can represent *both* a pear and a torso. This is analogous, on the cognitive plane, to the recognition that a child can be both an American and a Protestant at the same time. In both cases we have the intersection of two classes and the corresponding recognition that an individual can be a member of both classes at the same time. Perceptual schematization, therefore, can also be conceived as a semi-logical process.

Perceptual Exploration. Perceptual exploration has to do with the ability to systematically scan an array or figure so as to note all of its particular features. In order to assess this ability we employed cards upon which pictures of objects familiar to nursery school children were pasted (35). On one card, the pictures were pasted in a disordered array while on another they were pasted in the form of a triangle. Both cards were then shown to children at different age levels, from four to eight years, who were asked to name every picture on the cards. On the disordered array card there was a regular decrease with age in the number of errors of omission and commission (naming the same object twice). There was also a change in pattern of exploration with age and young children employed an unsystematic scattered pattern of exploration, while older children scanned the array systematically from left to right and from top to bottom.

With respect to the card upon which the objects were pasted in a triangular array, the results were surprising. While the young children and the oldest children followed the triangular pattern, the first grade children read the pictures from left to right. This suggested that in the course of learning the left to right swing required for reading, the first grade children spontaneously practiced it where it was not, at least from the adult point of view, appropriate. Among the older children, in whom the left-right pattern had become automatic, this spontaneous practice dropped out. Older children and adults follow the triangular pattern because they *choose to* while younger children follow it because *they have no alternative.*

It might seem, at first glance, that these patterns of exploration have nothing whatever to do with logic. To illustrate that logic-like processes are involved, consider the problem of scanning the disordered array card. To scan such an array in a systematic manner so as to avoid both errors of omission and of commission the child must, in effect, organize the various pictures into a *serial order*. Only if the child establishes such a serial order can he succeed on the task. But the establishment of a serial order is already a semi-logical process and corresponds to a rank order-ing of events: $A > B > C > D \ldots$ etc. Here again an apparently simple perceptual performance can be viewed as encompassing a much more complicated form of perceptual action.

Work on other perceptual activities such as transport and antic-ipation could be described, but the foregoing should suffice to illustrate the fact that many different types of perceptual per-formance can be viewed as involving a kind of logic. Indeed, as the following section will show, many of the simplest perceptual aspects of reading can be viewed as semi-logical problems.

PERCEPTUAL ACTIVITY AND READING

Once perception is regarded as involving its own form of logic, the perceptual hurdles in learning to read appear in an entirely new light. Consider, for example, the problem so prominent in English phonics, namely, that one and the same letter can repre-sent more than one sound, while one and the same sound can be represented by more than one letter. This is a hard fact to deal with from the discriminative response point of view, since it requires an explanation of how the subject comes to make different responses to the same stimulus at different times. That the problem is not primarily one of discrimination has been clearly demon-strated by the success of the Pitman International Teaching Alpha-bet (ITA) (14). From a purely discriminative response point of view, this alphabet should present the child with more difficulty than the English alphabet, first because it has forty rather than twenty-six characters and second because all of the characters are unfamiliar. Yet children find the ITA easier than the English alphabet.

If the Pitman alphabet does not aid discrimination, how does it help the young reader? One answer to this question comes from looking at the ITA from the point of view of the logical problem it enables the child to avoid. Looked at logically, the recognition that the same letter can represent different sounds and that the same sound can be designated by different letters poses a problem of logical multiplication analogous to that previously described in the discussion of whole-part perception. Once the child can perform logical multiplications (i.e. schematizations) on the perceptual plane, he can arrive at all possible combinations of letters and sounds and, on the basis of experience, rule out those which do not occur in his language. Prior to this stage, however, the child should encounter all sorts of difficulties in dealing with the multiple meanings of letters and sound combinations. In short, the Pitman ITA aids the young reader by eliminating the need for perceptual activities.

It should be said, however, that perceptual activities are important beyond the initial stages in the acquisition of reading skill. The ability to construct spatial seriations, for example, is clearly essential for comprehending the grammatical significance of word order. Reorganization, likewise, would seem to be important to the analysis and comprehension of new words. In the same way, schematization of part and whole would appear to play an important role in dealing with prefixes and suffixes, with the tenses, and with pluralization transformations of words. Finally, effective rapid reading would seem to require the ability to quickly explore and correctly anticipate (infer) words and sentences.

At all levels of reading skill, therefore, whether at the level of letter and sound combinations or at the level of advanced reading and comprehension, perceptual activities seem to be involved. This is not a mere supposition. In one study, children at different age levels were given a battery of tests which included measures of reading achievement as well as measures of perceptual activity (28). The measures of perceptual activity included, in addition to the figurative tests of reorganization and schematization already described, tests of the ability to read upside down and to unscramble words. A factor analysis of the data indicated that, at all age levels, there was a common factor which underlay performance on the various tests. That this common factor was not merely a general intelligence factor was shown by still another study in which slow and average readers, matched for intelligence, were pre-tested, trained, and re-tested with respect to reorganizing activities (31). The results showed that the slow readers were deficient with respect to perceptual activity both initially and after training in comparison with the average readers. It seems reasonable to assume, then, that perceptual activity—in the generic sense—is an important factor in reading achievement.

TRAINING IN PERCEPTUAL ACTIVITY

The foregoing analysis of the role of perceptual activity in reading, together with the research data, suggests that such activities are involved in reading failure as well as in reading success. Good readers appear to have well-developed perceptual activities whereas slow readers appear to be deficient in this regard. Accordingly, it seemed reasonable to suppose that training in perceptual activity might benefit at least some retarded readers. The exercises described below were specifically designed for such children. In one study (27), we found that black second grade children made more progress in reading as a result of perceptual training than did a control group that received equal time on a standard reading program.

Before presenting the exercises in detail, a few introductory remarks are in order. First of all, the exercises are by no means to be construed as a total reading program. Indeed, they are best thought of as comparable to playing scales when learning to play the piano. While the practice of such scales is essential for dexterity and control, such practice can in no way take the place of instruction in fingering, timing, expression and theory. In the same way, the exercises described here would seem to be beneficial in limbering up the child's perceptual muscles, so to speak, but they do not eliminate the need for training in phonics, vocabulary, and comprehension.

In addition, the exercises are designed for classroom use and as an adjunct rather than as a replacement for other classroom procedures. The exercises are non-verbal so that children are forced to attend to the blackboard and to use their eyes. Finally, the exercises require neither special teacher training nor any special materials. Once a teacher grasps the principles, it should be easy for her to construct additional exercises along the same lines. In short, the exercises are designed as a readily utilizable tool, which teachers can add to their existing storehouse of methods and use whenever they feel a need.

The exercises described here are specifically for second grade children but simpler exercises are available for younger age groups and more difficult exercises can be constructed for older age groups. Although the exercises are most effective with small groups, of perhaps fifteen children, they can be used with an entire classroom. In general the exercises are designed to get children to explore, reorganize, schematize, and anticipate perceptual figures and arrays. Furthermore, the exercises are designed so that the child's task is to find the nature of the problem as well as the solution. In these exercises, once the problem is known the solution usually follows as a matter of course.

To introduce the exercises, the teacher tells the children that "we are going to play a kind of game in which no one talks. I am going to put some things on the board and you have to figure out what should come next. If you think you know the answer

raise your hand and I will call on you by pointing to you with
the chalk. Then you come to the board and write the answer.
Remember, the important part about this game is that you cannot
ask questions and that I cannot tell you anything more than what
is on the board."

An easy exercise with which to begin is a simple series such as
the alphabet or number series. For example, it is helpful to begin
a session with the following series A B C D E⎯⎯ on the board.
After pointing to the vacant space with the chalk, a child who
has raised his hand can be called to the board. Most children get
the idea immediately but it is useful to continue for a number of
letters to ensure that all the children understand. The same procedure can be used with number series. This exercise can be varied
by moving backwards Z Y X W⎯⎯ or by putting down every
other letter A C E G⎯⎯. For younger children circle faces and
stick figures can be used; for older children more complex series
(e.g. ABC BCD CDE DEF) are appropriate. Note that these
exercises train children both in left to right exploration and in
serial relationships.

The following is an exercise in visual reorganization. Several
words are put on the board which are meaningful when written
either forward or backward. For example:

    WAS = SAW
    TAR = RAT
    PIT = ⎯⎯

A whole series of words of this kind can be used. Similar to this
exercise is another using scrambled words. Starting with a class
of words (an orienting set is helpful) the following task can be
presented:

        ENT = TEN
        RUFO = FOUR
        OTW = ⎯⎯

Second grade children seldom have difficulty with such problems,
which provide good training in visual organization and reorgani-

zation. The scrambled word exercises can be repeated with other classes of words such as fruits, colors, and so on.

To train children in transport activities a coding exercise is entertaining as well as effective. On the top of the board one puts the following:

1	2	3	4	5	6	7	8
E	T	S	H	A	P	L	I

and then:

$$482 = \text{HIT}$$
$$382 = \text{SIT}$$
$$452 = \underline{\hspace{1cm}}$$

Quite clearly, many different kinds of codes could be set up; this is an easy one that works well. These exercises train children both in transporting symbols across space and in vicarious symbolism and representation.

Still another class of exercises are designed to develop the child's schematizing abilities as well as his understanding of logical symbols and relations. An illustration of this type of exercise follows:

In addition to whole part schematization one can also move from pictographic to verbal representation:

Note that in these exercises the left to right and top to bottom patterns of exploration are also reinforced.

Additional exercises can be used to provide training in tenses, pluralization and phonics as well as in perceptual activities. Here is an exercise in rhyming:

RAT   HAT
LIKE BIKE
HIT   SIT
SUN   ____

And another in pluralization:

HAT   HATS
TOE   TOES
BOOT BOOTS
FOOT ____

And still another in tenses:

HAS   HAD
DO   DID
IS   ____

By making such exercises non-verbal one insures that the child is actually attending to the printed work and to the perceptual as well as grammatical relations involved.

Although many more exercises could be described, these should suffice to illustrate the method in a general way. Indeed, a teacher who understands the underlying principles can make up exercises as she goes along. To facilitate that, a couple of practical suggestions are in order. About one half-hour of such exercises a day is sufficient to produce some effect and not so long as to produce boredom and disinterest. It is also well to vary the nature of the exercise frequently within allotted time period. Finally, once the children are accustomed to the exercises and the procedures, it is instructive to allow the children themselves to go to the board and act as teachers.

These then are the non-verbal exercises in perceptual activity. All of the exercises have value in the sense that they force the child to attend to the visual materials and to uncover the relations involved. In a very real sense, then, these exercises could be regarded as a *discovery* method of reading instruction.

We are currently programming the exercises for use with teaching machines and developing group forms of the tests of perceptual activity for diagnostic and screening use by schools; this work is part of an ongoing research program which hopes to detail still further the significance of Piaget's theory of perceptual growth for reading instruction and achievement.

STUDIES OF EARLY READERS

Another way to assess the role of logical ability in learning to read is to look at the mental abilities of children who learn to read early, that is, before they enter kindergarten. If logical abilities are a necessary, if not a sufficient, condition for learning to read, then early readers should be superior to matched non-early readers in this regard. This essentially, is what was found in one study of sixteen pairs of matched early and non-early readers (Briggs and Elkind, 1973) and in a just completed study of forty pairs of matched early and non-early readers. That is to say, early readers, regardless of intellectual level, tended to be significantly higher than their matched controls on measures of perceptual regulations and concrete operations.

It should be said that the data also suggest that perceptual regulations may be essential primarily during the initial phases of learning to read and that mental operations become more important thereafter. In other words, as reading becomes more fluent, perceptual regulation skills become subordinated to cognitive abilities. But it is important to emphasize that both perceptual regulations and mental operations are logical in nature and that mental operations are really higher order regulations.

Still another finding was that a goodly number of the early readers had a close relation with an adult or older child who spent much time with them in reading-related activities. Moreover, significantly more of the fathers of early readers than of non-early readers read frequently to their children. Finally, the mothers of early readers tended to have more education than the mothers of non-early readers.

These findings suggest that there is a strong social-motivational component involved in learning to read. Learning to read is not something children do automatically, like walking and talking, once they develop the necessary abilities. Rather, learning to read requires concentrated effort and attention to materials and stimuli that are not intrinsically interesting. Accordingly, it seems likely that the primary motivation for learning to read is social and consists of attachment to, and desire to please, an adult or adults who model and reward reading behavior. The failure of many children to learn to read may result from a lack of motivation rather than from any lack of capacity or improper or poor instruction.

It is necessary to say that the requisite level of mental development and the presence of appropriate social motivation are not in and of themselves sufficient to guarantee that a child will learn to read. Instruction is required as well. But there is probably no one "best" way to learn to read because children are much too variable for one method to fit them all. For some children phonics will work best, while for others the "look-say" or "language experience approach" will be best. It is likely that teachers who offer children a variety of approaches to learning to read will be most successful because they will enlist the learning of the largest number of children. An alternative is to have different teachers offer different programs and allow children to shift to the program that suits them best.

In summary, it seems fair to say that learning to read probably involves at least three factors: the necessary regulational and operational abilities, social motivation derived from the example of, and rewards for, reading by persons to whom the child is attached, and a program of instruction. Obviously the presence of all three factors is still no guarantee that a child will learn to read since reading failure, like fever, can be a symptom of a wide variety of psychological maladies. Nevertheless, if we insure that the child has the requisite maturation and motivation before we undertake formal reading instruction (as opposed to informal instruction such as reading to him, having him identify letters by name, letting him print, and so on) the possibility of his becoming a successful reader is much greater than if we had left these matters to chance.

Stages in the development of beginning reading from a Piagetian or structuralist perspective are presented in this chapter. At the first stage, children construct letters and words much as they construct object concepts. At the next stage, identity decoding, letters and words are associated with sounds and meanings on the basis of a one-to-one correspondence. Then during the next stage, equivalence decoding, children learn to cope with multiple sounds for single letters and multiple meanings for the same word. It is concluded that the stages are compatible with many different teaching methods and that a theory suggests how best to use any particular instructional method, not which method is best.

12

Beginning Reading: A Stage-Structure Analysis

Discussions of beginning reading are most often concerned with pragmatics, with the methods to be employed in teaching children to read. In such discussions the particular method being advocated is usually justified by reference to some psychological theory or educational philosophy. The "look-say" approach to reading, for example, had its origins in Gestalt psychology, which argued that the whole (in this case the word) was greater than the sum of its parts (the letters that make it up). Likewise, a phonics approach assumes that language involves auditory as well as visual processes and that auditory discriminations are essential to successful reading.

In my opinion, the connections between theory or philosophy and teaching methods are much less direct and simple than they are often made to appear. This is true because a theory or philosophy, by the very nature of its generality, is subject to many different pragmatic interpretations. Piaget's (151) theory, for example, has been evoked to support both informal (Chapter 14, this book) and formal teaching methods (162). Such divergent conclusions can be arrived at because hidden assumptions are made to mediate between theory and practice.

These hidden assumptions have to do with the nature of pragmatics. In reality, *every classroom experience is a nonreplicable experiment.* This is true because each classroom is a unique combination of personalities, working together at a unique time and under a unique set of circumstances: A teacher changes as a function of his or her experience and never really teaches exactly the same way twice. And the combination of children in any classroom is never repeated. Accordingly when an educational theory is translated into practice, some erroneous assumptions are made. This happens because a theory deals in generalities and teaching practice deals with specifics.

There is, however, another approach to translating theory into practice that can avoid the distortions that result from hidden assumptions about classroom practice. This approach is to assume that the translation from theory to practice is indirect rather than direct. In effect, no educational theory can tell a teacher what to do on Monday morning. What it can do is provide guidelines that a teacher can use no matter what method he or she employs. This approach assumes that a translation from theory to practice has to involve the practitioner as well as the theorist. A meaningful translation only goes part way, and the teacher must do the rest. In other words, a theorist often does not fully understand practice and a practitioner may not always understand theory. What is required is a middle ground, a translation that is more specific than the theory but more general than the specific classroom.

Hence my present stage structure analysis of beginning reading. This analysis starts from Piaget's theory of intellectual development and applies it to children as they go about the task of learning to read. While this analysis takes us a step beyond the theory and a step closer to reading instruction, it does not prescribe a particular method of instruction. Rather it suggests certain guidelines or parameters that a teacher using any method of reading instruction should probably heed. The analysis can be presented as a sequence of stages of progressively more complex structural attainments.

THE CONSTRUCTION OF LETTER CONCEPTS

From a Piagetian standpoint, the child must arrive at a concept of a letter in much the same way that he or she arrives at any other entrance into reality. For Piaget the child never copies reality nor projects it, rather he or she always *constructs* it out of his or her experiences with the environment. This process of construction, however, is not a matter of abstracting "common features" from diverse instances. The abstraction theory is really a copy theory that insists that common features intrude themselves upon a child in such a way that he or she must take account of them.

But we know that this is not the case. In the first place, children spontaneously conceptualize the world in ways that adults do not. If the world intruded upon every one in the same way such naive conceptions could not occur. For example, a child that I know pointed to a hirsute male and said "Look, Daddy, a mouthbrow" (moustache). Likewise, some common features are not perceived by us. Raw meat and cherries are both red and juicy, but we do not conceptualize them together. When a child constructs a concept of a letter then, he or she is doing more than objectively noting common features.

The construction of the concept of a letter, like the construction of other concepts, requires the child's involvement. Looking at letters, tracing them with fingers, using one's body to copy their shape, recognizing sandpaper letters, and of course writing are all ways in which the child goes about constructing a *schema* or internal representation of the letter. As a result of this schema, the child can recognize new instances of the letter, not by identi-

fying common features, but rather by finding whether or not a
new instance fits into the letter schema, the set of actions by
which it is identified.

The construction of the letter schema, as it has been described
here, requires the same active construction that infants employ
in building object concepts. But it is a more advanced construction because letters are two dimensional and essentially nonfunc-
tional to the young child. Learning letters, in the sense of
constructing schemata of them as described here, is not easy and
takes time. It also requires motor coordinations, such as those
involved in tracing and writing, that may not be present until
the age of three or four. In other words, the child's ability to
construct the concept of letter is limited by his or her sensorimotor abilities.

IDENTITY DECODING

The construction of letters, then, and to some extent learning
their names, involves an advanced form of sensorimotor coordination and is an extension of the processes children use in constructing objects and labeling them. On the other hand, learning
a sound for a letter like *ma* for m involves new mental abilities
that emerge only during the preschool years. Piaget (151) terms
the operations of this period *functions* and says that they operate
in the manner of mathematical functions: $X = f(y)$. When children define words in functional terms (a hole is to dig, a bird is
to fly) they express this functional mode of thought. What they
are saying is that holes are a function of digging and birds are a
function of flying.

The attainment of preoperational functional thinking enables
young children to deal with transformations. An object that begins to fly is transformed into a bird, a piece of ground that is
dug up is transformed into a hole. And, at this stage, children
recognize that a single quantity that is changed in appearance

remains the same in amount (121, 133). It is the understanding of transformations that enables young children to comprehend how a letter can be translated into a sound. Such translations are what I have called *identity decoding*.

It has to be said, however, that the young child's ability to engage in identity decoding has an important limitation: young children believe that an object has one and only one function. This is most clearly seen in the young child's belief that every object or person has one and only one name because the name is the function of the object and every object can have one and only one name function. In the same way young children believe that each and every letter can have one and only one sound function. That, in fact, is why I have called this stage of reading "identity" decoding. At this stage young children see the sound of the letter as identical to (a simple transformation of) the letter that leaves it unchanged because it is, in fact, a part of it.

Another form of identity decoding is reading sight words. Young children can construct concepts of whole printed words much as they can construct concepts of letters. And they can learn what those words mean much as they can learn the sounds of letters. Learning sight words, like learning sounds for letters, is nonetheless limited by the child's preoperational functions. The child can learn only one meaning for a given word. So while children can learn sight words at the preoperational level, such learning is quite limited.

EQUIVALENCE DECODING

In largely phonetic languages, such as Japanese, children can learn to read at the preoperational stage and entirely by means of identity decoding. In a phonetic language the child is required only to learn a single sound transformation (function) for each letter. That may be why there are one tenth the reading failures in Japan that we have in the United States (147). Unfortunately, however, English phonics require more than identity decoding because the same letter can indicate different sounds, and the same sound can be representd by different letters. To understand the complexities of English phonics, children need more than the functions of the preoperational period. They need more advanced abilities that appear about the age of 6 or 7 and which Piaget (151) calls concrete operations.

Concrete operations enable the schoolage child to do many things that the preschool child is incapable of. He or she can engage in syllogistic reasoning ("Candy is sweet, this is candy, therefore this must be sweet"), to follow rules (which permits them to engage in group games), and to engage in systematic problem solving (that permits "discovery" learning at school). In addition, and most important for the present discussion, concrete operations enable the schoolage child to coordinate functions and to establish their equivalence.

When children engage in identity decoding they have, in effect, engaged in a kind of *functional* classification. This is an advance over the *structural* classification involved in the construction of letters. What concrete operations enable children to do is order and combine the functional classifications of the preschool period. For example, schoolage children can learn that a ball is not only to throw but also to be caught, that a story is not only to be listened to but also to be read. In other words, children learn that one and the same object can have more than one function.

It is this ability that enables children to understand the complexity of English phonics, a process I have called *equivalence* decoding. Basically, equivalence decoding involves the extension of the concrete operational processes of logical addition and logical multiplication to the identity decodings learned during the preoperational period. Logical addition involves adding two classes to form a third that includes the two that have made it up. For example, the class of boys + the class of girls = the class of children. Logical multiplication involves the coordination of two classes to arrive at a third made up by their intersect, by the members who belong to both classes. The class of Protestants × the class of Americans = the class of Protestants + the class of Americans + the class of Americans who are also Protestants.

When logical addition and logical multiplication are applied to identity decodings, children come to appreciate that one letter can indicate different sounds and that the same sound can be represented by different letters. Consider the long and short sound of the letter a. A child who knows the short sound of a, or that $s_{\check{a}} = f_1(a)$, is now taught the long sound for a, or that $s_{\bar{a}} = f_2(a)$. From the preoperational standpoint, this is an apparent contradiction. How is it resolved? It is resolved by logical addition, by the formation of a higher order function that encompasses the two lower ones. This new, higher order function might be symbolized as: $S_a = f_1(a) + f_2(a) + f_3(a) \ldots f_n(a)$, in which the general sound a, (S_a) includes the various particular sounds of a $(s_{\check{a}}, s_{\bar{a}}$, and so on). In other words, the "sound of a" is now a superordinate class that includes all of the sound functions of a.

In the same way, logical multiplication makes it possible for the concrete operational child to understand how the same sound can be associated with different letters. For example, the hard k sound is a function of both c and k, or $s_k = f(k)$ and $s_k = f(c)$. A logical multiplication of these functions gives the original sound symbol relations plus a new intersect sound, or $S_k = f(k) + f(c) + f(ck)$. That is, the hard k sound can be a function of c, a function of k, or a function of their intersect ck. Although this may seem an elaborate way to learn sound symbol relationships, it is necessary if children are going to learn equivalence decoding for English. It is because English phonics requires these complex mental operations that so many young children have difficulty in learning to read. This difficulty is increased if equivalence decoding is introduced before children have attained concrete operations.

As described above, stages in beginning reading deal primarily with the logical structures children need to break the linguistic code. They say nothing about comprehension. This is not because I believe comprehension to be unimportant, but rather because I believe that when children are "centered" on decoding they are not really concerned with comprehension. Comprehension becomes an important facet of reading only *after* decoding has become reasonably automatic either at the identity or equivalence levels.

Consider a child who is coping with equivalence decoding. His or her attention is focused or centered upon the multiple sound functions of particular letters and letter combinations and upon their coordination. In contrast, comprehension as it is conceived by some (119) is the assimilation of the meanings of printed words to complex conceptual frameworks or *schemata*. Put differently, decoding involves one kind of assimilation and accommodation whereas comprehension requires another. The young child cannot do both at the same time. It is only when decoding becomes automatic that children really begin to learn from what they read.

Research support for a stage structure approach to beginning reading has been growing. Francis (135), for example, found that children learned the concept of a letter before they learned the concept of a word and the concept of word before they learned the concept of sentence. This was true despite the fact that the method of instruction was look-say. And some of our early studies suggested that decoding of letters and words was an important corollary to reading success (130, 132).

More recently a number of investigators have found high positive correlations between measures of operativity and beginning reading. Lunzer (146) observed that measures of seriation and classification were positively correlated with measures of reading success in first and second graders. Scott (157) found that children's success on a seriation task at kindergarten correlated .50

with their reading success at third grade. Kaufman and Kaufman (143) reported that success in seriation at kindergarten correlated .58 with reading success at first grade.

A review of many different studies relating measures of operativity and reading has been provided by Waller (161). He concluded that in all of the studies he reviewed, measures of operativity were positively correlated with measures of reading success. Waller also noted that, of all the measures of operativity, those assessing seriation yielded the highest correlations with reading achievement. This latter observation is in keeping with the stage structure analysis. This follows because, in addition to logical addition and logical multiplication, seriation involves a directional or spatial orientation. In learning to read children learn not only how to reason about letters and sounds but also how to reason in particular directions.

A final experimental support for the stage structure analysis comes from our own investigations of early readers (123, 124). In these studies we compared children who read early (before attending kindergarten) with comparable children who did not. Of all the many different measures we used, the measures of operativity were the only ones that systematically differentiated the early readers from non-early readers. Early readers were significantly superior to non-early readers on measures of operativity.

In summary, then, there is a good deal of research evidence that directly, or indirectly, supports the stage structure analysis that has been presented here.

IMPLICATIONS FOR READING INSTRUCTION

In the introduction to the chapter I suggested that an analysis of reading from a particular theoretical perspective did not prescribe the specifics of how reading should actually be taught. Failure to recognize this point has produced a great deal of unnecessary controversy among theoreticians of reading. They assume that their different theories necessarily dictate different teaching methods. In contrast, as I have argued in this paper, I really do not believe this to be the case.

For example, Frank Smith (158) cogently argued that decoding is not an essential part of learning to read. He also suggested that this theoretical analysis has a pragmatic conclusion —that the teacher need not teach decoding skills. My impression is that this conclusion does not follow and that at best Smith's theory suggests how best to teach decoding, not its exclusion from teaching practice. Likewise Kenneth Goodman (139) and Gibson and her followers (e.g., 138) are probably going too far when they use their quite different theories of reading to arrive at direct prescriptions for reading practice. These theories would be much more useful to teachers if they were translated into guidelines for using existing methods rather than prescriptions for which methods to use.

For example, the stage structure analysis suggests that young children can learn some sight words and some phonics. Hence the analysis would support a phonics, or a look-say, or a language experience approach. But it would also suggest limitations. A look-say approach for preoperational children must be careful not to use words that have more than one meaning. Likewise, homonyms (e.g., dye and die) could cause trouble for children at the identity decoding level. Moving to these more complex decodings would require children to do equivalence decoding.

Similar guidelines would hold true for a phonics approach. What any phonics approach for young children has to guard against is the introduction of words that require equivalence decoding—words that present children with more than one sound for a given letter or more than one letter for a given sound. A similar caution would hold for a language experience approach in which children tell stories, have them written down, and then proceed to read them. The language experience approach has to guard against the dangers of equivalence decoding at both the whole word and the phonics level.

Accordingly, the analysis of beginning reading that has been presented here does not prescribe a particular reading method. It does suggest some basic guidelines as to what should be taught when, regardless of the particular pragmatics used. Perhaps if we recognize that theories do not prescribe methods, we will more fully appreciate the values and the limitations of all the methods we have available.

Montessori's famous dictum to the effect that "Play is the child's work" is challenged in the present paper. Her views on play are compared and contrasted with those of Erikson, following Freud, and Piaget. It turns out that Erikson, like Montessori (he was a Montessori teacher), equates play and work whereas both Freud and Piaget separate the two in parallel ways. It is concluded that the separation of work and play, of social accommodation and personal expression, is a necessary one and that the tension between these two modes of adaptation is essential to their later integration in science and art.

13

Work Is Hardly Child's Play

The role of play in human development has been interpreted and understood in many different ways and from the perspectives of several quite different disciplines. A comprehensive listing of the many divergent approaches to the origin of play has recently been offered by Bruner et al. (126). The focus of this chapter is much more limited and attempts to compare and to contrast the writings of Montessori, Erikson, and Piaget with respect to their positions on play. Their theories have a common bond because Erikson was trained as a Montessori teacher, and the Maison des Petits, the Lab School at Piaget's Institute in Geneva where much of Piaget's early research was done, had a modified Montessori program.

In addition to this theoretical connection, there is also an applied one. Although none of the three was an educator by profession (Montessori was a physician, Erikson gave up teaching for psychoanalysis, and Piaget is a psychologist), all three have had considerable impact upon educational practice, particularly at the early childhood level.

MARIA MONTESSORI

In 1896, Maria Montessori received her degree in medicine in Italy. She was just 26, and the first woman physician in that country. After achieving some remarkable results working with retarded children, she was given the task of rehabilitating a group of "slum" children in a day care center serving a housing development in a poor section of Rome. It was here that she began evolving the educational theories and practice that have since won her worldwide recognition.

It is a tribute to Montessori, perhaps the highest tribute that can be paid to an innovator, that many of her concepts and methods have become part of established educational practice and are no longer associated with her name. The use of child-sized chairs and tables, the concept of a "prepared" environment suited to the child's level of cognitive ability, and the ample provision of manipulative materials from which children can learn basic concepts, all derive from Montessori.

But there was one Montessori contribution that has not become assimilated to early childhood educational practice—her conception of play. And to this day, the greatest divergence between Montessori and non-Montessori child-centered classrooms resides in their handling of play and fantasy. What made this conception so unattractive when so much else of Montessori was swiftly taken over by those working with young children?

First of all, while Montessori was a revolutionary in an educational sense, she was not so in a political sense. She saw education, good education, as the best means for children to become good citizens of high character. To be sure, she advocated that children should be appreciated and respected as persons in their own right, and expected that such treatment would result in adults who were self respecting as well. But it is fair to say that the thrust of her educational method was social adaptation. The value of teaching at the child's level was that the child could learn the basic skills of the culture. Her image of the child was that he or she could be regarded as an immigrant "who goes to a new country ignorant of its products, ignorant of its natural appearance and social order, entirely ignorant of its language," and who is confronted with "an immense work of adaptation which he must perform before he can associate himself with the active life of the unknown people" (149, p. 35). This image reflects her view of education as primarily social adaptation. Montessori, working with slum children, wanted them to be good citizens who would accept rather than challenge the social order. Montessori's conception of play was therefore conditioned by her view of education as social adaptation.

But Montessori's conception of play was also grounded in the contemporary thinking of her time. Carlotta Lombroso, a prominent nineteenth century philosopher of education wrote: "Play is for the child an occupation as serious, as important, as study is for the adult; play is in his means of development and he needs to play, just as the silkworm needs continually to eat leaves" (145, p. 117). Likewise, Karl Groos argued that "the animal does not play because he is young, rather he has a period of youth because he must play" (141). From this standpoint play is the natural and essential activity of the young in preparation for adult life.

The conception of play which was in vogue when Montessori wrote held that it was the natural activity of the child and that its function was to prepare the child for adult life. Montessori wedded this conception to her view of education as social adaptation when she wrote that "Play is the child's work." In fact, she went much farther than did Groos. For Groos, play did serve as a socializing force in the sense of modulating instincts, but for him the modulation of instincts gave rise to art and personal expression as well as social adaptation. It was this dimension of play, its artistic and aesthetic dimension, which was somehow lost in Montessori's presentation. Very simply, play for Montessori had little value in and of itself and took on importance only when it was put in service of socialization.

Montessori's emphasis on the use of play and fantasy for

social adaptation rather than for artistic personal expression is shown in the following paragraph. "Imagination has always been given a predominant place in the psychology of childhood, and all over the world people tell their children fairy stories which are enjoyed immensely, as if the children wanted to exercise this great gift, as imagination undoubtedly is." But then she adds, "Yet when all are agreed that a child loves to imagine, why do we give him only fairy tales and toys on which to practice this gift? If a child can imagine a fairy and fairyland, it will not be difficult for him to imagine America. Instead of hearing it vaguely in conversation, he can help to clarify his own ideas of it by looking at the globe on which it is shown" (150, p. 177). As suggested here, Montessori regarded fairy tales as frivolous and felt that the child's imagination could be put to better use in the service of learning about the real world.

Why did this gifted woman, who had such brilliant insights into children and their ways of thinking and feeling, eschew the esthetic, the personal, the artistic side of children and of children's play? It would certainly make an interesting psychohistorical investigation. It is my own guess that the aesthetic was not very important to Montessori personally, or not something she took great pleasure in. One gets very little sense of aesthetic appreciation in her books. On the other hand, she was enormously productive and achievement oriented. In short, Montessori's view of play as social adaptation may have come from her own personal value system rather than from her observations of children. Perhaps that is why it has been less accepted than many of her other contributions.

ERIK ERIKSON

Erik Erikson is a student of Freud's as well as of Montessori's, and his conception of play bears traces of both his teachers as well as his own unique genius. In 1896 when Montessori received her medical degree, Sigmund Freud had turned away from neurology and began his investigations of the psychoneuroses. In 1895, he and Joseph Breuer published their classic *Studies in Hysteria* (122) and in 1904 Freud published *The Interpretation of Dreams* (136).

Not surprisingly, Freud too shared the conception of play as a kind of work. In *Interpretation of Dreams*, for example, he spoke of the "dream work," by which he meant the mental processes that transformed unacceptable, unconscious wishes and impulses into acceptable, if often undecipherable, conscious dream images. The dream work clearly has an adaptive function: it allows the person to sleep undisturbed by wishes and impulses which, if they were known, would awaken the person and cause distress.

The dream work, the mechanisms of displacement, condensation, and substitution are also the mechanisms of fantasy production, and also of play. In children's play one can see the very same mechanisms in operation that we can see in dreams. An analyst would say, for example, that in block play a child substitutes blocks for people, displaces feelings when he or she knocks them over, and condenses many different life themes into a particular form of play. Play-work is thus parallel to dream work.

It is important to recognize, however, that the Freudian identification of play and work is of a different order than the identification made by Montessori. First of all, for Montessori as for other psychologists such as Koftka (144), play was the dominant mode of child behavior. The child was, by nature, a playing creature. What Montessori argued was that this play was not, or at least should not be, frivolous. Play should be put in the service of social adaptation.

Freud, however, distinguished between primary and secondary process thought, and recognized that children were capable of both. Primary process thought included the processes of the dream work while secondary process thought was logical and mathe-

WORK IS HARDLY CHILD'S PLAY

matical. Freud, therefore, recognized two types of adaptation and two types of adaptative processes. One type of adaptation was directed toward the pleasure-seeking instincts and was called the pleasure principle. A second type of adaptation was directed toward the external world and was called the reality principle.

So Freud differed from Montessori in two major respects. First, children are not totally engaged in play because they operate according to the reality principle as well as the pleasure principle. Second, while play involves effort in the sense that it is an adaptation, it is not, or at least not directly, social adaptation. Play from a psychodynamic view has much less to do with mastery of the world than it has to do with mastery of the self. Play is the means by which we are able to control our own inner forces that threaten established social relations. Accordingly, Montessori said that children's play was subordinate to work whereas Freud said that children's work (at least the primary process work) was in the service of play.

This view of play extends to wit and humor as well. Jokes, from a Freudian position, always have a sexual or an aggressive content. Like dreams they permit the expression of unacceptable impulses in nonthreatening ways. Laughter is the release of hidden reservoir of tension built up from repressing anger and sexual impulses and feelings. So we laugh for the same reason that we play, it allows us to express in acceptable, if disguised, ways deep-seated conflicts, anxieties, and wishes.

Erikson attempted to integrate the Montessori and the Freudian positions. The desire to integrate diverse positions, to create an ordered whole or an identity, is characteristic of Erikson's work. And he would be the first to acknowledge that his concern with the integration of apparently unrelated or contradictory conceptions stems from his own efforts to construct a unified whole from the disparate parts of his own professional and personal background.

In the chapter "Toys and Reasons" in *Childhood and Society*

(134) Erikson makes explicit his conception of play and how it differs from that of Freud and the psychoanalysts. He offers the passage from *Tom Sawyer*, where Tom is starting to whitewash the fence and one of his friends appears. Ben Rogers, the friend, is imitating a steamboat, its captain, and its crew. Erikson asks how this sort of imaginative play is to be interpreted and offers in response some typical psychoanalytic explanations he received from a class of social workers he was teaching. The answers suggested that Ben Rogers was expressing, and working through, some family trauma such as an overbearing father and bed wetting.

Erikson, in contrast, offers an alternative explanation epitomized in the statement "Ben is a growing boy." Erikson writes:

> To grow means to be divided into different parts which move at different rates. A growing boy has trouble in mastering his gangling body as well as his divided mind. He wants to be good, if only out of expediency, and always finds that he has been bad. He wants to rebel, and finds that almost against his will, he has given in. As his time perspective permits a glimpse of approaching adulthood, he finds himself acting like a child. One "meaning" of Ben's play could be that it affords his ego a temporary victory over his gangling body and self by making a well functioning whole out of brain (captain), the nerves and muscles of will (signal system and engine) and the whole bulk of the body (boat). It permits him to be an entity within which he is his own boss because he obeys himself. (134, p. 211)

For Erikson, therefore, play has a much broader function than it did for Freud. Play is not just an outlet for dangerous wishes and impulses. It can also be a means, a symbolic tool, for coping with the normal asynchronies and contradictions inherent in mental and physical growth. Ben's play, to put it simply, was an expression of health and not of illness. While play can have curative powers for children suffering from emotional disturbance, it goes beyond that.

Growing up in a particular society at a particular time in history and in a particular ethnic milieu presents every individual with problems of adaptation that are part of his or her human condition. Not all of a young person's conflicts derive from disturbances of childrearing, and some are evidence of growth and adaptation to particular social circumstances. Play, then, cannot be reduced to an expression of familial trauma, and has to be seen more broadly as symbolizing many different facets of a child's growth and problems of adaptation to self and social milieu.

While one can applaud this broadening conception of child's play, it is less easy to applaud Erikson's slip back to the Montessori identification of work and play, of social adaptation and personal expression. Oddly enough, after showing the value of play as personal expression in Ben Rogers's case, he concludes with the following sentence: "At the same time, he chooses his metaphors from the tool world of the young machine age, and anticipates the identity of the machine God of his day, the captain of the Big Missouri." Play is social adaptation as well as personal expression. That Erikson intends this identification of work and play is clear from his use of an anthropological example from Ruth Underhill which sounds a lot like Montessori: "The man of the house turned to his little three-year-old granddaughter and asked her to close the door. The door was heavy and hard to shut. The child tried but it did not move. Several times the grandfather repeated, "Yes, close the door." No one jumped to the child's assistance. No one took the responsibility away from her. On the other hand there was not impatience because the child was small. They sat gravely waiting until the child succeeded and her grandfather thanked her. It was assumed that the task would not be asked of her unless she could perform it, and having been asked, the responsibility was hers alone, just as if she were a grown woman" (134, p. 236).

Erikson argues that this child is early conditioned to social participation by tasks geared to her level of ability. In our society, he argues, this is not the case and the child does not make a contribution to society unless it competes with adults. And he concludes: "It dawns on us then, that the theories of play which are advanced in our culture and which take as their foundation the assumption that in children too, play is defined by the fact that it is not work, are really one of the many prejudices by which we exclude our children from an early source of a sense of identity" (134, p. 237).

According to Erikson the separation of work and play in childhood is a "prejudice." Hence, we are back to Montessori by way of Freud. Montessori argued that play was social adaptation where Freud argued that it reflected personal adaptation. Erikson extended Freud's notion to show that play could be an expression of personal growth as well as personal conflict, but then he gives up the important distinction between the individual and the social and argues that it is a prejudice. He says that if personal adaptation is separate from social adaptation in our society, this is regrettable. Apparently, for Erikson, children attain a healthier sense of ego identity in a society where play is a child's work than in one where these two activities are separate.

JEAN PIAGET

Piaget was born in 1896, the same year that Montessori became a doctor of medicine and a year after the publication of *Studies in Hysteria*. Piaget was thus of a different generation than the other two investigators, although he was greatly influenced by them. This influence however was tempered by a healthy minded skepticism grounded in an empirical mentality. Piaget was unwilling to accept what others said about the development of child life without first checking it against his own observations and analytical evaluation.

It was in this mode that Piaget attacked the problem of children's play (152). He was extraordinarily well read in this field, as in others which he investigated, and his challenges to the theory of Karl Groos, and of Claparede his mentor (128), were based on a solid understanding of those positions. Indeed, Piaget often saw broader implications in a writer's theory than the writer had himself.

However that may be, Piaget set himself three major tasks, the basic ones of scientific inquiry. He first sought to classify play behavior, regarding this as the first and essential step in any scientific investigation. Second he attempted to describe the rules that operated in the development of these behaviors. And third, he sought a general explanation by reference to general principles of human development. Piaget's work on play, although it was begun in his first exploratory stage of his career, was completed during his second period when he sought to trace the origins of intelligence to the sensorimotor coordinations of infants. More specifically, his aim was to explain play in terms of its place in the evolution of intelligence.

Piaget argued that classifications based on content (e.g., sensorial, motor, or intellectual games) or on functions (fighting, counting, family games) were bound to be inconsistent and inadequate. What is critical in Piaget's view to a general classification of play behaviors is what today we would call a deep structure in opposition to a surface structure classification. The deep structure analysis would group play behaviors on the basis of their underlying structural differences.

Using this type of analysis and the meticulous observations of his own three infants as his primary data, Piaget distinguished three types of play: practice play, symbolic play, and games with rules. Practice play occurs early in life, during the first few months, and can be observed whenever the child acts for the sake of acting. An infant who sucks his thumb or who grasps and lets go of an object is engaged in practice play. What characterizes this activity and why it is play, in Piaget's sense, is that it is almost entirely assimilative. The infant who is sucking its thumb has transformed that thumb into an object to be sucked. It has transformed the object so as to meet personal needs.

In Piaget's view practice play is usually short lived and gen-

erally appears after the mastery of one or another type of sensorimotor coordination. At the same time the child is engaging in
practice play, however, he or she is also engaging in imitation.
And it is through imitation that the child begins to be able to
represent objects and to differentiate signs from signifiers. At
about age two this distinction becomes fully operative and the
child becomes capable of representing his or her experience at a
temporal and spatial distance from it. The delayed reaction, or
the ability of an infant to respond to a hidden object after a time
delay, is an example.

After about age two until about age four or five, children are
primarily engaged in representational activities. These activities
move in two directions. One is toward conventional representations, concepts, verbal signs, and the socialization of experience.
The other is toward distorted representations, symbols, and the
expression of personal feelings and conflicts. The preschool child
is learning signs and becoming socialized, but he or she is also
creating symbols that reflect individuality.

It is evident that Piaget, like Freud, distinguishes between
work and play in early childhood. The young child is working
and accommodating to social reality a great deal of the time. He
or she is told not to get dirty, to say please, to eat more slowly,
to talk more rapidly, and so on. At the same time children engage
in symbolic play that is really not accommodative. The boys and
girls playing house and store are really *not* learning adult roles.
Symbolic play is not merely imitative because it has many transformational components, such as endowing dolls with life and
empty cups with coffee. Such play reflects personal needs for
mastery and control and is not primarily social adaptation.

The critical distinguishing feature of symbolic play in young
children, then, is not its function nor its imitative components
but rather the presence of symbols. For Piaget a symbol is a
personal representation as opposed to a sign that is a conventional
and a social representation. Because the child is still far from

mastering the complex world of signs and the concepts they represent, children have need of symbols to represent their personal needs and conflicts. For Piaget, symbolic play is important in its own right as a necessary means for dealing with wishes, desires, and conflicts by one who is not completely socialized and thus does not have socialized means of expression and of conflict resolution.

As children attain concrete operations, at about the age of six or seven, symbolic play diminishes in frequency and is replaced with games with rules. Social play comes to replace individual play and socially constructed game rules come to replace personally constructed symbols. Game rules, in Piaget's view, are collective symbols in the sense that they still distort reality while they are shared by several individuals. Games with rules can be handed down by oral tradition, such as marbles and jacks, or can be made up spontaneously by a group of children, such as tossing around a child's hat to keep him from getting it.

The appearance of games with rules makes, for Piaget, a dimunition of egocentrism and a new level of social integration. In his view, as a consequence of the maturing child's increasing size and competencies he or she finds other, socialized avenues for expressing personal needs or wishes. In games with rules, for example, the child can express competitive needs in a socially prescribed way. More generally, play, in the pure sense of assimilation unmodified by accommodation, becomes increasingly less common as children grow older and become socialized beings.

Piaget does not deny, of course, that some form of symbolic activity still goes on in later life. Dreams and fantasy are an example because these still reflect distorting assimilation. But even dreams and fantasies are much more socialized in the older child and adult than they are in early childhood. The majority of the child's play activity, and the adult's for that matter, is socialized and reflects a healthy integration of the personal and the social. There are, of course, numerous exceptions in this regard, notably those tennis and bridge players who give evidence that they have not yet been able to subordinate the personal to the social.

IMPLICATIONS

In reviewing this discussion of Piaget's theory of play an educational implication can be derived. Piaget alludes to the fact that children's artistic expression also becomes more socialized during childhood proper, as do his or her personal scientific preoccupations. Children begin to draw in much more conventionalized ways, and individual collections (e.g., teddy bears) give way to social collections such as coins, stamps, and comic books, which are traded from one young person to another.

Although Piaget does not emphasize it, I believe that we see in the socialization of these two facets of play the beginnings of art and science. Both art and science provide a unique integration of the personal and the social. Good art is at once personal and social and provides a unique vision of the world which can nonetheless be shared and enjoyed by others. The artist, in a sense, creates collective symbols through which many can express their personal feelings and desires. The scientist does the same thing in a somewhat different way. He or she creates a new concept that allows others to see the world in new ways.

Science and art, therefore, grow out of the separation between work and play in early childhood. Indeed, I would like to venture the hypothesis that the tension between play and work, between personal expression and social accommodation, is essential for their later integration. It is for that reason that I oppose the identification of work and play in early childhood, and why I urge that young children have the opportunity to play as well as to work.

SUMMARY AND CONCLUSION

Montessori equated work and play in early childhood inasmuch as she argued that play should be put in the service of social adaptation. Erikson, who was a student of Montessori's but also of Freud's, attempted to reconcile the Freudian theory of play, as a kind of personal catharsis, with the Montessori notion that play should be social adaptation. Erikson suggests that play can express healthy growth processes and need not always be a disguised expression of hidden impulses. But he also argued that play was a means of relating to one's culture and argued that the distinction between work and play in childhood is a prejudice.

Piaget takes a developmental perspective on play and sees it as having different forms at different age levels. In infants one sees a form of practice play where action is repeated for the sense of function pleasure and where accommodation is subordinated to assimilation. In the preschool period, thanks to the construction of personal symbols, assimilation becomes differentiated from accommodative activities and symbolic play becomes the means by which the child expresses unsocialized desires and impulses. In childhood proper, assimilation and accommodation, play and work, are reconciled in games with rules. Such games are social, inasmuch as they involve mutual obligations, but also personal by involving individual competitiveness. In addition, games also involve collective symbols—distorted representations of the world. In marbles, for example, the glass balls can represent many different things to different children. They are collective in being shared, personal in that they have no specific shared meaning other than their role in the game.

I have argued that the distinction between work and play in early childhood—advocated by Freud and Piaget, opposed by Montessori and Erikson—is important and should be maintained. It is really not a cultural prejudice as Erikson suggests. For example, Vytgosky (160) writing from a Marxist perspective describes play (the subordination of the object to meaning) and work (the subordination of the meaning to the object) in terms similar to Piaget's. The importance of the distinction between play and work, between personal assimilation and social accommodation, is that it provides the necessary tension for the sorts of integration that we call science and art. Good art, like good science, is a unique integration between the particular and the universal, between what is unique to the individual and common to mankind.

The recognition of the distinction between work and play is really the recognition of our biological heritage. Each of us has a unique combination of genes that will never be repeated. But we also have the same number of chromosomes, at the same loci as everyone else. We are like everyone else but different too. At its simplest level, then, play and work reflect our existential dilemma of being both one and many. It is, as I have argued here, a mistake to deny or ignore this dilemma since it provides the tension out of which man's lasting achievements emerge. More particularly, in young children we should encourage play for its own sake since it provides an avenue for expressing himself or herself in personal ways. Paradoxical as it may seem, personal expression in early childhood may be the best possible preparation for social accommodation later. Play is not the child's work and work is hardly child's play.

It is often said that informal or child-centered British Pirmary educa-
tion reflects a Piagetian philosophy of education. Nonetheless, the con-
crete relationships between informal infant-school practice and Pia-
getian theory have not yet been spelled out. An attempt in that
direction is made here. A brief sketch of some of the major features of
informal education such as its emphasis upon expression, integrated
day and multi-age grouping is presented first. Next, two basic tenets
of Piagetian theory, constructivism and equilibration, are shown to be
consonant with informal educational practice. It is concluded that in
many ways informal educational practice is, in fact, a concrete em-
bodiment of the educational philosophy implicit in Piaget's theory.

14

Piaget and British Primary Education

WITH DONNA HETZEL AND JOHN COE

BRITISH PRIMARY EDUCATION*

Over the past half century, a distinctive approach to early childhood and elementary school education has evolved in England.
The movement generally began in English infant schools (for 5-
to 7-year-old children), which were for the most part separate
from the junior schools (for 8- to 11-year-old children). Most
English primary-school teachers have been trained at colleges
of education and not at universities. Thus they have tended to
be more child centered and less subject-matter oriented than the

---

* This description is a composite portrait of good teaching practices in
British primary schools. It is derived from the extensive experience of two
of the authors (Donna Hetzel and John Coe) who have spent many years
observing, teaching, and advising in different primary schools in Britain.

secondary teachers. At first small group of pioneering infant-schools emerged. The success of the new methods could be clearly seen at these schools and over the years their influence and example spread upward and outward so that today very few English infant and junior schools are untouched by fundamental change.

As we have suggested above, the growth of child-centered practices has primarily been dictated by work with children and only secondarily by theoretical concerns. And yet one frequently hears, in both England and America, that the informal education practiced in the schools is consistent with and constitutes a concrete embodiment of the work and theory of Jean Piaget. This chapter articulates for the first time the assumed relationship between informal school practice and Piagetian theory.

What makes informal education in England unique and what sets it off from other child-centered approaches (such as that of Montessori) are its original insights regarding child nature and the learning process. These fresh insights were derived primarily from the observations of teachers who were working with children and who were unfettered by preconceived notions as to how children live and learn.

One unique insight about children that informs all of the child-centered education practiced in England is the belief that children learn best by experiencing the world directly and then reconstructing, reconstituting, or representing it in ways that are appropriate to their individual talents and abilities. By recasting it in a mold of his own thinking, the child integrates it into his own personal conceptual system and makes it his own. Informal education thus provides the child with many opportunities to experience his world and with the time and means for re-presenting that experience.

This view of child learning differs considerably from the theory of learning that pervades the traditional classroom. Much traditional learning holds that children learn best by copying the reality that is presented to them. In more recent years, there has been an emphasis on more active "discovery" learning or problem-solving approaches to dealing with subject matter. What these approaches to learning miss, however, and which is critical to the kind of learning characteristic of informal schools, is the process of assimilating and integrating new material to the child's existing body of knowledge and understanding.

Coupled with this insight into the nature of learning is another that consists of a recognition of the child's fundamental aesthetic propensities. Not only does the child appreciate beauty in nature, art, and craftsmanship, but he has the desire and the talent to express himself in ways that are aesthetically pleasing and gratifying. Informal education tries to create an aesthetically pleasing world for the child and one in which he can acquire the skills of formal education in pursuit of aesthetic expression. The child's task is to give sense and meaning to his world, and this task is most enjoyable and satisfying when there is an element of beauty inherent in its execution.

It is important to recognize that this is a radical departure from traditional views regarding education and aesthetics. In most of our schools in America, aesthetics are considered a luxury to be indulged in when there is time and money available. More important, however, is the tacit assumption that the appreciation of the finer things of life (art, music, drama) is the preserve of the well-educated and is the consequence of formal education. In contrast, English child-centered education assumes that the appreciation of beauty is within the powers of every child and that formal skills should be a natural outgrowth of the child's desire to appreciate and express his experience in aesthetically pleasing ways.

These fundamental insights into the child's need to learn by reconstituting experience and his aesthetic propensities are the root stock out of which all English child-centered practices grow and which gives all the varied facets of this practice their organic wholeness and integrity. That is to say, the organization of the classroom, the way in which the teacher relates to the children, the vertical grouping of children, and the use of the world surrounding the school are inexplicably bound up with one another. Indeed, all of these practices support and reinforce one another so that their combined educational impact is far greater than the sum of their effects considered separately and alone. Accordingly, it is only for purposes of exposition that these practices are presented apart from one another.

To encourage children to observe, explore and to represent their world the traditional classroom has given way to a very different, informal, environment. Gone are the rows of desks all focusing on the teacher at the head of the room. Instead the room arrangement is based upon the needs and activities of the young learners. A wide range of materials to facilitate communication and expression are ready to hand alongside living creatures and man-made artifacts that provoke interest and curiosity from the children. The learning environment is designed to promote the making of choices by each child, to encourage personal learning through the exploration of materials while working in small groups or alone.

The materials are arranged to stimulate the child and to help him to see what options he has. In many cases such arrangements do not coincide with the traditional "subject" grouping of materials into "math," "science," and "reading" areas. Rather the room is arranged so that there are places for reading, surfaces for writing, drawing, and painting, space for coming together to talk and discuss with or without the teacher. The environment is rich with books, objects, animals, and other living things. Available too are materials such as rulers, tape measures, scales, and objects to be weighed and compared. Cooking centers are a vital part of the practical math approach and recipe following is a natural way to learn reading as well as math skills. A class store where real items are bought and sold is yet another way in which academic skills can be acquired while engaging in interesting activities.

In the informal classroom the child encounters the need for academic skills (reading, writing, arithmetic) as a means of expressing or re-presenting† his experience. After catching a fish for the first time, a child wants to tell about it and is delighted if that telling is written down as a story that can be read again. Writing is a natural and desired activity in the context of the child's need to put his experience into words and to make that experience permanent on paper. In the same way, a child will feel the need for numbers and measurements once he becomes interested in problems such as the length of time it takes a snail to cross a table. In this, as in many other ways, the child's spontaneous needs, interests, and curiosities lead him to the attainment of academic skills through the acquisition of artistic and craft skills, as a means of deriving sense and meaning out of his rapidly expanding world. Closely intertwined with the organization and layout of the informal classroom is the teacher's mode of interacting with the children. She is less often an instructor than she is a catalyst, releasing the powers of the children.

In child-centered rooms the teacher encourages, even at times prompts a child to make choices from the learning environment. She moves about the classroom observing how children are working within it, trying to understand the children and using her training and experience to see the varied learning experiences as the children see them. Then she uses her insights to help the children forward, sometimes by explaining, sometimes by offering a skill, often by asking questions thus provoking fresh thought and responses by the children. What is implicit in this mode of interaction is the teacher's respect for the child's sense of industry and of autonomy (to use some Eriksonian terms) and her fundamental belief that the child's own interests and motivations are the best gauge of how to help him to make sense out of his world.

Another way in which the teacher's mode of interaction in the

† Re-presentation of experience is regarded as the basic mode of learning. By translating his experience into his own words or graphic expression, the child assimilates the experience and makes it his own.

informal classroom differs from that of the traditional classroom is in the flexible time scale followed by the class. In general there are few if any fixed time points to interfere with the flow of activity. Children begin a project and work at it until it is complete or they have had enough of it for that day. Accordingly, there is the opportunity for an intense commitment to a task without the threat of it being interrupted to conform to some arbitrary schedule of activities. Such an intense commitment is one of the keys to the astonishing quality of the work, in terms of both content and skill, characteristic of present-day child-centered education. The free-flowing time scale calls for considerable openness on the part of the teacher, who must constantly adapt to the children and whose long-range planning is most concerned with providing continual opportunity for spontaneity and choice.

In general, children and teachers snack and go to the toilet when they feel the need rather than at some pre-established time. There is generally a long lunch at which teachers join the children for meals and conversation. Usually there is no break in the afternoon, but before the children go home there is a quiet gathering that is used as a time of reflection upon what has happened, for planning the next day's activities, and for the teacher to tell or read a story. This "integrated" day allows both the teacher and the child to see the connection and relatedness of all the child's activities.

There is considerable variability in informal classrooms as to the demands and expectations presented to the children. In some classrooms the children understand that they are to undertake some reading, some writing, and some work in math each day. In others there are similar demands and expectations but these are much more loosely defined. The time scale may be different, as the children may balance the curriculum over a week rather than within a day. The rhythm and pace of learning evolves more flexibly from the changing nature of the learning environment.

The informal classroom is a dynamic, changing one in which the teachers as well as the children are always learning from one another and are continually looking for innovative ways to represent and reconstruct their experience. Still another characteristic of the informal school is the use of the surrounding world. In such a school not only is real life recreated inside classrooms, but the children go out of school with parents and teachers to learn directly from the environment. Such excursions are much different from the "field trips" with bus loads of children running through the zoo or museum while teachers rush about trying to maintain order. In the informal school small groups of children might go to a nearby village, the ruins of a church, to a bird sanctuary for a weekend, or to the heart of a big city. As much as a quarter of the learning activities may take place outside school in the real world.

On such excursions the children have an opportunity to observe, explore, question, and reflect at a leisurely pace about their experience. Alongside the children, as a participant in their experience, the teacher might suggest an appropriate response and offer techniques to facilitate that response. The children might collect specimens, take photographs, make rubbings to take back to the classroom. Or they might make sketches and tape recordings of sounds and of other children's reactions. Descriptive and reflective writing about any aspect of the excursion experience is thought to be most worthwhile and is encouraged. So also is accurate recording and tabulation of observed phenomena, since this is an essential beginning to scientific method that bears fruit in later education.

The grouping of children in informal schools also differs from the traditional classroom. Heterogeneous vertical grouping of children (particularly of the 5- to 7-year-olds) has proved most helpful to the development of both older and younger children. The former present a living model of skills and attitudes to younger ones who later become the senior members of the learning group. Children are enabled to respond at different levels on different occasions according to their particular stage of development, sometimes regressing from or reinforcing previous learning, sometimes leaping ahead of their chronological peers. The vertical grouping permits continuity over a number of years, strengthening the essential bond between the teacher and the child upon which so much depends. Competitiveness is played down; instead children attempt to surpass their own previous best and, more generally, to cooperate with others both in living and learning.

The foregoing description of informal educational practice details some of its highlights, but hardly does justice to its richness in practice. Child-centered education regards the years of childhood as an important and valuable stage of life and not as a waiting room through which the children must pass as quickly as possible on their way to the real world. Consequently informal schools try to make each day a satisfying and happy one for children. The quality of life that is created promotes not only the acquisition of vital basic skills but also the growth of positive attitudes to learning itself so that the children are eager for more achievement in the future. Indeed it has been found that the best way to prepare for the future is to live richly today.

PIAGETIAN THEORY

To what extent are the educational practices described above consonant with the educational theory implicit in the work of Jean Piaget? In particular, to what extent does Piagetian theory support the two related insights (that the child learns best by representing this experience and by doing so in aesthetically pleasing ways) that distinguish British primary education from other child-centered pedagogies? To answer this question we have to look first at what Piagetian theory has to say about knowing and representation and then at what it implies about the necessity for aesthetic judgments in mental development.

Knowing and Representing. From a Piagetian standpoint, knowing the world is always an active process in which the child constructs reality out of his experiences with the environment. This process of construction is not so much a straight line progression as it is a continually expanding spiral. At each successive level of development the child must reconstruct his existing concepts of space, time causality, etc., in keeping with his new level of mental abilities. In fact, therefore, the child does not construct one reality but rather a series of realities that progressively approximate the world view known to adults. At each stage of development the child reconstitutes his reality by actively manipulating and exploring his environment either motorically or mentally and by abstracting schemes or concepts from these activities. Knowledge, looked at in this way, is the system of schemes or concepts derived from the child's active encounters with the environment.

It has to be emphasized that, in Piaget's theory, constructing knowledge of reality is not at all the same thing as acquiring re-presentations (such as words and images) of it. While the construction of knowledge comes about as a result of the child's actions upon the environment, representations are acquired as a consequence of the environment's actions upon him. Knowledge is thus a more general and integrated system than is the system of representations. Knowledge is acquired by rational processes that involve logic—deduction and induction—whereas representations are acquired largely by imitative processes that primarily involve observation and modeling.

Children all over the world acquire, at about the age of 6 or 7, the knowledge that quantities (such as the number of pebbles in a pile, the amount of a liquid or a solid substance) remain the same despite transformations in their appearance (140). Children acquire this knowledge by reasoning about (acting upon) their experiences. In contrast, the particular language a child learns, his vocabulary, and his accent are very much dependent upon the immediate environment in which he is reared. The child learns the articulatory aspects of language by modeling the language patterns of persons with whom he interacts.

The relative independence of the systems of knowledge and of representations can be shown in other ways. Deaf children (137) demonstrate adequate knowledge of concrete reality despite the fact that they lack the system of verbal representations. Blind children, in contrast, who lack knowledge about concrete reality are nonetheless proficient in dealing with abstract representational systems (142). Clearly deaf children possess nonverbal means of representation and blind children have some notion of concrete reality. The point is that in deaf children the absence of the traditional representational system (verbal language) is not indicative of a lack of knowledge about reality, nor does the verbal ability of blind children indicate an entirely adequate knowledge of the immediate world about them.

This distinction between the child's need to construct *both* a system of concepts about the world (knowledge) *and* a system of representations has important educational implications. Traditional education often equates the system of representations with the system of knowledge or vice versa. When it proceeds in this way, traditional education provides the child with a lopsided pedagogical experience. That is to say, under such an educational regime the child is either taught representations for which he lacks the appropriate concepts or he is encouraged to form concepts without being provided the opportunity to represent them in personally appropriate ways.

For example, in America second-grade children are often taught the names of planets, their sizes, and their relative distances from one another and from the sun. But children of 7 or 8 years lack the mental ability to comprehend the size and distance concepts involved in planetary configurations. Hence their learning is merely representational (Piaget calls it "empty verbalism") and is necessarily short-lived inasmuch as it is not integrated within a broader conceptional system of spatial and temporal concepts.

Likewise, when children are taken on a field trip and the teacher's efforts are directed at keeping them quiet rather than at helping them to represent their experience, their new knowledge remains implicit and without a representational counterpart.

The Piagetian distinction between acquiring knowledge and acquiring representations does more than highlight some fallacious educational assumptions. Perhaps its greatest value is to point to a central task of education that the traditional identification of representation with knowledge has caused us to overlook. This task involves helping children to construct *meanings*, the relations between knowledge and representations. As the forgoing arguments demonstrate, the relations between knowledge and representations are not given but have to be actively constructed by the child. In contrast to knowledge, which is acquired by rational processes, and representations, which are acquired by imitations and associations, meanings are acquired by discovery and by invention.

From a Piagetian standpoint, therefore, the task of education is to facilitate the child's acquisition of knowledge, of representations, and of meanings. To accomplish this, education has to provide the child with opportunities: to continually interact with the real world; to interact with sympathetic adults who are skilled models of various systems or representation; and to relate their conceptualizations of experience to their developing representational skills (to acquire meanings). From the standpoint of Piagetian theory the most neglected task is the last one, providing children with the opportunity to represent their experience in a variety of different ways. In the end, the truly educated person is the one who can articulate what it is he knows and has learned.

Clearly, the child-centered educational program practiced in some British primary schools closely parallels the educational program suggested by Piagetian theory. The insight of British, informal education that children learn best through re-presenting their experience in multiple ways highlights the Piagetian distinction between knowledge and representation. Rather than equating knowledge and representation, as is so often done in traditional education, it separates them and designates their coordination as a primary educational task. In other words, a prime aim of British child-centered education is to help children to acquire meanings and not just to acquire knowledge or representations. By providing children with an environment rich in things to observe and to manipulate, by providing teachers skilled in a variety of representational media, and by encouraging children to relate experience and representations, British informal education fulfills the three pedagogical tasks suggested by the Piagetian model of effective education.

THE DEVELOPMENTAL NECESSITY OF AESTHETIC JUDGMENTS

The relationship between cognitive development and aesthetics is very complex and can be dealt with at many different levels of discussion and from many different perspectives. For our purposes, which are educational rather than philosophical, we can limit our treatment to the child's aesthetic judgments, his evaluations of what is pleasing and beautiful. From an educational point of view, the question that has to be answered is not the quality of the child's aesthetic judgments but rather *his need to make them*. To what extent are the child's aesthetic judgments necessary judgments? If aesthetic judgments are necessary, if they are an integral part of the child's thinking, then aesthetic values must play part in all facets of education.

To assess the developmental necessity of aesthetic judgments, we must first describe their nature and their function. From the standpoint of our earlier discussion, it is reasonable to define an aesthetic judgment as one regarding the adequacy, or appropriateness, of the relation between knowledge and its representation. Conceived in this way, aesthetic judgment has to do with the beauty of meanings. When a representation does full justice to the idea or concept it connotes, the meaning is pleasant. But when the representation does not do justice to the thought, the meaning is unpleasant.

It follows, from the forgoing definition, that aesthetic judgments, conceived as judgments of the appropriateness of meanings, are affected by personal, social, and developmental considerations. To some extent, a person's judgment as to whether a word, a painting, or a poem adequately expresses a particular thought is a matter of personal inclination and taste. Aesthetic judgment always contains a subjective component. But it also involves a social or objective component. Many meanings, such as the dictionary definitions of words, are socially determined and proscribed. Other representations, such as red lights and street signs, are also social in origin. While such social meanings do not usually convey a great deal of aesthetic pleasure when used correctly, they sometimes cause considerable displeasure when used incorrectly. Words that are used incorrectly, and traffic signals that are disobeyed, convey a certain unpleasantness even when the misuse has no dire consequences.

There is, in addition to the personal and social dimensions to aesthetic judgment, a developmental dimension as well. As children grow older and develop more elaborate mental abilities, their ideas become more complex and abstract and their representational skills become more refined and elaborate. Consequently, there is a developmental transformation in the kinds of relations that exist between representations and thought. In young children, the relations between concepts and representations are likely to be fairly global and personal. Children of 3 and 4 may describe size differences in personal metaphors and call the biggest chair the "daddy" chair while they label the littlest one a "baby" chair. By the time children reach adolescence, however, the relations between thought and representation are much more objective and social. Currently, for example, the word "heavy" is used by young people to describe difficult or awkward social situations.

Accordingly, one might expect the aesthetic judgments of children to change with age. And there is evidence that such changes do occur. In one study, Subes and Auzet (159) found that while children preferred literal art, adolescents preferred more abstract modes of graphic representation. Likewise, it is a common observation that most children give up drawing about the age of 9 or 10. Usually this occurs because older children, in contrast to younger children, become disturbed at the discrepancy between what it is they wish to represent and the quality of what they have actually produced. Indeed, this phenomena exemplifies the nature of aesthetic judgments at all levels of development, namely, evaluations of the adequacy of the fit between concept and representation. At any given level of development *beauty is a thought that is totally represented at the child's level of understanding.*

To what extent, however, are aesthetic judgments necessary in mental development? Are such judgments mere frills, occasioned by adult requests, or do they have adaptive significance for mental growth? In order to answer this question we have to look at Piaget's concept of equilibration. Although Piaget has not, to the best of our knowledge, looked at equilibration from the standpoint of aesthetics, it does appear to have aesthetic implications.

In Piaget's (153) view, equilibration is an overriding developmental principle that is inherent in all mental functioning. It is a dynamic principle that regulates the individual's interactions with the environment and insures that he is neither enslaved by the environment nor by his own egocentrism. Equilibration takes many different forms and operates in many different facets of mental development. One manifestation of equilibration occurs in the relations between representations and thought. Disequilibriums occur in these relations because the child sometimes acquires representations (such as certain words) before he acquires the appropriate concepts and because he sometimes acquires new concepts before he acquires the appropriate representations (such as certain graphic skills). As the child matures intellectually, he must not only reconstruct reality but also the relations between his knowledge and his means of representing them. The motivation for this reconstruction of meanings is aesthetic judgment. When a representation no longer adequately expresses a child's idea, this is unpleasant and he is motivated to alter and to modify its relationship to his understanding. Aesthetic judgment is thus a necessary, even essential, determinant in the evolution of meanings.

For example, suppose children at different age levels are shown two identical glasses filled equally high with juice. The children are asked to say whether there is the same amount to drink in the two glasses. After they have agreed that there is just as much to drink in the one container as in the other, the contents of one glass are poured into another taller, thinner container so that the level of the drink is higher in it, than in the glass. Now the children are asked whether there is still the same amount to drink in the glass as there is in the tall narrow container.

The reactions of the children will be different depending upon their ages. Young children simply say that the amount in the tall glass is more and that even pouring it back into the smaller glass will not make the amounts equal again. At about the age of five, however, children begin to show some discomfort regarding the relation between the representation and the concept. A five-year old may say that the amount in the narrow container is more because it is higher but then he looks at the width and says that the glass has more because it is wider.

This situation is aesthetically unpleasant because the relation between the representation "more" and the child's concept of "greater amount" is ambiguous. When the word "more" is used to describe either the heights or the widths of the two quantities, it does not adequately convey what the child understands by his concept of greater amount. For the child knows that one amount

cannnot be both more and less than another amount. This discrepancy encourages the child to integrate height and width and
arrive at a multidimensional concept of amount. Now the child
realizes that the liquids in the two differently shaped containers
are equal in quantity because he is taking both their heights and
widths into account at the same time. The elimination of the am-
biguity in his concept of "greater amount" leads to a more appropriate use of the term "more" and so is aesthetically pleasing.

One can then, on the basis of Piagetian theory, make a case
for the necessity of aesthetic judgments in cognitive development. Such judgments operate in the service of equilibration by
generating new cognitive coordinations that eliminate ambiguities
in the relations between concepts and representations. Far from
being something extrinsic to cognitive growth, aesthetic judgments constitute an integral part of its internal dynamics. From
an educational perspective, therefore, aesthetics, as it has been
defined here, has to be regarded not as a luxury to be indulged
in when there are sufficient funds, but rather as a critical component of the educational process.

Here again, this conclusion from developmental theory supports an insight of British informal education. When, in British
child-centered schools, children attempt to express their experience in aesthetically pleasing ways they are, in effect, striving
for a new level of cognitive equilibration. They are working for
a more appropriate fit between their concepts and their representations, for more pleasing meanings. In short, the construction
of meanings is simultaneously cognitive and aesthetic for what is
true cognitively is also pleasing aesthetically. "Truth is beauty"
is both an abstract aesthetic principle and a very practical rule
of mental growth.

There are many other, less formal links between Piagetian
theory and informal educational practice. They share a common
conception of child nature and learning, and this gives rise to
comparable attitudes and orientations. Piaget respects the child's

point of view and regards his ideas as different rather than as wrong. He believes in the child's ability to make judgments and choices and believes that the child can use his intelligence to guide and direct the course of his own learning. And Piaget, like the teachers in informal classrooms, believes that the aim of education is to grow children who will think for themselves and who will not accept the first idea that comes to them.

It seems, therefore, that child-centered education, as practiced in England, is a reasonable, concrete embodiment of Piagetian theory. In some respects this mutuality reinforces both positions. Informal educational practice grew out of work with children in the classrooms while Piagetian theory grew out of experimental studies of children. That both endeavors should arrive at comparable ideas about child nature and about the learning process adds to the impression of their validity, and to their value as guides to educational theory, research, and practice.

One of the most significant contributions Piagetian theory can make to education is in the domain of curriculum. For this contribution to be fully realized, however, some basic ideas of Piagetian theory such as externalization and automatization, the intellective unconscious and the logical substructure of the task, have to be recognized. Failure to deal with these ideas leads to curriculum errors in which materials are not suited to the intellectual level of the students for whom they are prepared. Examples of curriculum analysis at the secondary level are then presented to illustrate how Piagetian constructs and observations can guide the writing of curriculum geared to the intellectual level of the students using them.

15

Adolescent Thinking and the Curriculum

Innovations in American education tend to have a life cycle that is easy to chart and that parallels our behavior in other domains. Generally we are captivated by a new idea and tend to accept and to apply it uncritically and with considerable distortion. Then, when it does not fulfill the promise it never held out, it becomes the focus of criticism and eventual disregard. This was the fate of many of Piagetian ideas translated into elementary curricula during the 1960s. In fact, many of the so called Piaget based curricula were, if anything, in contradiction to the Piagetian notions.

For example, Bruner's (125) hypothesis (purportedly based on conclusions from the Woods Hole Conference where Piagetian concepts were a major theme) that "we can teach any child, any body of knowledge at any age in a intellectually respectable way" is completely at variance with Piaget's emphasis upon the limitations of learning imposed by the child's level of intellectual development. In Piaget's view the most efficient learning takes place when there is a match between the logic embedded in curriculum materials and the structure of the child's thought. Nonetheless,

Bruner's hypothesis became a beacon guiding much of the curriculum development in the sixties. These curricula (such as the "new math"), while said to be informed by Piagetian research and theory, were in fact quite contrary to a developmental position. And when these curricula failed, Piaget took much of the blame. Today, Piaget is regarded as passé in elementary curriculum writing where "Back to Basics" is the latest fad.

Not so in secondary education, fortunately. Secondary education teachers came to Piaget late, and on their own, rather than through new mass-produced curricula materials. Accordingly, there has been a sort of grass roots interest in Piaget, with individual instructors attempting to revise curricula in keeping with their reading of Piagetian theory and research. I find this sort of development most healthy because it combines curriculum innovation with scholarship and with experimentation in the classroom.

In the interests of furthering the utilization of Piaget in secondary curriculum writing, I would like to suggest a way of looking at curriculum materials that might help those who would like to analyze and revise them. This means introducing some constructs that provide a linkage between the Piagetian theory of cognitive development and curriculum analysis: externalization and automatization, the intellective unconscious, and the logical substructure of the task. Examples of developmental curriculum analysis at the secondary level will be provided at the end of the chapter.

SOME PRELIMINARY CONCEPTS

Externalization and Automatization. From a Piagetian perspective, our knowledge about the world is neither entirely innate nor entirely learned but is always constructed as a consequence of our interactions with the environment. All human knowledge, whether of the simplest objects about us or the most abstract physical elements, are constructions. Any bit of knowledge possessed by an individual is a unique creation derived from interaction of a subject and his or her environment, but reducible to neither. For example, a boy who called an airplane a "choo-choo bird" had created a new concept that derived from his language and everyday experience but also from his or her own thought processes. The resulting concept (its unique idea) cannot be reduced to either one of these, however, and must be considered a new whole which is greater than the sum of its parts. In a very real sense a new concept is a work of art.

Piaget's demonstration (e.g., 154, 155, 156) of the idea that knowledge is a construction is not widely accepted. For example, some of Piaget's most widely known observations are those on conservation—the demonstration that young children believe that the amount of something changes with a change in its appearance. Young children, to illustrate, believe that a clay ball weighs more when it is made into a sausage; that liquid poured from a low, wide container becomes more when it is poured into a tall, narrow one. Only as children attain the appropriate mental operations are they capable of constructing true quantity concepts that enable them to recognize that quantities do not change as a result of change in their appearance.

Nonetheless, many investigators do not accept the demonstration that young children literally see the world differently than we do. These investigators (e.g., 120, 127, 148) have tried to show that children attain conservation at earlier ages than Piaget described. In each instance, however, the investigator altered the conservation task so that it was capable of being solved by perceptual rather than logical processes. (For Piaget conservation is always an index of the victory of reason over perception, and if these are not put into conflict, the task does not measure conservation.) These investigators mistakenly conclude that because they have made a task easier, they have thereby made children brighter.

The reason that we have difficulty accepting the constructive nature of knowledge has to do with the processes of automatization and externalization. (My terms for what I believe to be implicit in Piagetian discussions.) Once we construct a concept or acquire a skill, the constructive process becomes automatic (that is, unconscious) and the product is externalized (seen as independent of the self). Consider a simple analogy. When a house is in the blueprint stage, it is clear that the proposed house is a matter of intelligence and imagination since it does not yet exist in fact. Likewise, as the house is being built, the construction process is clearly visible. Once the house is completed, however, neither the plans nor the constructive process are any longer in evidence and the house is treated as an external reality, quite independent from human intelligence and imagination.

A similar process occurs as we construct concepts of the world. A student who begins a foreign language, for example, is painfully aware of his or her ineptness in pronunciation, grammar, and vocabulary. At that stage, the psychological complexities of learning a language are very much in the student's mind. Likewise the constructive process, the memorizing, listening, speaking, are quite conscious activities. But once the student masters the language, it becomes automatized and externalized. In using the language, whether in speaking or in reading, the student is no longer aware of the constructive process he or she underwent. And the meaning of the language is also externalized. Words in the new language, whether heard or read, have an immediate meaning that seems to reside in them and not in the student's head. The same is true, of course, with one's native language. To an advanced reader of English the meaning of words seems to rest on the page and not in the mind.

The Intellective Unconscious. As the preceding discussion has suggested, much of the constructive activity of knowing becomes unconscious and makes up what Piaget calls the "intellective unconscious." The intellective unconscious, like Freud's affective unconscious, is revealed by errors, but of a different sort from "Freudian" slips. If you are typing and suddenly focus attention upon your fingers, you begin to make mistakes (or more mistakes). The same is true for any skilled action that has become automatic, including reading. If you are an advanced reader and try to sound out letters as you read, you find yourself making errors of pronunciation. We know that a skill has become part of the intellective unconscious when any attempt to focus attention upon the mechanics of the skill results in disruption of the skilled action. In other words, skilled action requires automatization and externalization.

Getting at the intellective unconscious, however, presents a very special problem. Once a person becomes truly skilled in a particular action, there is no way to get back to the intellective unconscious. The processes have become so rapid and automatic that it is impossible to become conscious of them to any great extent. Errors of skilled action reveal the presence of automatization and externalization, but they reveal nothing about the structure of the intellective unconscious.

What this means is that to learn the intellectual and/or motoric components of a particular skill and how these components are put together, we cannot rely upon the introspections of those who are adept in that skill. It is for this reason that many people who are skilled in a particular area, whether it be playing the piano or doing research or doing therapy, may, nonetheless, be poor teachers. Being skilled does not imply knowledge of how we became skilled. On the other hand, many people who are not the best performers can nonetheless be good teachers. A voice coach or piano teacher will be able to train individuals who are much above his or her own level of proficiency.

This puts a whole new meaning on the old adage "Those who can, do; those who can't, teach." It is not, as the adage suggests, that teaching is a kind of second choice, but rather that good teaching requires different skills and abilities than does performance. To be sure, the teacher must be able to perform the skill to be taught because this ensures that the teacher can assess the learner's progress. But it does not ensure that the performer can teach the skill. Basically, the good teacher in any field has learned the cardinal rule about the intellective unconscious, namely, that it cannot be gotten at by reflection after the fact. The good teacher knows that to understand the structure of a skill (its components and their organization) and the process of acquiring it, one has to observe the skill being acquired. *The good teacher watches the learner.* Whether it be a ski, or tennis, or piano teacher, *the person who wants only to demonstrate* is less effective than the teacher who observes carefully and who relates his or her demonstrations to these observations.

The same holds true for academic skills. To discover the difficulties children are encountering, say, in learning math, one has to observe the errors they make as they go along. For example, consider a child who puts the following answers into the boxes on his worksheet.

$$3 + \boxed{4} = 7 \qquad\qquad \begin{array}{r} 3 \\ + \boxed{10} \\ \hline 7 \end{array}$$

To the adult, who has automatized and externalized the processes involved, the tasks appear the same. The teacher might, therefore, be tempted to demonstrate again the addition/subtraction routine for finding the hidden addend. But the child's real difficulty is of a different order. What is causing the child difficulty is the transformation of an equal sign ($=$) into a straight line ($-$), and the transposition of an operator ($+$) into a new visual alignment. In moving from a horizontal to a vertical format, the

$$\begin{array}{r} 3 \\ + \square \\ \hline 7 \end{array} \qquad \begin{array}{r} 3 \\ + \\ \square \\ \hline 7 \end{array}$$

child is required to engage in additional transformations that make the vertical format more difficult—hence the child reverts to the easier operation of addition.

One more word about demonstration. The use of demonstration in teaching is necessary and appropriate. The real question is *when* in the teaching learning process it should be introduced. Demonstration evokes imitation, so the question is *When* is imitation important in the learning process? This is really an empirical question. For example, in learning certain formulas in mathematics, it may be best to learn them in a rote, imitative way first and arrive at a conceptual understanding later. On the other hand, in writing and reading a certain fluency ought to be encouraged before an emphasis upon accuracy (spelling and pronunciation) is introduced. Correct spelling and pronunciation are acquired through demonstration and imitation, but these are best introduced after the child has attained some basic mastery and fluency in the skill.

This, in effect, is the central lesson Piaget has been trying to teach us. What each of his books, filled with studies of how children acquire various skills, tells us is that if you want to know how children acquire certain concepts or skills, you must study how children acquire those concepts or skills. It is only by observing children's struggles to learn that the psychological difficulty of the task and the mental operations required for its completion are revealed.

Reading is a case in point. If we really wish to know the underlying structure of reading and how this structure is acquired, we have to study children who are learning to read. I am afraid that, too often in the past and in the present as well, investigators have made the assumption that a reflective analysis would reveal something about the nature of reading. *Information processing models* of proficient reading are an example. While these models may be suggestive, they often seem to be spoken of as if they truly represented what goes on in the child's head. But since these models were not derived from a careful observation of children who were learning to read, this assumption is very suspect. What we must avoid, and what Piaget constantly cautions us against, is the substitution of reflective analysis for careful observation.

The idea that the best teaching derives from careful observation of the learner is an old maxim that is given fresh support with the concept of the intellective unconscious. It challenges again the assumption that one can arrive at learning sequences by logical analyses and reflection rather than by empirical observation.

But insightful observation of children requires knowledge about the task as well. It is for that reason that we turn now to the logical substructure of the task.

The Logical Substructure of the Task. In the last section I argued that we cannot learn about learning just by reflecting on our own past learning experiences. We can, however, employ the knowledge arrived at by the observation of children in some learning contexts to their performance in others. Indeed, Piaget's empirically derived stages of cognitive development provide us with powerful tools for analyzing various tasks and for guessing at the intellectual operations required to attain them. In a sense, the Piagetian stages provide a set of principles for judging the developmental correctness of curriculum materials in any discipline. Each stage or cognitive development has its own set of mental operations and these provide the analytical tools for that stage. If curriculum materials for children at that stage are consistent with the mental operations of that stage, then they are appropriate. If they are too simple or too complex, then they are not appropriate.

Consider the following example. We know that the set of concrete operations attained at about age six or seven enables children to coordinate two variables at a time. Concrete operational children understand that one quantity can be greater in height but less in width than another and that the two can be equal in amount although they appear unequal. Knowing this, we can look at different curriculum materials to see what demands they make upon children's thinking. If, for example, we see a phonics instruction in a first grade reader that says: "Color all the balloons with a short *a* blue, color all the balloons with a long *a* green except those that have a silent *e* which you are to color purple," we might judge this inappropriate. It demands that the child coordinate three different ideas, when we know that two ideas is about his or her limit.

Such an analysis, however, needs to be tested. In the above example, one might simplify the instruction (Color all the balloons with a short *a* blue and color all the balloons with a long *a* green) and see whether more children succeed than with the first instruction. Using an understanding of the child's mental operations (the concrete operations of the elementary school child in the above example) to analyze the cognitive demands of the task (how many ideas it asks the child to coordinate simultaneously) is what I have called finding the "logical substructure" of the task.

It is important to understand that the logical substructure of a task can be explicit or implicit. In the example of the phonics instruction, the substructure of the instruction was explicit because the various ideas to be coordinated were given in the instruction itself. But the logical substructure can also be implicit. This occurs when a concept is employed that presupposes multiple coordinations but does not demand these directly. The concept of a "century," for example, involves complex coordinations of temporal concepts (minutes, hours, days, months, years) that are really not possible until a child attains adolescence. Yet, because the coordinations required are implicit, their logical substructure may not be appreciated, and they may be introduced to children who lack the mental operations to grasp them.

Accordingly, this approach to task analyses of necessity looks at the form (the complexity of instructions, illustrations, format) as well as the content (the concepts, materials, examples) of curriculum materials. It tries to determine what level of reasoning is demanded by a given curriculum material (its logical substructure) and whether that level of reasoning is appropriate to the age group being served. To differentiate this logical substructure approach to task analyses from other approaches (a useful exercise because it is at the level of task analysis that the different theories of learning can best be differentiated) I will explore the analysis of reading.

One approach to a task analysis of reading is that of information processing. In this approach computer terms and technology are employed to analyze the reading process. It is assumed that the child uses, or might use, parallel processes. An important concept is that of *redundancy,* the extent to which the same information is given in different ways. For example, at rapid exposures a letter is recognized more readily when it is embedded in a word than when it is displayed alone or embedded in a random collection of letters or meaningless symbols. The difficulty with the information processing analysis, from a developmental perspective, is its lack of a base in the logic of the child. That is to say, an analysis of a task in terms of redundancy still ignores the child's capacity to deal with redundancy. It may be, too, that what is redundant on the basis of formal analysis may not be redundant for the child. Redundancy may not exist at the time the child is constructing letters and words but only after these are fully attained. The analysis of written language as a total system for the child who has not yet constructed such a system is an example of the danger of externalization—it presupposes that which is to be constructed.

Task analysis has also been approached from the standpoint of behavior modification. Looked at in this way, reading involves a set of visual stimuli (letters and words) to be discriminated and a set of responses (verbal) to which they must become associated. Correct discriminations and responses are rewarded or reinforced while wrong discriminations and responses are not. The advantage of this type of task analysis is its simplicity. But that is also its difficulty. The adult who is deciding what the stimulus is has already constructed and externalized it. Hence what the adult sees as the stimulus may not be what the child sees. Fortunately, adjustments are made because behavior modification is an empirical system, but the complexity of the child's task in learning to read is badly oversimplified.

From a developmental point of view, printed language has a complex logical substructure that requires a certain level of mental development to decode. For example, to truly comprehend English phonics the child must be able to grasp that one and the same letter, say a, can give rise to two different sounds, say *cat* and *ate*. But such a comprehension presupposes a "logical addition" of letters and sounds (i.e., the formation of a superordinate class A that encompasses the two subclasses $\overset{.}{a}$ and $\overline{a}$ or the class of sounds of A = the class of sounds $\overset{.}{a}$ + the class of sounds $\overline{a}$). There is now considerable research (see Chapter 12, this book) to support this interpretation of the logical substructure presupposed by printed English and the requisite mental operations required to decode it.

SOME EXAMPLES OF CURRICULUM ANALYSIS

The previous sections have made the argument that we need to systematically explore the psychological difficulty inherent in the curriculum materials that we use. As indicated above, this difficulty is not self-evident and must be arrived at by careful task analyses. I have made a case for using the Piagetian description of stages of mental development as a tool of task analysis. I argued that curriculum materials should first be examined to determine their logical substructure—the necessary mental operations required for their comprehension. This examination would then suggest whether the materials should be modified to better fit the cognitive level of the young people for whom they were designed, or whether they should be presented at earlier or later grade levels.

For purposes of discussion, the argument for a Piagetian analysis of curriculum was left at the micro level, namely at the level of specific instructions, illustrations, tasks. But curriculum analysis can also be undertaken at the macro level and would include the sequencing of subject matter, for example, within elementary math instruction (when "number lines" or "coins" ought to be presented) or when a subject matter should be presented (at what grade level should algebra, history, etc., be taught). In the examples of secondary curricula below, I will give some macro as well as micro analysis to suggest the potential breadth of the approach advocated here.

Health Education. The past ten years has been witness to a broad expansion of health education at the secondary level. Material on human reproduction, nutrition, human development, and health care have become mandatory for most junior high school or middle-school students. While the attempt to present this material to young people is laudatory, the presentation of the materials in the texts shows little appreciation of the logical substructure imbedded therein.

One text currently being used is called *A Healthier You* and in a brief span covers nutrition, basic psychology, human development, human reproduction, the psychology of disease, and more. Perhaps the authors never heard, or don't believe, that a little knowledge is a dangerous thing. The first problem with the book is that it presupposes much too much background on the part of the reader. That is to say, part of the substructure of a body of subject matter is the prior knowledge or concepts required to comprehend it. Providing, as this book does, phonetic pronunciations for new words does not really facilitate their comprehension. It is reminiscent of talking louder to someone who doesn't speak your language.

But consider some of the thought questions that are posed to seventh graders:

Tell what you think is meant by this statement: "Personality is a blend of self and society."
What is meant by maturity?
How does a person's self-concept affect the degree to which he achieves total health?
What must you do, to become more mature?

The problem with these questions is rather obvious. The concepts involved—self, personality, maturity—are complex and have an elaborate logical substructure.

Consider the concept of personality. To truly grasp this notion, the young person must have some comprehension of temperament, of traits (kindness, selfishness), and of different situations (frustrating, demanding, boring) that bring out these traits. Also, a true understanding of personality presupposes some sense of the interaction of these variables. Clearly, a true understanding of the personality concept requires a level of formal operational thinking that the majority of young adolescents have not yet attained. To assume, in addition, that young people can deal meaningfully with the interaction of self, society, and personality—or with the other questions—simply denies the logical substructure of these concepts and treats them as simple descriptive terms.

Does this mean that nothing can be taught about the health sciences at this age level? Not at all. The psychology of growth and development is concrete and demonstrable and some of the best writing in this text deals with that material. Even some psychological concepts like the "self" can be presented if this is done with many concrete examples and without reference to the complex sociocultural determinants of that concept. My own sense is that much of the material in a book such as this miseducates. Young people must, of necessity, deal with it with the logical substructures they have available. Since these are inadequate, they construct their own interpretations, which are usually wrong.

For example, most young people over-concretize concepts such as self and personality. The self is often thought of in terms of a single trait such as "selfish" or "he always thinks only of himself" rather than in terms of a broad complex of interacting attitudes and behaviors. Likewise young people tend to have a global undifferentiated sense of "personality" and will say that another young person has a "good" or a "bad" personality. But when they are forced, by a question, to break this conception down and to illustrate it, they can come up with only a couple of behaviors of attributes.

Geography and Social History. The study of geography and of social history, which is often taught in the seventh grade, presupposes abstract conceptions of space and time. Such abstract conceptions require the attainment of *formal operations.* Formal operations are the new set of mental abilities Piaget says appear at about the age of eleven or twelve. These operations enable young people to deal in possibilities, to grasp simile and metaphor, to handle multiple variable interactions, to comprehend abstract conceptions of space and time, and to think about thinking (see Chapters 1, 6, and 7, this book). Formal operations bring about a Copernican revolution in thought that moves young people from the here-and-now thinking of childhood to the vastly extended spatial, temporal, and figurative world of adult thought. The conception of 1,000 miles, for example, is a kind of second-order concept that requires formal operations for its comprehension. A young person must be able, mentally, to extend the concept of immediately present distances to distances that are beyond the limits of perception. The same is true for historical measures, such as a century. A century is a second-order temporal conception inasmuch as it can never be directly experienced.

In most secondary level texts, however, the spatial and temporal concepts are taken for granted as being readily understood. For many young adolescents, however, this is not the case. Even though they can identify countries on a map or globe, or talk about "centuries," they may not truly grasp geographical space or historical time. At the very least such students need clear-cut markers so as to be able to sequence historical events and to gain an impression of geographical distance. For example, it might help a preformal operational adolescent to say how long it would take, by car, to drive across a particular country. Since most young people have taken trips by car, this ties in with their own experience and gives them an intuition of the distances involved.

Unfortunately, even in well written and interesting texts, such as the one from which the following excerpt is drawn, this is not done. What is a young person without abstract concepts of historical time and geographical space to make of the following paragraph:

> The first great series of books describing the lands and peoples of the known world was the work of the Greek Herodotus (484–425 B.C.). Like Thales he was a great traveler and especially keen observer. During his lifetime, he went as far north as the Dnepr River on the north bank of the Black Sea; he traveled over land into Persia (present day Iran) and visited the ancient city of Babylon; he saw the ruins of the old Phoenician part of Tyre and he spent many years traveling in Egypt.

It is, of course, not only the spatial and temporal concepts that pose difficulties for young people. Some social science concepts like "slavery" require the understanding of many different variables like social values and prejudices, economics and geopolitics, interacting at the same time. Such understandings, we know, require the utilization of formal operations. Yet, perhaps because the concepts are represented by single words, the difficulties posed in their comprehension often seem to be ignored by textbook writers. Consider the paragraph below taken from the same textbook as the earlier one. Although the ideas are presented simply, the ideas themselves are far from being simple.

In the capitalist system, Marx believed, profit was the difference between the wages paid to a worker and the price for which his product was sold. Profits, according to his theory, would be invested in new capital (machinery, factories, and other tools of production) for the purpose of making more profits. But the owners of capital, he thought, would keep the wages paid to the workers at the lowest possible level. Production would increase until more goods would be produced than the people would be able to buy. Eventually, he believed, the system was bound to collapse. He urged the workers to rise up against the owners of capital.

In these examples from a text on geography and social history, it is easy to see how the logical substructure of the material has been overlooked. For adults, to whom geographical space, historical time and economic concepts are well automatized and externalized, these ideas appear simple and not in need of further explication. Moreover, inasmuch as the content of the discussion is presented simply and directly, the material seems easy. In fact, however, such simplicity is deceptive, and the material is much like a series of proverbs. The proverb is simply stated ("Shallow brooks are noisy"), but its interpretation requires abstract cognitive skills. Simplicity of language, we need to learn, does not necessarily connote simplicity of concepts.

Mathematics. This is not the place to go into a detailed discussion of mathematics education. All that I hope to do is, again, suggest that the logical substructure of some of the mathematical material we present to young people may be more difficult than it seems on the surface. Perhaps this point is nowhere more evident than in "thought problems." In such problems the curriculum writers may not always be aware that conceptual difficulty is confounded with mathematical difficulty. A young person's failure on such a problem could be a result of failure of logical comprehension as much as mathematical sophistication.

Consider the following thought problems:

Three friends visit the library on different days: the first, once every 3 days; the second, once every 4 days and the third, once every 5 days. The last time they were together at the library was on a Tuesday. In how many days will they again be at the library together.

To solve this problem the student must first be able to comprehend it. Conceptually, it is a four variable problem dealing with three visitation times and the seven days of the week. Even to begin to deal with this problem the student has to be able to comprehend multiple interactions before these can be translated into mathematical formulas.

Take another example:

A mother is three times as old as her daughter. Ten years from now she will be twice as old as her daughter. What is the mother's age?

This second problem requires an algebraic solution. But prior to that the student must cast the content into algebraic form. This means that the mother's age has to be defined in terms of the daughter's (e.g., 3x) and that the daughter's age is understood as being a variable. So both the mother's age and the daughter's age are variables and at two points in time, now and ten years hence. This introduces a third variable. Accordingly, as in the preceding example, the task is conceptually a multivariable one. Without formal operations, the problem could not be understood, much less translated and solved.

The material we present young people may be difficult in ways we do not and cannot appreciate because of the automatization and externalization of our own mental processes. Only by working alongside young people as they struggle with the materials can we begin to get some insight into the logical substructure of the curriculum we are using. Such insights should help us to revise our curriculum materials so as to make them more accessible and interesting for the students to whom they are directed.

There is one last problem. Many readers may feel that materials such as those illustrated here are important because, even if students don't understand them, they present an intellectual challenge. Making materials easier removes the challenge and the intellectual struggle essential for cognitive growth. My reply is that challenge is indeed useful, but we need to distinguish between intelligent and unintelligent challenge. If the challenge is too difficult, so that no amount of struggle produces success, then the result is failure and frustration. What we need in education is intelligent challenge—a reasonable match between the logical substructures of the task and the current cognitive developmental level of the student.

SUMMARY AND CONCLUSION

I have tried to point out some of the valeus of Piaget's research and theory for curriculum writing at the secondary level. The concepts of externalization and automatization, the intellective unconscious, and the logical substructure of the task were introduced. These concepts illustrate how, when a skill or knowledge is acquired, the process of acquisition is lost to conscious reflection: once we have acquired a given skill or body of knowledge, its acquisition may seem much simpler than it actually was. This blinds us to the difficulties curriculum materials can pose to young people.

Then some examples from contemporary curriculum materials were analyzed from the standpoint of their psychological difficulty. Materials in health education were often seen to be too abstract or complex to be meaningful to young people. Likewise materials in geography and social history, while simply written, were seen as difficult to interpret and comprehend. Examples from mathematics illustrated how, in thought problems, conceptual complexity was confounded with mathematical difficulty.

The point of these analyses was that to determine the difficulty of curriculum materials, we have to try them out on those for whom they are being written. A careful analysis of the errors young people make helps reveal the logical substructure of the task. It is here that the levels of thinking described by Piaget are useful. They are tools for the analysis both of tasks and of children's thinking. Used as analytic tools, the Piagetian formulations can help us to provide a better fit between young people's thinking and the curriculum materials that we would like them to learn. Piaget's work, then, does not provide us with a new curriculum, but rather with powerful tools for curriculum analysis.

Epilogue

Jean Piaget died on September 18, 1980. He was 84. His death marks the end of an era, of the first hundred years of psychology, and of the great psychologists, Wundt, Hall, James, Freud, Jung, and Piaget. With these men, Piaget shared a vision of psychology as a discipline that necessarily drew upon and contributed to other fields of study. And with these men he shared the faith that man could best come to understand himself and others through the disciplined and rigorous methods and constraints of science.

In many ways Piaget's work parallels that of Freud rather than that of the others. Like Freud, Piaget shared a biological orientation and like Freud he sought to understand the nature of mental processes. But while Freud was concerned with how needs and motives regulated man's thinking, Piaget sought to show the ways in which thought was regulated by developing human intelligence. Together these two men have helped us to grasp both the rational and the irrational propensities of human thought. They have brought us closer to realizing Plato's admonition "know thyself" than the ancient philosophers ever dreamt might be possible. Together Freud and Piaget have opened paths to understanding the worst as well as the best of man's potential. Together, and without the aid of technology, they have made psychology a true science. As their work bears witness, science rests upon the bedrock of human intelligence and creativity, not arid methodology nor sophisticated equipment. True science is always a product of human, not mechanical, genius.

Piaget's death was to me, and to his other students and colleagues, a personal as well as an intellectual loss. In the press, Piaget was sometimes depicted as rather cold, foreboding, and unapproachable. That was far from the case. It has to be re-membered that Piaget was much sought after and that strangers from all over the world were constantly asking to see him—more out of a desire to say they had met him than because of any pro-fessional or scientific matters they needed to discuss with him. Consequently, Piaget cultivated a particular demeanor when he felt intruded upon. His voice would drop and become flat and affectless. At such times you knew he had withdrawn into him-self and could not be reached. Certainly, to those who did not know him this would appear to be a cold and distant man.

On the other hand, when he was with friends and colleagues, he was relaxed and charming. And at parties he could, in a child-ishly flirtatious way, play the clown. It is true that he did not relish small talk and much of his waking time was spent thinking about the current research effort. But when the day's work was done he could be a most charming and gracious host. And I still re-call with great pleasure the moment when, after having eaten din-ner at his home, he invited me into his study and welcomed my questions about his theory of concept formation. He answered with warmth and amusement and acknowledged that a little asso-ciationism had sneaked in to his formulation.

It is too early, we are too close, to make a fair and objective assessment of Piaget's contribution to psychology and social sci-ence. It is certainly the case that contemporary developmental psychology in America would be much less visible and much less vigorous had he never been on the scene. The real impact of his work in applied fields like education and child psychiatry has yet to be truly felt because the translations are only now being made. But if a man's place in history is judged by the extent to which his contributions have become part of the accepted wisdom of his time, then Piaget has already attained greatness.

Bibliography

1. Anthony, E. J. The significance of Jean Piaget for child psychiatry. *The British Journal of Medical Psychology, 1956, XXIX,* 20–34.
2. Berlyne, D. E. *Conflict arousal and curiosity.* New York: McGraw-Hill, 1960.
3. Berlyne, D. E. Curiosity and education. In J. D. Krumboltz (ed.), *Learning and the educational process.* Chicago: Rand McNally, 1965, 67–89.
4. Bertalaffny, Ludwig von. *Modern theories of development.* New York: Harper & Bros. (Torchbook edition), 1962.
5. Bloom, B. S. *Stability and change in human characteristics.* New York: Wiley, 1964.
6. Blos, P. *On adolescence.* New York: The Free Press, 1962.
7. Bearly, Molly, and Hitchfield, Elizabeth. *A guide to reading Piaget, 1968.* New York: Schocken, 1968.
7a. Briggs, Chari, and Elkind, D. Cognitive development in early readers. *Developmental Psychology,* 1973, *9,* 279–80.
8. Bruner, J. S. *The process of education.* Cambridge, Massachusetts: Harvard University Press, 1960.
9. Burt, C., and Howard, M. The relative influence of heredity and environment on assessments of intelligence. *British Journal of Statistical Psychology,* 1957, *X,* 33–63.
10. Burt, C. *Mental and scholastic tests.* London: Staples Press, 1962 (4th edition).
11. Charlesworth, W. R. Development of the object concept in infancy: A methodological study. *American Psychologist,* 1966, *21,* 623. (Abstract)
12. Cowan, P. A. Cognitive egocentrism and social interaction in children. *American Psychologist,* 1966, *21,* 623. (Abstract)
13. Davidson, Audrey, and Fay, Judith. Fantasy in middle childhood. In Mary R. Haworth (ed.) *Child psychotherapy.* New York: Basic Books, 1964, 401–406.
14. Downing, J. A. The augmented Roman alphabet for learning to read. *The Reading Teacher,* 1963, *16,* 325–36.
15. Elkind, D. The child's conception of his religious denomination,

I: The Jewish child. *Journal of Genetic Psychology,* 1961, *99,* 209–25.

16. Elkind, D. The child's conception of right and left. *Journal of Genetic Psychology,* 1961, *99,* 269–76.

17. Elkind, D. The development of quantitative thinking. *Journal of Genetic Psychology,* 1961, *98,* 37–46.

18. Elkind, D. Quantity conceptions in junior and senior high school students. *Child Development,* 1961, *32,* 551–60.

19. Elkind, D. The child's conception of his religious denomination, II: The Catholic child. *Journal of Genetic Psychology,* 1962, *101,* 185–93.

20. Elkind, D. The child's conception of his religious denomination III: The Protestant child. *Journal of Genetic Psychology,* 1963, *103,* 291–304.

21. Elkind, D. Ambiguous pictures for the study of perceptual development and learning. *Child Development,* 1964, *35,* 1391–96.

22. Elkind, D. Conceptual orientation shifts in children and adolescents. *Child Development,* 1966, *37,* 493–98.

23. Elkind, D. Middle-class delinquency. *Mental Hygiene,* 1967, *51,* 80–84.

24. Elkind, D. Piaget's conservation problems. *Child Development,* 1967, *38,* 1967, 15–27.

25. Elkind, D., Barocas, R. B., and Johnsen, P. H. Concept production in children and action in adolescents. *Human Development,* 1969, *12,* 10–21.

26. Elkind, D., Barocas, R., and Rosenthal, B. Combinatorial thinking in children from graded and ungraded classrooms. *Perceptual and Motor Skills,* 1968, *27,* 1015–18.

27. Elkind, D., and Deblinger, Jo Ann. Perceptual training and reading achievement in disadvantaged children. *Child Development,* 1969, *40,* 11–19.

28. Elkind, D., Horn, J., and Schneider, Gerrie. Modified word recognition, reading achievement and perceptual de-centration. *Journal of Genetic Psychology,* 1965, *107,* 235–51.

29. Elkind, D., Koegler, R. R., and Go, Elsie. Effects of perceptual training at three age levels. *Science,* 1962, *137,* 755–56.

30. Elkind, D., Koegler, R. R., and Go, Elsie. Studies in perceptual development II: Part-whole perception. *Child Development,* 1964, *35,* 81–90.

31. Elkind, D., Larson, Margaret, E., and Van Doorninck, W. Per-

ceptual learning and performance in slow and average readers. *Journal of Educational Psychology*, 1965, 56, no. 1. 50–56.

32. Elkind, D., and Scott, Lee. Studies in perceptual development I: Re decentering of perception. *Child Development*, 1962, 33, 619–630.

33. Elkind, D., Spilka, B. and Long, Diane. The child's conception of prayer. *Journal for the Scientific Study of Religion*, 1967, 6, 101–9.

34. Elkind, D., Van Doorninck, W. and Schwarz, Cynthia. Perceptual activity and concept attainment. *Child Development*, 1967, 38, 1153–61.

35. Elkind, D. and Weiss, Jutta. Studies in perceptual development III: perceptual exploration. *Child Development*, 1967, 38, 553–61.

36. Erikson, E. H. Identity and the life cycle. *Psychol. Issues*, I, No. 1, New York: International Universities Press, 1959.

37. Fowler, W. The effect of early stimulation in the emergence of cognitive processes. In R. D. Hess and Roberta M. Meyers (eds.), *Early Education*. Chicago: Aldine, 1968, 9–36.

38. Freud, Anna. *The ego and the mechanisms of defense.* New York: International Universities Press, 1946.

39. Freud, S. Three contributions to the theory of sex. In A. A. Brill (ed.), *The basic writings of Sigmund Freud.* New York: Modern Library Edition, 1938, 553–632.

40. Furth, H. G. *Piaget and knowledge.* Englewood Cliffs, New Jersey: Prentice-Hall, Inc., 1969.

41. Gagné, Robert M. Contributions of learning to human development. *Psychological Review*, 1968, 75, 177–91.

42. Ginsburg, H., and Opper, Sylvia. *Piaget's theory of intellectual development: An introduction.* Englewood Cliffs, New Jersey: Prentice-Hall, Inc., 1969.

43. Glick, J., and Wapner, S. Development of transitivity: Some findings and problems of analysis. *Child Development*, 1968, 39, 621–38.

44. Goodenough, Florence. New evidence on environmental influence on intelligence. *Yearbook of the National Society for the Study of Education*, 1940, 39, 307–65.

45. Goodenough, Florence L. *Mental testing.* New York: Rinehart & Co., 1949.

46. Goodnow, Jacqueline J. Problems in research on culture and thought. In D. Elkind and J. H. Flavell (eds.), *Studies in cognitive*

development. New York: Oxford University Press, 1969, 439–64.

47. Goodnow, Jacqueline J., and Bethon, G. Piaget's tasks: The effects of schooling and intelligence. *Child Development,* 1966, 37, 573–82.

48. Gosse, E. Father and son: *A study of two temperaments.* London: Heinemann, 1909.

49. Gourevitch, Vivian, and Feffer, M. H. A study of motivational development. *Journal of genetic Psychology,* 1962, 100, 361–75.

50. Greco, P. L'apprentissage dans une situation à structure opératoire concrète: les inversions successives de l'ordre linéaire paré des rotations de 180°. In J. Piaget (ed.), Études d'épistémologie génétique. Vol. 8. Paris: Presses Universitaires de France, 1959, 68–182.

51. Harlow, H. F. The formation of learning sets. *Psychological Review,* 1949, 56, 51–65.

52. Harvey, O. J., Prather, Misha, White, B. J., and Hoffmeister, J. K. Teacher's beliefs, classroom atmosphere and student behavior. *American Educational Research Journal,* 1968, V, 151–66.

53. Hebb, D. O. *The organization of behavior.* New York: Wiley, 1949.

54. Hunt, J. McV. *Intelligence and experience.* New York: The Ronald Press, 1961.

55. Hunt, J. McV. Intrinsic motivation and its role in psychological development. In D. Levine (ed.), *Nebraska symposium on motivation.* Lincoln: University of Nebraska Press, 1965, 189–282.

56. Inhelder, Bärbel and Piaget, J. *The growth of logical thinking from childhood to adolescence.* New York: Basic Books, 1958.

57. Inhelder, Bärbel. *The diagnosis of reasoning in the mentally retarded.* New York: John Day, 1968.

58. Jennings, F. G. Jean Piaget: notes on learning. *Saturday Review,* May 20, 1967, p. 82.

59. Jensen, Arthur R. How much can we boost IQ and scholastic achievement? *Harvard Educational Review,* 1969, XXXIX, pp. 1–123.

60. Jones, H. E. The environment and mental development. In L. Carmichael (ed.), *Manual of child psychology.* New York: John Wiley & Sons, Inc., 1954, 631–96.

61. Kendler, Tracy S., and Kendler, H. H. Reversal and non-reversal shifts in kindergarten children. *Journal of Experimental Psychology,* 1959, 58, 56–60.

62. Kittlewell, H. B. D. Selection experiments on industrial melanism in the lepidoptera. *Heredity*, 1955, *9*, 323–42.

63. Koffka, K. *Principles of gestalt psychology*. New York: Harcourt, Brace, 1935.

64. Kohlberg, L. Cognitive stages in preschool education. *Human Development*, 1966, *9*, 5–17.

65. Köhler, W. *Gestalt psychology*. New York: Liveright, 1947.

66. Lambert, W. E. and Klineberg, O. *Children's view of foreign peoples*. New York: Appleton-Century-Crofts, 1967.

67. Lehrman, P. R. The fantasy of not belonging to one's family. *Archives of Neurology and Psychiatry*, 1927, *18*, 1015–23.

68. Lynd, Helen M. *On shame and the search for identity*. New York: Science Editions, 1961.

69. Montessori, Maria. *The Montessori Method*. New York: Schocken, 1964 (first published in English, 1912).

70. Montessori, Maria. *Spontaneous activity in education*. Cambridge, Massachusetts: Robert Bentley Inc., 1964.

71. Moore, O. K. Orthographic symbols and the preschool child: A new approach. In E. P. Torrence (ed.), *Creativity: 1960 proceedings of the 3rd conference on gifted children*. Minneapolis: University of Minnesota, Center for Continuation Studies, 1961.

72. Newell, A., and Simon, H. A. Computer simulation of human thinking. *Science*, 1961, *134*, 2011–17.

73. Opie, Iona, and Opie, P. *The lore and language of school children*. London: Oxford University Press, 1959.

74. Peel, E. A. *The pupil's thinking*. London: Oldhourne, 1960.

75. Phillips, J. L. *The origins of intellect: Piaget's theory*. San Francisco: W. H. Freeman, 1969.

76. Piaget, J. *The psychology of intelligence*. London: Routledge & Kegan Paul, 1950.

77. Piaget, J. *The child's conception of the world*. London: Routledge & Kegan Paul, Ltd. 1951

78. Piaget, J. *Judgment and reasoning in the child*. London: Routledge & Kegan Paul, Ltd., 1951.

79. Piaget, J. *Play, dreams and imitation in childhood*. New York: Norton, 1951.

80. Piaget, J. *The child's conception of number*. New York: Humanities Press, 1952.

80a. Piaget, J. *The child's conception of time*. New York: Basic Books, 1970.

81. Piaget, J. *The language and thought of the child.* London: Routledge & Kegan Paul, 1952.

82. Piaget, J. *Les relations entre l'affectivité et l'intelligence dans le développement mental de l'enfant.* Paris: C. D. U., 1954 (mimeographed and bound lectures given at the Sorbonne).

83. Piaget, J. *The construction of reality in the child.* New York: Basic Books, 1954.

84. Piaget, J. Apprentissage et connaissance (première partie). In P. Greco and Piaget (eds.), *Études d'épistémologie génétique.* Vol. 7, *Apprentissage et connaissance.* Paris: Presses Universitaires de France, 1959, 21–67.

85. Piaget, J. Apprentissage et connaissance (seconds partie). In M. Goustard *et al.* (eds.), *Études d'épistémologie génétique.* Vol. 10, *La logique des apprentissages.* Paris: Presses Universitares de France, 1959, 159–88.

86. Piaget, J. *Les mécanismes perceptifs.* Paris: Presses Universitaires de France, 1961.

87. Piaget, J. *Comments on Vygotsky's critical remarks concerning "The Language and Thought of the Child" and "Judgment and reasoning in the child."* Cambridge, Massachusetts: M.I.T. Press, 1962.

88. Piaget, J. Development and learning. In R. E. Ripple and V. N. Rockcastle (eds.), *Piaget rediscovered.* Ithaca, N.Y.: School of Education, Cornell University, 1964.

89. Piaget, J. Genesis and structure in the psychology of intelligence. In D. Elkind (ed.), *Six Psychological Studies by Jean Piaget.* New York: Random House, 1967, 143–58.

90. Piaget, J. *On the nature and nurture of intelligence.* Address delivered at New York University, March, 1967.

91. Piaget, J. Intelligence et adaptation biologique. In F. Bresson *et al.* (eds.), *Les processus d'adaptation.* Paris: Presses Universitaires de France, 1967, 65–82.

92. Piaget, J. The mental development of the child. In D. Elkind (ed.), *Six Psychological Studies by Jean Piaget.* New York: Random House, 1967, 3–73.

93. Piaget, J., and Morf, A. Les préinferences perceptives et leurs relations avec les schemes sensori-moteurs et opératoires. In J. Piaget (ed.), *Études d'épistémologie génétique.* Vol. 6. Paris: Presses Universitaires de France, 1958.

94. Radin, P. *Primitive man as a philosopher.* New York: Dover, 1957.

95. Rapaport, D. The theory of ego autonomy. *Bulletin of The Menninger Clinic*, 1958, 22, 12–35.

96. Reitman, W. R., Grove, R. B., and Shoup, R. G. Argus: An information process model of thinking. *Behavioral Science*, 1964, 9, 270–81.

97. Shaffer, L. F. *Children's interpretation of cartoons.* Contributions to Education, No. 429. New York: Teacher's College, Columbia University, 1930.

98. Skeels, Harold M. Adult status of children with contrasting early life experiences. *Monographs of the Society for Research in Child Development*, 1966, 31, 3, No. 105.

99. Smedslund, J. Apprentissage des notions de la conservation et de la transitivité du poids. In J. Piaget (ed.), *Études d'epistémologie génétique.* Vol. 9. Paris: Presses Universitaires de France, 1959, 85–124.

100. Spearman, C. *The nature of "intelligence" and the principles of cognition.* London: Macmillan, 1923.

101. Spelt, D. K. The conditioning of the human fetus in utero. *Journal of Experimental Psychology*, 1948, 38, 338–46.

102. Standing, E. M. *Maria Montessori.* Fresno: Academy Library Guild, 1957.

103. Strodtbeck, F. L. The hidden curriculum of the middle class home. In H. Passow, Miriam Goldberg, and E. J. Tannenbaum (eds.), *Education of the disadvantaged.* New York: Holt, Rinehart & Winston, 1967, 244–59.

104. Terman, L. M., and Merrill, Maud A. *Stanford-Binet intelligence scale: Manual for the third revision.* Boston: Houghton Mifflin Company, 1960.

105. Waddington, C. H. *The nature of life.* New York: Atheneum, 1962.

106. Waddington, C. H. *How animals develop.* New York: Harper & Bros. (Torchbook ed.), 1962.

107. Watson, J. B. *Psychological care of infant and child.* New York: Norton, 1928.

108. Wechsler, D. *The measurement of adult intelligence.* Baltimore: Williams & Wilkins, 1944.

109. Wechsler, D. *Wechsler intelligence scale for children.* New York: Psychological Corporation, 1949.

110. Weir, M. W. Development changes in problem solving strategies. *Psychological Review*, 1964, 71, 473–90.

111. Wertheimer, M. *Productive thinking.* New York: Harper, 1945.

248 CHILDREN AND ADOLESCENTS

112. Wertheimer, M. *Productive thinking.* New York: Harper, 1959 (2nd edition).
113. White, R. W. Motivation reconsidered: The concept of competence. *Psychological Review,* 1959, *66,* 297–333.
114. White, S. H. The hierarchical arrangement of learning processes. in L. P. Lipsitt and C. C. Spiker (eds.) *Advances in child development and behavior* II. New York: Academic Press, 1965, 187–220.
115. Wohlwill, J. F. Un essai d'apprentissage dans le domaine de la conservation du nombre. In J. Piaget (ed.), *Études d'épistémologie génétique.* Vol. 9. Paris: Presses Universitaires de France, 1959, 125–35.
116. Wohlwill, J. F. A. A study of the development of the number concept by scalogram analysis. *Journal of Genetic Psychology,* 1960, *97,* 345–77.
117. Wolfenstein, Martha. *Children's humor.* Glencoe, Illinois: The Free Press, 1954.
118. Woltmann, A. G. Mud and clay, their functions as developmental aids and as media of projection. In Mary R. Haworth (ed.), *Child Psychotherapy.* New York: Basic Books, 1964, 349–63.
119. Anderson, R. C., Spiro, R. J. and Anderson, M. C. Schemata as scaffolding for the representation of information in connected discourse. *American Educational Research Journal,* 1978, *15,* 433–440.
120. Bower, T. G. R., *Development in infancy,* San Francisco: W. H. Freeman, 1974.
121. Brainerd, C. J., and Hooper, F. H. A methodological analysis of developmental studies in identity and equivalence conservation. *Psychological Bulletin,* 1975, *82,* 725–737.
122. Breuer, J., and Freud, S. *Studies in hysteria.* Boston: Beacon Press, 1937.
123. Briggs, C., and Elkind, D. Cognitive development in early readers. *Developmental Psychology,* 1973, *9,* 2, 279–280.
124. Briggs, C., and Elkind, D. Characteristics of early readers. *Perceptual and Motor Skills,* 1977, *44,* 1231–1237.
125. Bruner, J. *The process of education.* Cambridge, Mass.: Harvard University Press, 1962.
126. Bruner, J., Jolly, A., and Sylva, K. (eds.) *Play: Its role in development and evolution.* Hammondsworth: Penguin, 1976.
127. Bryant, P., and Trabasso, T. Transitive inference and memory in young children. *Nature,* 1971, *232,* 456–458.
128. Claparede, E. *Education functionelle.* Neuchátel: Delachaux, 1946.

129. Elkind, D. Stages in the development of reading. *Eighth Annual Symposium of the Jean Piaget Society* (in press).
130. Elkind, D., and Deblinger, J. Perceptual training and reading achievement in disadvantaged children. *Child Development,* 1969, *40,* 1, 11–19.
131. Elkind, D., Hetzel, D., and Coe, J. Piaget and British primary education. *Educational Psychologist,* 1974, *11,* 1, 1–10.
132. Elkind, D., Horn, J., and Schneider, G. Modified word recognition, reading achievement and perceptual decentration. *Journal of Genetic Psychology,* 1965, *107,* 235–251.
133. Elkind, D., and Shoenfeld, E. Identity and equivalence in children's conservation judgments. *Child Development,* 1972, *6,* 529–533.
134. Erikson, E. *Childhood and society.* New York: Norton, 1950.
135. Francis, H. Children's experience of reading and notions of units in language. *British Journal of Educational Psychology,* 1973, *43,* 17–23.
136. Freud, S. The interpretation of dreams in *The basic writings of Sigmund Freud.* New York: Modern Library, 1938.
137. Furth, H. G. *Thinking without language: psychological implications of deafness.* New York: Free Press, 1966.
138. Gibson, E. J. *Principles of perceptual learning and development.* New York: Appleton, 1969.
139. Goodman, K. S. A psycholinguistic guessing game. In H. Singer and R. B. Ruddell (eds.), *Theoretical models and processes of reading.* Newark, Del.: International Reading Association, 1976, 497–508.
140. Goodnow, J. J. Problems in research on culture and thought. In D. Elkind and J. H. Flavell (eds.), *Studies in cognitive development.* New York: Oxford University Press, 1969, 439–62.
141. Groos, K. *The play of man.* New York: Appleton, 1901.
142. Hatwell, Y. *Privation sensorielle et intelligence.* Paris: Presses Universitaires de France, 1966.
143. Kaufman, A. S., and Kaufman, N. L. Tests built from Piaget's and Gesell's tasks as predictors of first grade achievement. *Child Development,* 1972, *43,* 521–535.
144. Koffka, K. *The growth of the mind: An introduction to child psychology.* New York: Harcourt, Brace & Co., 1927.
145. Lombroso, C. L'instinct de la conservation chez les enfants. *Rev. Philos.* 1896, XLIII, 379–390.
146. Lunzer, E. A., Dolan, T., and Wilkinson, J. E. The effectiveness of measures of operativity, language and short-term memory in

the prediction of reading and mathematical understanding. *British Journal of Educational Psychology*, 1976, *46*, 295–305.

147. Makita, K. The rarity of reading disability in Japanese children. In S. Chess and A. Thomas (eds.), *Annual progress in child psychiatry and child development.* New York: Brunner/Mazel, 1969.

148. Mehler, J., and Bever, T. G. Cognitive capacity of very young children. *Science*, 1967, *158*, 141–42.

149. Montessori, M. *Dr. Montessori's own handbook.* New York: Schocken, 1965. (first published 1914)

150. Montessori, M. *The absorbent mind.* New York: Delta, 1967.

151. Piaget, J. Piaget's theory. In Paul H. Mussen (ed.), *Carmichael's Manual of Child Psychology.* New York: Wiley, 1970.

152. Piaget, J. *Play, dreams and imitation in childhood.* New York: Norton, 1963.

153. Piaget, J. *Six psychological studies.* New York: Random House, 1967.

154. Piaget, J., and Inhelder, B. *The origins of the idea of chance in children.* Leake, Lowell Jr. et al. trans. Norton, 1976.

155. Piaget, J., and Inhelder, B. *The child's conception of space.* London: Routledge and Kegan Paul, 1963.

156. Piaget, J., and Inhelder, B. *The child's conception of number.* New York: Humanities, 1952.

157. Scott, R. Perceptual skills, general intellectual ability, race and later reading achievement. *The Reading Teacher*, 1970, *23*, 7, 660–69.

158. Smith, F. *Psycholinguistics and reading.* New York: Holt, Rinehart and Winston, 1973.

159. Subes, J., and Auzet, J. Tentative d'etude objective de sens esthetique chez l'enfant. *Enfance*, 1950, *2*, 160–67.

160. Vygotsky, L. S. *Mind in society.* Cambridge, Mass.: Harvard University Press, 1978.

161. Waller, T. G. *Think first, read later! Piagetian prerequisites for reading.* Newark, Del.: International Reading Association, 1977.

162. Weikart, D., Rogers, L., Adcock, C., and McClelland, D. *The cognitively oriented curriculum. A framework for preschool teachers.* Urbana: University of Illinois, 1971.